079772

W9-CMB-318

SOMETIMES I WONDER

A Da Capo Press Reprint Series

THE ROOTS OF JAZZ

General Editor: Christopher W. White

Director, Rutgers Institute of Jazz Studies

Newark College of Arts & Sciences

SOMETIMES I WONDER
The Story of Hoagy Carmichael

by
Hoagy Carmichael
with
Stephen Longstreet

DA CAPO PRESS • NEW YORK • 1976

Library of Congress Cataloging in Publication Data

Carmichael, Hoagy, 1899-
    Sometimes I wonder.

    (Da Capo Press reprint series)
    Reprint of the 1965 ed. published by Farrar, Straus and
Giroux, New York.
        1. Carmichael, Hoagy, 1899-   2. Musicians—Corres-
pondence, reminiscences, etc. I. Longstreet, Stephen
1907-   II. Title.
    [ML410.C327A27   1976]   780'.92'4   76-7577
    ISBN 0-306-70809-4

This Da Capo Press edition of *Sometimes I Wonder*
is an unabridged republication of the first edition
published in New York in 1966. It is reprinted with
the permission of Farrar, Straus & Giroux.

Published by Da Capo Press, Inc.
A Subsidiary of Plenum Publishing Corporation
227 West 17th Street, New York, N. Y. 10011

SOMETIMES I WONDER

SOMETIMES I WONDER
The Story of Hoagy Carmichael

by Hoagy Carmichael

with

Stephen Longstreet

FARRAR, STRAUS AND GIROUX

NEW YORK

Published simultaneously in Canada by
Ambassador Books, Ltd., Toronto

Manufactured in the United States of America

Contents

ONE   *"But That Was Long Ago"*   3

TWO   *"The Little Stars Climb"*   73

THREE   *"When Stars Are Bright"*   161

FOUR   *"The Music of the Years Gone By"*   245

FIVE   *"The Purple Dusk of Twilight Time"*   311

ONE

"But That Was Long Ago"

I

The world I was born into on a rainy day, November 22, 1899, in a small four-room cottage at the southern end of Grant Street in the college town of Bloomington, Indiana, was a million light years away from the world of today. But it was a pleasant world, and after weighing in at eight pounds Grandmother Robison (always known as Ma) grabbed me and began to rub my head into shape.

"It should be rounder."

It was a lazy golden age; hard times sure, and troubles, but the pace was easy and the Indian summers of Indiana made a cozy frame for a way of life once tested by Indian raids and educated by McGuffey's readers. A young man didn't mind that his hands were callused from gripping a plowhandle, and many a young girl could milk a cow.

Popular music was mostly ragtime, a bouncy kind of thing that served as the two-step when couples danced in the Masonic Temple. Some music publisher in Chicago sent out free copies every month of the latest rags in booklet form with a crude drawing of Uncle Sam on the cover. Mother couldn't wait to receive the new copy and practice the pieces on the piano.

Along about this time New Orleans had sportin' houses and was bringing in the first jazz combos, but of course no one knew about that in Indiana. Gilbert and Sullivan songs traveled the countryside, a land innocent of stereo, bop, and even the blues. I heard my family talk the blues, but they couldn't sing them. They did have early hand-cranked talking machines that produced tinny sounds from cylindrical records. Motion pictures were something back East where one ground out flickering snap-shots for a penny while peering through an eye piece. A motor car was a rich man's toy and was greeted by shouts of "Get a horse!"

That was the kind of world I inherited, and I was happy to get it. My people were just folk, which didn't mean they didn't have their pride and their tall stories about floods, frontier raids, and about moving West. Everybody, it seemed, was moving West for generations before I was born, and Indiana with its rivers and meadows, its strong sun that brought up the corn plants with a shout in one night, seemed good to my forefathers. The Robisons, my mother's family, had made it in a couple of jumps, and my grandmother as she rubbed my head into shape was already comparing me to the forest runners and the trail markers and the town settlers who had come before me.

Grandfather Taylor Carmichael was a cattle trader. Dad used to drive cattle to Indianapolis when he was a young man. Grand-ma Carmichael was a Campbell and could really sing. The Camp-bells were related to Queen Anne, but Grandma set more store by the Carmichael plaid than she did by royal connections.

2

My father, Howard Clyde Carmichael, was a wiry, feisty young fellow; everybody called him Cyclone. He had been middle-weight champion of his regiment during the Spanish-American War and while he didn't charge up San Juan hill or ride with Teddy Roosevelt's Rough Riders, still he came back cocky and ready to take on the world.

You could call my father a livery stable man—we did. He was a horse-and-buggy owner, advertising his rubber-tired hacks for hire in the local college publications, and driving the waltz-heated students of both sexes around the dark streets after the proms and balls were over. He had courted my mother, Lida, while banging a whip into the rump of a fast-pacing horse. My mother had promised to marry him if he'd only slow up.

My mother was a shy, poetic young girl, fashioning herself after the Gibson girls who were appearing then in the magazines as the ideal of how an American girl should look. They were tall, classical-faced beauties, smart under their piled-up hair, with studied, superior smiles ready to trap a male. Their stockinged curves and long black jersey bathing suits caused sighs in every young girl's heart and taught country boys anatomy.

Yes, Mother and Dad were once very young and I remember their talking about it. Just as my father, born on a stock farm near Harrodsburg, ten miles south of town, never did approach John L. Sullivan in size and skill, my tiny mother never fully succeeded as a Gibson girl. She was dreamy, musical, and could rattle the eighty-eight keys of a piano with a speed and expertness that showed she wasn't fooling. She could play sweetly classical even as a child, I was told, and could play any ragtime tune by ear or pick out Stephen Foster melodies or numbers from such light operas as *Robin Hood*, *The Mikado*, and early Victor Herbert. When motion pictures grew to be a popular entertainment, my mother became the piano player at the local vaudeville house, The Wonderland, and she accompanied the flickering celluloid epics of the day, busting out in fragments of Wagner for train wrecks and fires, bringing in the sobbing notes for *Way Down East*, and giving the *Indian Love Call* its most cloying chords whenever the plot hinted of outdoor men enmeshed in turn-of-the century sex. There was always *The Stars and Stripes Forever* for the charge of the horse soldiers and the big ride in a stone-age western.

3

We were an ordinary poor family, eager and honest, just living our lives, trying to make ends meet, paying the rent, hiring a piano, or paying for one over too long a period of time. I remember the family getting together on Thanksgiving, watching autumn turn the trees golden and red, exchanging simple gifts at Christmas, hearing the hounds bark at foxes in the next county, sitting in the livery stable or the freight agent's shack at the depot, telling wild yarns of the war in Cuba or gold in the Klondike. I suppose I absorbed this information in my first few years, yet somehow I once thought I was born with a full knowledge of it all.

"Get out the cigars!"

"What is it?"

"A boy. Good lungs."

"Odd looking head."

The doctor's fee was twenty-five dollars, but Dad had to promise it to him, the hack business being poor at that time of the year.

I was a big baby, and made the family proud. In proportion to my size, it was the heaviest I ever weighed. I've been a rangy, lean man of no great heft. But I began jumbo size.

A few days later, Grandma Robison, still rubbing my skull into shape, asked, "What will we call him?"

Grandma Carmichael, a sharp-nosed, pointed-chin lady, waiting her turn to polish me, looked up. "It's up to Lida."

My mother, resting after her ordeal, thought about names.

There was a new railroad spur being built on the Monon line near Harrodsburg, and some of the surveyors were living in our neighborhood. One of them named Harry Hoagland lived with one of the Carmichael family, who advertised for "Gentlemen Boarders." Mother liked the unusual and had the imagination and the temperament of a poet, or a piano player. "Well, Hoagland sounds grand!" she said.

My father didn't mind. "Sure, we can always use my name in the middle."

Grandma Carmichael raised her hands in horror. "Lida, dear, please don't name him Hoagland. They'll nickname him Hoagy for sure. And besides, I like Taylor better." Grandma did like Taylor. She bore him five sons and two daughters. Ma Robison bore Alex five daughters and two sons.

But Mother remained solidly for Hoagland Howard Carmichael. The name won, and so did the nickname. However, Mother never called me anything but Hoagland.

For a woman barely five feet tall, Lida Mary Robison Carmichael could put her size 3A foot down when she had to. Her height was no indication of the strong temperament that governed all her life. She never weighed over a hundred pounds, even when carrying an eight-pound baby. But as Dad once said: "She has spunk and most of the time I listen."

My father was the opposite of my mother. Howard "Cyclone" Carmichael was firm in temperament and build and a little light-footed. He tipped the hay scales at 185 pounds and he never let anything much ruffle him. Proud of his agility, his nickname was derived from his skill and speed in handling horses, fast horses, outlaw horses—any kind of horses—with the assurance of today's jet pilot. When the horse, in good odor, passed into history, Dad became a linesman and electrician. His abilities in this field were mediocre and he admitted, "I'm no Tom Edison." He was well-liked in the local electrician's union which he helped to found, and was known as a great guy, an easy mark, and a soft touch. I remember him as a man who was always being bamboozled into something yet not getting riled up about it. He had the patience of a good loser. He also had a lot of native intelligence and a primitive instinct that made him a fighter when he was enraged. Grandma told me once that when he was eight he was sent by horseback on an errand to borrow a tree-saw from a neighbor who lived several miles away across a river that had to be forded. It was bitterly cold and a storm was in the making. On the return trip it hit, a real old-time Indiana blizzard. He wouldn't turn back to the safety of the neighbor's house. He hung on and the horse eventually brought him home, across the cold, swollen river and through the blinding snow. They had to break the ice to get him out of the saddle: he was frozen to it, stiff as a board.

"Stubborn, but not smart. Couldn't use the saw in that weather anyway."

4

The years of his marriage were hard ones. A wild young man doesn't settle down easy. There were children to feed and raise, and his livelihood, the horse and buggy, was losing ground. Dad was sensitive in spite of his rough-and-ready style. I remember, with shakes, the death of my three-year-old sister Joanne. The loss of that sweet, innocent child was almost more than he could bear. He was away in Alabama on a boom-time job and he walked into the house to the news of her illness after a thirty-four-hour ride in a cold day-coach. It was diphtheria, a terrible disease in those days. He found my sister dead, laid out in her little white dress. Only a week before he had given us kids a prolonged farewell before he struck out for Alabama, hoping to make enough money so we could get enough to eat. Because she died of an infectious disease, there were no services. But my mother played a hymn on the old upright piano. My sister's death aged Dad who, at 40, took pride in doing a fast handspring and a right smart back shuffle step if the music was hot enough.

I never really got to know my father, probably because of my own childhood doubts and sensitivities. His wild, shouting personality overwhelmed me. As a boy I never gave myself a chance to find out his real worth. During the last years of his life, I had matured enough to appreciate him more and we did have some good times together, when his finer qualities got through to me.

He tested my mother's love by his desire for moving and wandering, tearing up roots to try new places, new ideas, new plans. He was born too late: he belonged with the wagon trains in the gold rush days.

Mother suffered on these journeys.

"Now, Howard, I just unpacked."

"Then you still have the barrels. Good."

"Where to this time?"

"You'll see, eh Hoagy?"

"His name is Hoagland."

I didn't mind piling the paper-wrapped china on an express wagon. I remember a time when Dad was outside, tying the weights on the family clock. The family dog, Duggan, was looking out the second story window. Dad turned his head away for a second and Duggan, who followed his master's lead at all times, thought the motion meant to jump. The dog landed at his feet and died. We stopped to bury the faithful (and like his master), impetuous pet.

Soon we'd be resettled—but not for long. After spending some pleasant period of time in a place, Mother would see Dad looking absentmindedly at the wide blue sky and jingling the change in his pants pocket. This jingling of coins was a never-failing sign. Whenever we heard them clinking together in his pocket, we got out the crates and barrels.

"Now Lida, big things are happening. This is a hick town. Wait till you see where we're going."

"I'm taking our things with us, Howard."

During the ensuing days she would try to decide what to sell, what to store. We learned from experience it was best to patronize the storage places rather than the used furniture market. Yet there was always one piece of household goods she would never surrender.

"I *must* have music, Howard."

So our one treasure was the piano. Whenever the time came to take the road, we always called a dray and had it taken to Ma Robison's house. She kept it for us till nostalgia won out and, heads held high, we drifted back to the old neighborhood, battered *and* hungry.

5

The first of these ventures into the outside world came a few years after I was born when we moved to Indianapolis, the nearest big city. At the turn of the century it held promise of earning better money than Dad was making in Bloomington following the horses and buggies, or so he thought.

"You'll see tall buildings, son."

It wasn't far, only fifty-two miles, but there were no super-highways and fast automobiles in those days, so Indianapolis to me at the age of four seemed a million miles away, and a place where one wore shoes every day. I was old enough to feel heart-broken at leaving "Blooring," as I pronounced our home town.

My father found us an apartment on the corner of East and Lockerbie Streets, and we moved in with a few cherished items salvaged from our first big shattering wrench from home.

"It's called a flat."

"It sure is," said Mother, fighting back tears while laughing at her little joke.

It was a long, empty-looking dismal place on the second floor of a shaky house. We got out of it as often as we could. Mother and I took long walks and played dull games in the yard. Three houses up Lockerbie Street was the home of James Whitcomb Riley, the Hoosier poet, then at the height of his fame. I saw him often, a fat, fine figure of a man, riding by on his bicycle. He nearly always wobbled a little.

"He has a penchant for the cup that cheers," our landlady told us.

One morning, walking by the house, Riley saw me and my mother sitting on the grass—you couldn't say it was a lawn—and he called me over to the gate. He talked to me and he asked Mother if he might take me to the grocery store around the corner. Since it was Mr. Riley, whom everyone knew, Mother sniffed the air for any whiskey odor and said "yes." He lifted me to his shoulder and marched to the store where he bought me bananas and a bag of candy. ("The worst combination he could think of," Mother said later when I got a stomach-ache.) On the way back, fire engines clanged by and Mr. Riley, watching me out of the corner of his smiling eyes, counted quickly as they went rushing on: "One, two, three, four, five"—up to fifty, which was absurd. But always afterward I insisted I saw fifty fire engines go by because Mr. Riley said so.

Dad frowned. "Poets are poets, I guess, and never a word a lie."

II

It wasn't long before the Carmichaels had to admit that Indian-apolis was just bigger, not better than home. I grew moody, with-drawn, and began to suspect my father wasn't God. Ma Robison came from Bloomington to visit us, bringing boxes of fruit, jars of jam, and a hog joint to add to our meager larder.

"Shucks, folks have to eat—just like any place."

As she was leaving, I staged a heartrending scene at the station, letting everyone know how plain unhappy I was. The engineer held up the train till I recovered and Dad promised to take us back to Bloomington soon.

I was too young to understand fully the feeling for Blooming-ton that was always with me, the compulsion to get back there, to take from Bloomington the security it offered: things I knew later were more fundamental than just happy kids and safe streets and broad meadows where you could run and roll panting in the thick cool grass as you gasped "Safe!" I felt there were things there that I must have, and the more my father scattered his hopes afield, the more I wanted to go back.

We moved back, Mother retrieved the old piano, and a year later I entered school. Well, I was dragged. The information from books never seemed quite so important as the associations of the place and the time. Mother understood. She had grown up in the neighborhood and it hadn't changed much since she was a girl. She used to finger out some ragtime beat on the piano as she sighed and told me how good it was to be home.

"Do we have to leave again?"

"Your father is getting restless."

"He isn't rattling any change in his pants pocket."

"Maybe he hasn't any to rattle."

We lived within a stone's throw (a good-sized stone) of Indiana University. I could stand on our front porch and throw the stone across the road right into the campus and I was tempted to do that on numerous occasions just to release some personal pressure within myself. With my cousins and the neighbor boys, we played in Dunn's Meadow, just to one side of the bell tower on the campus. There was a small creek (which we were warned could drown us) called the Jordan River. We waded and fished with bent pins for fish we never caught. There were pawpaw trees along the path next to the campus wall, and we lay in the tall grass and had big dreams about the future and ate green fruit. Naturally, we couldn't wait until it ripened.

Dunn's Meadow was the community pasture, and when my mother was first married, she used to drive her cow, Molly, to pasture there after the evening milking. There was a big wide gate that swung heavily on its rusting hinges just beside the entrance to the campus and she said she always enjoyed slamming it shut, just to annoy the professors. I never had that happy chore because by the time I was born we were buying milk from a farmer who came around in an old wagon with a dipper and tin pail.

The university stadium was built on that meadow later; the place is so packed with Indiana limestone buildings now that one can barely make out the original lay of the land.

2

Change always upset me. My music is often about things lost to me. Simple things like rocking chairs, the weather of my childhood, moods and memories, and landmarks. The Jordan River, named for David Starr Jordan (an early president of the university), became a covered sewer and is hardly more than a smelly memory today. I suppose this is progress of sorts.

My cousin Hugh Campbell and I haunted Nicholson's apple orchard. It stood where Campus Hill is now and Old Man Nicholson, all whiskers and overalls, was always generous with his Baldwins and Pippins and his fresh cider. We could have all we could drink. Once I was showing off and drank five full glasses. I don't recall that I had any aftereffects besides feeling like a bursting frog for a while. Somehow I never liked cider much after that.

One day Mother noticed me running my hand through my hair in a pattern of irritation, and she suspected bugs. I had them free from the boy who sat next to me in the second grade. "Hoagland!" my mother cried. "You're infected."

I was cheerfully unperturbed.

"How?"

"Hoagland. Nice people don't have bugs in their hair."

"Oh."

The only real disaster I felt was breaking an arm or leg and I never did that. But she drenched me in coal oil, and I smelled like a leper for a week. No bug could live within ten feet of me. I could hardly stand myself. Another time I caught chiggers while picking berries and for two days I walked around in a suit of long underwear coated with lard.

About this time motion pictures began to be really popular and the first film palace in town—a converted dusty store stocked, at first, with kitchen chairs—hired my mother to make the music for the flickering screen. Later real seats were put in.

I can still remember walking with bare dusty feet into the cold parlor and standing beside the upright golden oak piano on which Mother practiced her movie music. How I used to love hearing her play! Outside life on the quiet tree-lined street moved at a modest tempo, not like her train-wreck and girl-tied-to-the-tracks music. I remember at the movie house the long chromatic runs my mother threw off with ease when the redskins bit the dust. Because she played picture-show music, I was admitted free. I was the most important kid in town; I got into the picture show on the cuff. Except one night a new ticket taker wouldn't let me in and I first learned embarrassment and hate.

Everybody at that time called me Hoag except my mother and

my grandparents. Hoag didn't become Hoagy till much later, and a girl did that.

My mother also played for local dances and often nights I slept stretched across two chairs beside the dance hall piano while she pounded out ragtime for college proms. Oh that *Maple Leaf Rag!* Her talent came in handy as Dad's income barely covered the five or six dollars a week we needed for groceries. Living was cheap, Dad said.

"But it's never free."

When I was six years old, someone sold us an Armstrong piano on time payments. It was a pretty brown and very shiny.

At that time I never thought of touching the keys or trying to play. It was an instrument sacred to Mother—I'd as soon touch it as try on her hat.

The town had contact with the outer world. We kids would go past a beer garden, full of glamor for us, and watch the older kids whistling impolitely at some of the girls.

A cousin would say: "There used to be six bartenders at the Windsor Beer Garden. And naked lady oil paintings. Buffalo Bill and John L. Sullivan always drink there when they're in town."

"Really?"

"They sure do, Hoag. Buffalo Bill was so drunk in the last street parade of the Wild West show he dang near fell off his horse."

I protested, "But he busted them glass balls they threw into the air. Never missed a shot." I was defending my first folk hero.

"Shucks, he had a large gauge shotgun scattering so far he could have hit them in the next county with his eyes closed."

Our town was a boy's idea of fun; it was not too neatly geared to teach him manners and spoke not too strictly of a quiet life of duty and hard honest work. There were political banners to carry for ten cents a day; chemical pink lemonade; posters featuring Bryan's bear-trap mouth, bird's nest hairdo, and his slogan for Free Silver (which most of us mistook for a platform to help one's self at every corner bank when Bryan was elected). The

Cadets Light Artillery—the local militia—in their Civil War caps paraded smartly or pushed back election-day rioters. Elections were more fun before TV coverage. The fat mouths and boodle hunters really made the eagle scream in those days.

When raucous vaudeville acts, French girlie shows, tramp comics came to town, there was my poetic little mother knocking out the *zoom, zam, boffs* and *socks* on the theatre piano. I read show business papers before I read Bo-Peep.

It was like signing our lives away to take on the heavy obligation of the monthly payments on that new Armstrong piano. Raising the six dollars every month was never easy. We were always discussing *where* we would get the six dollars a month.

I said, "Mom, when I get big, I'll pay for the piano, don't worry."

"Don't sweet talk. I'm not overlooking the dirty footprints on my freshly scrubbed kitchen floor."

"Aw—play me ragtime."

If we didn't eat at times, at least somehow we always managed to hold on to the piano. I was becoming hooked on music, although I didn't realize it. Home was such a pleasant place— and my father hadn't been jingling his coins of late. The high picket fence divided the backyard from the adjoining lot and the maples flourished. Once I went over the fence in a hurry and caught the seat of my pants on one of the sharp pickets. The ensuing hullabaloo I made on being impaled brought all the neighbors out to help dislodge me. Surgery was not called for, but I did get my ears boxed.

Often the cry would go up, "One of the chickens fell into the privy!" Then all hands would go to work with hoes and rakes to try to save the poor thing. Besides, chickens were exceedingly valuable.

3

Bucktown, the colored community, full of spirituals and early blues, was only a short way from our house and since color prejudice was something only adults knew, the Negro kids,

Klondike Tucker, Beano Brown, Abner Shivley, and Collett Johnson were part of the neighborhood gang. There were wild games, but I managed to survive.

So while Mother hit ragtime on the golden oak, me and the gang romped through the house playing Indian-and-Cowboy, and on cookie-making days we all gathered at the back step for handouts, like a moocher's picnic.

When the razzle-dazzle Barnum and Bailey circus came to town the whole gang had a part in setting up our corner lemonade stand. Before daylight on the morning of the big street parade, I would drag the family washtub to a strategic corner while the rest of the gang brought ice and lemons and sugar and a few spare glasses. It was a sickening sweet brew, and with the number of partners entitled to drinks on the house, the profit margin was never very good.

I loved the *wha wha* jackass sound of circus music, the smell of elephant droppings, peanuts, sawdust, the sight of the tight-fitted bareback girl riders, the strut of animal trainers—but the faces of the clowns I found sinister and sad. I always disliked violence and theirs was mad. To me they weren't funny, except the rube who rode the trick mule and got kicked in his padded pratt. I laughed, but only because you were supposed to.

The circus pitched their tents in Dunn's Meadow, where at other times we fished and played baseball and football. The bigger kids would let me play baseball because they didn't have enough guys to make up two full teams. Football was different. I was the smallest line backer in the game, but they feared my shoe-string tackles! North of the meadow the tall ironweeds made wonderful Indian tepees when cut and stacked in the right manner. But as I found out, they were no good in the rain and I caught a cold. Indiana rains are solid and persistent. And how it did rain! Sometimes even long enough and hard enough to cause a drenched, teeth-chattering baseball game to be called off.

Once when this happened, I had such a feeling of frustration I didn't know what to do with myself. I wanted to break or beat something. I came home disconsolate and wandered into the icy parlor and banged my fists on the old upright piano. And a miracle happened, a new world opened up. Standing there watching the rain drip through the maples beside the house, I heard Mr. Foley over at the University tolling *Indiana Frangipani* on the college tower bells. Each separate note as it came winging through the rain hit me right in the solar plexus. I stood transfigured, a small boy, mouth open, in the ecstasy of revelation. (Frangipani is a red jasmine—*Plumiera rubra*—and the only reason I could ever ascribe for its use in the University's song is that it was the only word the composer could find that came anywhere near rhyming with Indiana).

Mr. Foley finished, and shivering with a strange glow, I went back to the piano. With one finger I began picking out the notes. Suddenly I was amazed, shocked at myself. I was picking out the notes correctly! I hadn't thought about doing it but I had done it. I had been exposed to the piano all my life but no one ever told me to try it, to touch its keys. It was the first time I knew I had some special talent. You can say the moment was propitious. Yes. I had discovered a whole new world, had found a new true love. And so the Dunn's Meadow Demons lost an incompetent sixty-pound third baseman that day and the piano found me—for life.

My mother coming home at dusk discovered me sitting on the stool in the dark picking out tunes and chords.

"Oh, Hoagland, this is *so* wonderful."

"I'm playing."

"Of course you are."

"*Really* playing."

"Yes, Hoagland."

She put her arms around me from behind, and held me ever so tightly and I felt her tears falling on my shaggy neck. I didn't turn around. I went on playing. I knew then that my mother had realized a secret goal and that neither of us would be lonely again, as long as we kept that piano.

III

At first it was the discovery of self that mattered most in my piano playing, but slowly it became the opening of a cave into the sunlight. And that light was music. Not just as I heard it but as I now wanted to play it. Most children are alike, but each child is only himself, too, and I came awake to music, to the wonder and the glory of chords. And to the creative ache of making clusters of sounds. Not that my family ever used the word creative. Neither town boy nor country boy, I was not very sure of myself: shy, somewhat ashamed of my family's way of living, not too impressed by the image of my father, and living in agony every time the family packed to move on. Still I was like other kids, belonging to their games and talk, only having feelings under my breastbone that they didn't have.

I was aware they would mock at my reactions to colors and sunsets, to village and country sounds: the purr of running water, the smooth *clop clop* gait of a trotting horse, the special baby-green color of new leaves, the feel of bark and dog hair, the smoothness of polished stones.

To me it was all something in key with music, and while I couldn't make the music to express what and how I felt, I knew someplace in the welter of wire and felt-covered hammers and yellow keys on the piano were the notes to say what I sensed about the external world and the deep dark internal secrets of a boy groping for something no one was teaching him.

I couldn't express my feeling in words. I lacked the ability for that. But I knew it was how most boys must feel, though only a few could grasp or want to express it. I hoped I was a grasper, one who could some day hold on and make tangible the emotions that came over me when I walked surrounded by the wonder of things, the pattern of shapes. I didn't know what an absolute was then, or the line between reality and the spirit. Yet I was wise enough to catch on early that one had to separate the reality from the fancy in broad daylight or one would end up like the village idiot.

"He don't know piss from vinegar."

Only at the piano could I guess at ways to join reality and spirit without fear of being called names. Now that Mother and I shared a simple musical world of our own, I let myself go a little more. I wasn't even too annoyed at my father's loud ways, his hunt for a crazy rainbow at the end of some uprooting journey. I was learning to observe, and to file away my emotions, the way a big-eyed silent kid will.

From my mother I have a poet's feeling for the simple, easy things of earth and sky, and I came by it all as doggone naturally as growing up, only no one told me. Like the autumn day I saw the wild geese flying over.

There was me and my cousin Hugh, and Klondike and Beano from Bucktown. We were struggling across Dunn's Meadow in a crisp wind with an express wagon load of walnuts we had looted in the woods when we heard the wild geese honking. We had come a long distance with the wagon, all the way from the hills northeast of the campus. Hunting walnuts, hazelnuts, and hickory nuts was the big belly-filling adventure of the fall weather. We had a little wagon with a badly deformed wheel. Every time the wheel turned the wagon wobbled and because we had a big load, some of it was falling off.

"Easy over the rocks."

"You pull, Hoag."

"I'm steering."

"You pick up the falling-off stuff."

It was a fine day, with cotton candy clouds on a crayon-blue sky, loosely hung like a curtain—and the specks flying. I was lagging behind to pick up fallen nuts, and was the first to hear the wild geese. "Lookie!" I yelled, pointing skyward with one hand while with the other I clutched staining walnuts against my shirt. "Big birds."

"Heck, Hoag, they do that every year."

But our eyes sparkled just the same. It was always a thrill to see the first wild autumn geese going over.

The birds, honking far off, passed swiftly in long lines, the spearhead of leaders in a wide-spreading V, their beautiful, lonely sounds easily heard by us below. They flew diagonally over the field, heading south, undulating like a dark ribbon pulled through the air.

"Boy," I said, "that's something!"

The words weren't profound, but they were felt.

In a moment the sight was lost to us. But that line of wild birds flying with unerring instinct south and the sound of their strong raucous voices became, for me, part of the recurring symphony of the Indiana autumn, a favorite theme of mine, one tinged with melancholy. I knew suddenly why my father was always thinking of moving on.

My cousin Hugh, a realist, said, "If I had a shotgun I'd a got us each a real fat one."

But I didn't feel at all hungry for those wonderful travelers. Following the load of walnuts in the chilly dusk, I became aware of the theme of autumn being repeated in many variations around me. The fragrance of the crisp air, the sound of dry maple leaves crushing under my feet, the distant whistle hoot of a Monon line freight engine at a crossing, the quiet, soft colors around me, the fall haze of burning leaves that hung low over the umber hills, even the brown walnut ooze that stained my hands and pants. I didn't let on how I felt; the gang might think me daffy.

I was beginning to be more fastidious about my hands. I might have to be scolded to take a bath, in the round uncomfortable family washtub in the kitchen Saturday nights, but no one had to tell me to wash my hands. My growing love affair with the piano had a lot to do with it. You don't paw your love with dirty fingernails.

The wagon and its load moved on. I was sorry to leave the spot. I couldn't express what I felt about the swift passage of life and season, and I knew that a boy isn't supposed to feel these things anyway. Boys were judged by chores, wood chopping, lawn mowing, school marks, and skill in marble shooting.

Dad once told a story of a grimy, sweaty, dust-soaked coal miner who found a little flower on his way home from his work-shift. It was so pretty and yellow and he so filthy with muck that he didn't know what to do: so he ate the flower! Like the miner, I wanted a gesture. I wanted to say something to my pals. But I couldn't think of the right words, and they wouldn't have understood me if I had. So it was just something to store up within myself.

Maybe it was this storing up of early impressions that caused me all the loneliness and longing I suffered when we were away from Bloomington following one of Dad's gypsy trails.

2

When I was ten years old we were living in Montana in a bleak and strange place. Mother, as usual, had been against the move, but as always we moved in Dad's shadow. We sold some furniture, borrowed money and with an aunt and uncle who were also wandering souls, we pooled our meager resources and away we went on the day coach. A telephone company was running a new line from Missoula to Hamilton along the Missoula River. And Dad as a lineman felt he could make more money stringing wires down the Bitteroot Valley (General Custer also made a big mistake near here) than he could around Bloomington. Besides, it was always an experience for him to see new hills. One morning I was looking out of the dirty train window and for the first time I saw mountains on the distant horizon. It took us all day to reach them and my excitement increased by the hour as I played at being the engineer. It was the only interesting distraction I had, free from the thoughts of our old home.

It was winter and cold when we arrived in Montana. Even the

half-wild horses had shaggy coats. It seemed a mean and hard place to a boy raised in the intimate, neatly settled country of Indiana. Montana was raw and unfriendly and there was no piano. There was little to break the monotony of school and house-bound winter weekends. When the river froze over, I went skat-ing and playing on the ice with the bigger boys. It was frontier life in many ways. My father said, "Why, there are folks here-abouts still have Indian arrows imbedded in their hides."

The weather moderated; the ice cracked up and began to push its floes down the river. One Saturday morning Mother missed me and went looking for me. In a panic she thought of the river and ran a quarter-mile down the railroad tracks to the bridge that crossed the icy Missoula. I was with a group of small boys, each of us on an ice floe, poling our way around with long poles. She managed to get my attention, as I stood there teetering on the ice, waving my arms.

"Look, Mom," I yelled. "Uncle Tom's cabin. Eliza crossing the ice to escape the bloodhounds!"

"Come here," she said, trying to hide her anxiety. "I want you to run an errand for me."

"Sure—watch! Simon Legree is after me!"

Jumping from one cake of ice to another, I reached the bank, sopping wet to the knees. She grabbed me and my stick and she used the latter to impress on me the danger of ice-floe shenani-gans.

"Suppose you had drowned, Hoagland?"

I rubbed my stinging rear and said, "You'd be sorry *then* you beat me."

I sensed her loneliness and her need of me, and I shivered and cried as we walked home. That night I washed and dried all the dishes to make up for throwing a big scare into her.

Escapades like this were the exception. In the main, it was a period of loneliness and childish introspection. I played alone a lot. I built a whole farm, in miniature, out of old cartons—houses, barns, fields, stock—all in our backyard. Maybe it was an expres-sion of subconscious desire to return to my familiar Indiana country; certainly it resembled nothing in Montana. I was busy for weeks with this country project, and also with an ingenious underground bank into which I dropped every penny I could scrounge. Mr. John D. Rockefeller was much in the news. Saving was fashionable. (If I had held on to those 1909 pennies they'd be worth hundreds of dollars today.)

I had some compensations. When we moved into the rented house in Missoula I found a gold ring under a leg of the rusty stove. It was the first piece of jewelry I ever owned and I kept it for years.

3

A neighborhood girl named Flo was my first love. To my young eyes she had an alluring build, an engaging walk, and a bold manner. I didn't carry my study of this new subject very far. I wanted a bicycle, instead. Dad managed, by some sacrifice, to buy me a used one and what with the frequent flat tires and constant repairs, I was very busy.

I didn't play mamma and pappa. I suppose this set back my sexual education. But there were always opportunities in those pre-Freudian days for living encounters with the subject. It was by no means the rigid, repressed era that some writers have made it. In farm country, one didn't talk about it with grown-ups, but with the barnyard begettings and couplings, it was a backward child who didn't grasp the first and easiest principle of the system, and didn't do some kind of personal research on the matter. But at that time, it couldn't compare with a twenty-two-inch wheeled bike and a real coaster brake.

When I returned to Missoula in 1957 to star in the movie *Timber Jack*, I took a taxi out to the old neighborhood. The little house still stood but the cherry tree that bore the big purple fruit was gone—as I remember it, the only worthwhile thing on the property.

Spring saw all us Carmichaels back in Bloomington, and Dad doing odd jobs again and occasionally getting paid for them.

They were finishing off the new county courthouse and he got a few days' work there, too.

The new courthouse was made of Indiana limestone and was prettier than the old bird-soiled one, but for us it didn't have the charm the old building had. The old courthouse had been of weathered red brick, with a green copper roof and fine pillars—all surrounded by tall trees. They cut down the trees when they started to build the new one.

What I enjoyed most were the band concerts on the courthouse square on Thursday nights—kids, families, fireflies, moths, horses *and* John Philip Sousa.. The band would play on one corner one week and on another the next week, so the small businesses around the square got their share of the crowds. Saturday was the big shopping day for the farmers, all spit and polish in the best wagons, but Thursday nights were for us townspeople a sort of social block party. I never missed any of these band concerts if I could walk. They gave me themes and ideas to try out on the piano.

We made our own music in those days—we weren't flooded by mechanical recordings of everything. Somehow, good as these can be, they come too easy and too often. Village music fifty years ago—you had to work for it.

I wasn't growing much but I was maturing. Life was real and it was sure earnest and it was part of the Hoosier philosophy to impress the hard fact of existence upon the youngsters of hard working parents.

The summer after our return from Montana, I got the idea that I should get a job. I badgered everyone in the family within reach to give me work. Grandpa Robison, my mother's father, and her two brothers were carpenters. Many homes and buildings in Bloomington were built by Pa Robison and his sons. The first sawn lumber house ever built in Brown County, Indiana, was built by my great-grandfather as a change from log cabins. He drew the line on indoor toilets. "Isn't fitten to have an indoor jake. Ungodly and unsanitary."

When I begged my grandpa for a job, Pa Robinson said,

"Well, you might have inherited some inclination to be a carpenter. All right, son. You do what the men tell you to do. Carry things, make yourself useful. Don't climb ladders, though."

"Can I carry a hammer, Pa?"

"Long as you don't use it—sure."

I worked the whole week right along with the men. I got sawdust in my hair and dirty fingernails. Saturday morning I was up early and went to work. The men hadn't showed up yet. It was a fine day, the half-completed house smelling of pine pitch and wet plaster—the fresh-cut lumber pale sepia and yellow. It made an exciting background.

I was never one to sit around and twiddle. Besides, I was thoroughly convinced I was a full-fledged carpenter. I got an apron, a pocket full of shingle nails, a hammer, and a bundle of shingle shakes, then climbed the long narrow ladder to the skeleton roof of the house. I nailed footholds in place as I had seen the men do, stretched a chalk line and proceeded to nail on the shingles. I didn't dare look down at the ground.

I had shingled a strip a yard wide clear across the roof when I heard my grandfather shouting. "What in the name of tarnation are you doing?"

"Shingling."

"Come off *that roof!*"

Meekly I came down, my elation fast running out of my heels.

Pa climbed the ladder to survey the roof. He stood there a moment, nodding his head and looking down at me. "I never would have believed it."

"Not bad?" I asked.

"Not bad."

And he didn't change a shingle. The men began laying them where I had left off. The house and roof are still standing but I can't take all the credit for that survival. A year, and several houses later, I shingled a whole roof by myself. By then it was just a hard job and a sore back to me. There wasn't much boyhood for me from then on. I was muscle for hire in my spare time. So from ten to fourteen the world passed as it does for a boy—gaining knowledge, losing a few illusions, and working on the piano.

4

I became aware just before the First World War that there was a new kind of music coming up from the south. It had been coming north, both east and west. Some called it the blues, some whore-house music, some jass or jazz. I had heard very little of it, but that little fascinated me in the next few years. Called coon songs or race records, this music was not yet fully jazz.

There was a white strain of popular music that was close to the roots of jazz. I had heard it came from the poverty of white people, from the life of the hillmen and the shanty and shack boatmen of the rivers and bayous. It came from the camp meetings and the turkey shoots and it was as real and true to the people who made it as the Negro music of the same time. The two streams weren't pure, weren't kept apart, and each took from the other what was liked or needed.

Nobody owned this ragtime tinged with jazz because nobody really wanted it. It was the poor man's tennis and foxhunt. Out our way, folk music didn't need more than a jug, a homemade fiddle, a jew's-harp or a wooden sweetpotato. You could cut a willow branch flute in no time and the banjo was no problem to transport under one arm.

When the white men made music with the Negro stuff, something was bound to happen. And that new folk music was the music of both black and white men.

But at the time when all kids wore knee pants, my problem was to get into longies—the badge of true youth, not figure out any native musical history.

I liked to go to Bucktown and hear them sing things that later somebody claimed and copyrighted as their own but which were then unknown. Those faces, solid bronze, and a blues someone took hold of with two big hands gave the tune a meaning of its own. Early versions of *Jazzbo Brown, Careless Love, Put It Right Here, Spider Man Blues, Empty Bed Blues, Hard Drivin' Papa,* and *Black Water Blues* floated up over the Negro shacks.

> Love O Love O careless love
> You flood into my head like wine,
> You wrecked the life of many a poor gal
> An' you left me fault this life of mine.

I'd listen and wonder how a people could get so musical—and no one in the white part of town to care. I didn't ask too many questions, just sat and heard them singing what became later on *Shave 'em Dry, Slow-Drivin' Moon, Jelly Bean Blues* and *See See Rider.*

The basic background instrumentation was the horns, sometimes a beat-up piano and banjo. The trombone was often played by a black man who later froze to death in a doorway, a not unusual fate for the early jazz player.

It got real funky and blue, but to a kid—all he got was the mood and the music, and a sense that it was true and sad.

> I'm gonna buy me a pistol
> Just as long as I'm tall
> Lawd, Lawd, Lawd
> Gonna kill my man
> And catch the Cannon Ball
> If he don't have me
> He won't have no gal at all.

IV

I had started high school in 1914, still in short pants. I didn't earn my first long pair for a year. I completed the freshman year without much difficulty or paying attention. At the beginning of my sophomore year I got into trouble. It was the sort of thing any young kid, feeling his vigor and approaching manhood, could get into.

Naturally, it concerned a girl—a blue-eyed blonde with a baby stare, brain to match—and a body she didn't fully admit to yet. She sat in front of me in study hall. I said something that had been said to girls millions of times. She ran screaming in outrage and told. The principal of the school did not feel kindly toward me. My father had worked on the electrical wiring for the high school and the wiring job was not to the complete satisfaction of the politically appointed school board. I felt some of the responsibility for the imperfect wiring. Dad came to school on several occasions while I was there and rummaged around from room to room looking for the trouble in the crazy electrical system. One embarrassing afternoon he spent hours in the study hall trying to repair a major electrical fault. It was very humiliating to me when someone said, "Send for Ben Franklin and his lightning kite."

So the principal gloated over every word he pulled from the shaking girl. As he repeated them, they took on the color of Sodom and Gomorrah. My simple question about her notion of the differences between boys and girls became in his mind the vices of Rome, of Oscar Wilde, of lust uncontrolled in innocent Indiana. I was called to his office. He looked and acted like the movie version of a First World War German sergeant. Silent and strong in black broadcloth, he didn't bawl me out or utter a single word. Under the pressure of his fierce stare and ominous silence he could get a fourteen-year-old boy like me to admit to anything. He stared—I went pop-eyed. I felt ground glass in my stomach. I admitted I had said a *dirty* word. In victory he panted, white-faced and excited: "I expel you from this high school."

"Please," I whimpered.

"You may go."

I went.

I spent a lot of time in exile with Grandma Robison. I loved her and she was very fond of me. I always wanted to be a "nice boy" so she would think well of me.

"Now Hoagland, any man who does this to a boy is sick himself."

Which didn't help my state of mind. I could see it was safer to think of bicycles than girls, although by this time the female shape was becoming more interesting to me than even a red English racing bike with extra long handle bars.

Eventually, through Dad's efforts and his pull with some political member of the school board, I was given the privilege of going back to the principal to cry again and beg to be put back in school.

"I have learned my lesson," I lied.

"You'll be the better man for it," he replied with distaste.

But I didn't finish that second year of high school. Dad was stirring to move again. We were living in a nice little house with an indoor bathroom (coming up in the world) and we had our old upright piano sitting in a small parlor room, right on Fess Avenue in Bloomington. I continued to pound out notes on the piano like a madman, trying to impress the peg-legged college boys in tailored clothes as they walked past our window. I wanted to make them see how refined I was. I was amazed that they never seemed to pay any attention to me. I thought I was good; at least I played loudly, and in stylish ragtime. No one discovered me.

I had my own tiny bedroom with a slanting ceiling and I would lie on my bed nights, listening to the college boys carry on in the Beta Theta Pi house. Hube Hanna, the pianist, was there at the time and so was Wendell Willkie, Harry Shackelford, and Paul V. McNutt. They made a lot of country-boy racket. It was Hube Hanna I listened to. He had a wonderful right hand on the keys and could run octaves faster than chain lightning. I admired his fine bass too.

Harry Hostetter lived right next door. He was a few years older and at that time Harry took no special joy in my music. He was only faintly interested in his sister Hilda's music. Hilda Hostetter was a fine pianist, but I was the only one in the block that appreciated her.

Harry and I played football a lot and that kept me hardened and healthy and in good standing with male society. Harry liked me because I was slight and yet was a good tackler. But he wouldn't take an interest in my piano.

My experience with the tattling blonde hadn't soured me on romance. My sexual drives didn't give a damn what they did to my high school standing. I remember dressing up for my first date. The crisp feel of white duck trousers, the thrill of going out with a pretty girl. It didn't matter that she was my cousin. I sweated a lot, mopped myself with a square-folded handkerchief, and later pressed her arm and bought us both ice cream sodas. *Wow!*

2

Dad was restless again. Life was dull. We moved to Indianapolis. It was duller until I found Reggie Duval. The only bright moments of that cheerless period in my life were at Reggie's house. Reggie Duval was a young Negro, long-fingered for good piano. He had a pretty wife who fed me while I listened to Reggie play the piano as if he were part of it.

"Listen to this rag, boy. Catch that melody!"

Reggie was playing professionally in a crumbum dive. But he didn't care. "A brown man plays where he can."

He hit keys where they shouldn't quite be hit, but it came out right.

"Keep the fingers going."

He laughed like a hyena over the keys. "Boy, don't ever hold back."

Reggie had the new black music tricks and he made ragtime sound old hat. With his head hanging to one side, as if overcome with ecstasy, he'd play and play—and grin. "You listening, boy?" I would sit, absorbed, watching the movements of his crazy hands. The new music from New Orleans held me. He looked at me. I was small and very thin, even at sixteen. I was tired, too, and getting on. I was working twelve hours a night running a cement mixer.

"I like it, Reggie," I said. "I want to play it."

"If you got it, you'll play it."

"Like you, Reggie."

"No, like Mr. Carmichael." He always called me Mr. Carmichael.

I wanted to hear more, actually hear a big band play it, and there wasn't much chance of that happening just then. I was itching to catch on to the new beat.

I had listened to the early scratchy recordings—called race records in those days. It sounded very good then and even better much later, in the recordings made by Sam Morgan's Jazz Band and Louie Dumaine's Jazzola Eight. The polyphony was well integrated and only the piano was really hit hard by acoustical recording and lost in the background. Reggie explained it all to me. Other good recordings were by Halfway House Orchestra and Tony Parenti's Famous Melody Boys. Dixieland never was a mere hybridization of western music and Negro jazz, as Reggie showed. All men are brothers, the spirituals sang, all flesh is grass. So what was handy and around makes folk-art, and jazz was alive. Like everything else, it has its tricky flashy forms and grandstand players. But music isn't as racial as blue eyes and a musty membership in the D.A.R.

It was music pretty much a world of its own, pretty much

Dixieland by the time the big trek started for Chicago. Soon—
in a year or so—that was the place to be, as Reggie told me, the
place where there was money for jazz, nightclubs and torch singers and roadhouses; where later the big bootleggers threw it
around, where the torch singers were to give out with great
blues, where a jazzman could live, make his music, and have a
session now and then with his friends. It wasn't a healthy city and
the booze, Reggie said, was bad.

"Rotgut kills faster than anything but a bullet."

I liked to hear Reggie explain it all while he noodled the keys
with themes and chords all new then.

"You learnin'."

Hick kid that I still was, I *was* learning things. The world of
a small town, my father's moving around all fell away. It was a
cold dirty world Reggie spoke of, but with a flavor and a juice
of its own, and if they froze in doorways, slept in bug-joints, got
taken by demanding dames, there was always a way to blow it
out of their horn as music or finger a piano with it.

So I knew where it came from even then, but I didn't as yet
know where I was going myself. As my father said so often,
leaving an old home, "The train whistle's calling."

3

For me it was a new music I didn't fully understand; only some
of its history and sounds had come through to me. It began in
New Orleans, Reggie had said, where the black man became in
time a little lighter and the white men often a little darker. The
French and the Spanish, the African tribesmen, and even the
Indian, the men off long boats from Kentucky and the Yankee
mountain men in buckskin fringes come to town for a big bust
on untaxed whiskey, all wanted music and made it. Reggie made
me sense the frontier in this music.

New Orleans mixed it all up and churned it around and was
part of a South that was part of a new time and a new world
where anything could happen. Just people, wild people, pioneers

and men on their way up in a hurry, all sang a lot and stomped around to music, according to Reggie. It came from the hills and from the polite music masters' minuets and string sections. But the best of it came out of New Orleans, came first from those who had lost their birthright there. Here classic jazz began and here it came to its full growth: New Orleans the way it was, and even the way the tourists and the thrill-hounds saw it. The way we all saw it later, sporting house, pleasure town, graveyard, slum, bayou outpost, all added up to the fun and the gamy quality of the music Reggie played.

"What are you doing there?" I asked Reggie, pointing to his hands on the piano.

"I bring my thumb down, like that," Reggie said. "I dunno, it just makes it."

"You bring your thumb down on the chord right after you've hit it with your right hand."

"Yeah," he grinned. "I want that harmony to *holler*."

"To laugh?"

"Look, Mr. Carmichael," Reggie said. "I want it so it sounds right to *me*. And that is the way is sounds rightest."

"It's wonderful."

"No, but it's *right*. Never play anything that ain't *right*. You may not make any money, but you'll never get mad at yourself."

I looked at him in wonder and awe.

By 1916 our house was the thin dark side of a double-fronted place in the West End of Indianapolis. I had started at Manual High School but I was filled with rebellion rather than a yen for learning. One course, designed to be practical, I had to take— they tried to teach me how to shingle a house.

"I've already shingled a whole house, singlehanded, for my Pa Robison."

"Just do as you're told. Hold the hammer *this* way."

"Roof men don't. They—"

"Leave the room."

"You still don't know how to shingle a roof."

At Manual High School I took other subjects. Some I liked and

some I felt I ought to have liked but didn't. The ones I didn't
like were languages. Except for roofing, I did well in manual
training. A couple of the little things I made that winter still
exist. They show pretty good workmanship. I'd have made a fine
carpenter. A cedar chest I built was one of my mother's treasures
all her life. Wood, I found, was a friendly thing.

The playground at Manual High was a hard, paved courtyard
of crazy cement. We gathered here at lunch time and stood
around in groups, eyeing each other. There was no team play,
no encouragement to form friendships. For a year and a half
there I never had a friend or knew a girl or boy as a human being.
At that time, I didn't have anything to give. I was not attractive
in a collar-ad way, I had an inferiority complex as long as a tape
worm, I was homesick. It was going to school under the worst
possible conditions, and I didn't make them better. I was too unhappy to let the outside world in or to find inspiration from
others. I was a mixed-up kid, living at school like a monk with a
vow not to talk or enjoy anything if he could help it. Today I
suppose I would have become a beatnik—if I had more beard-
growing areas.

So when the teacher tried to show me how to shingle a roof,
I knew my school days were numbered. I went to work. I had
to make some money so I could get back to Bloomington and
maybe go to high school there where I belonged. I needed nearly
two years of high school to get into any college, which was a
secret desire I had, thinking college life would get me out of my
downbeat world. It made my attitude toward work healthy, even
my pretty menial jobs.

I helped build the Union Station in Indianapolis. A cousin,
Sammy Dodds was living with us at the time and we worked together on that job. We called ourselves "engineers," wore muddy
hunting boots, beat-up hats, and carried dollar watches. We held
transits, tape measures, and marking stakes for the surveyors. I
gained weight and I needed it. Five full pounds.

The head man of this construction crew was a good Joe. He
loved music and took a great interest in my musical ideas. He

played piano himself, and that was a common bond. My cousin, Sammy, was a tomcat with a lot more on the ball than I had. He was very attractive to women. I was not. He was a roughneck in a fascinating way and the sporting women were always giving him the goo-goo eyes—as the term was then. The foreman and Sammy and I went out together a lot. Young men on the town, we'd go to the foreman's house and play his piano, trying out the new music, then we'd drift down the back alleys of Indianapolis' red-hot night spots—and it had them—like Illinois Street, and we'd play the rattle-trap pianos in the Greek restaurants and cheap little joints. We'd go to the whore houses full of smoke and night faces, where they'd have the best music. One of the great experiences I had was in a sporting house, all Victorian red plush, on North Illinois Street. I wasn't much interested in the sexual attractions of these girls. What I wanted was a good audience for my ragtime jazz. The girls would gather around the piano and listen and clap for more.

They smiled at me just like real nice girls on the outside. I didn't see much wrong with these girls. Perhaps I was shock-proof, or maybe it was just that any girl who wanted me to play music and said nice things about it seemed like any other girl to me.

It's easy to paint too dark a picture of one's unsettled youth, and I don't want to grime up my own early life as nothing but a struggle, all dark edges and hard times, with me fighting on-ward and upward against odds. Actually it was living and feeling very much alive, it was having a family, a place where my child-hood had happened and to which I could always return. The sun shone, life felt good, I smiled and laughed, we enjoyed our food and took our little pleasures. Hard times would pass and there was always Christmas with family and relatives. And alone I could dream, rig up hopes, knit together plans. But it wasn't an agony and dark despair.

There has been much said about Mother and Dad but little about my sisters. I guess it is because they were so much younger and I felt they were of another generation. Sister Georgia is five

years younger, almost blackeyed and very petite. Martha arrived when I was twelve. I was keen on a girl down the street
named Martha Ragsdale and when they asked me what name I
thought would be nice for the new baby, I said Martha.

I remember feeling proud of baby sister Georgia because
cousins Sam and Hugh had only older sisters. I was the only one
in the gang who had to baby-sit and my method was unique.
Hugh, Sammy, and I would take Georgia out in her buggy and
when we got around to Indiana Avenue we would let the buggy
coast down the hill taking turns standing on the rear axle and
guiding it. It is a credit to luck that she lived.

A few months after Martha was born we moved *again*, this
time to Bedford, Indiana, and I had my baby-sitting chores to
repeat. One of my hips is a little larger than the other, which is
probably the result of carrying Martha around on that hip like
a sack.

"Hoagland, you'll drop her!"

But I was too busy catching flies to feed to the spiders in the
windows of the woodshed to hear mother's constant admonition.

Joanne came along when I was fifteen. Once when Dad was
out of town on one of his job trips, mother was sick. I acted as
head of the household. Joanne took advantage of the fact to have
one of her temper tantrums; she would hold her breath and scare
us to death.

One night she became impossible and I decided to take matters
in hand. Grabbing her up fiercely, I threw her into bed with me
and held her in a vice-like grip. She could understand the King's
English and I told her, "Joanne, go ahead and howl but I'm going
to win." Almost two hours of struggle and howling took place
and then all of a sudden there was quiet. I kissed her on the
cheek and said, "I love you," and she kissed me back and said in
a small voice, "I wove you." That was the end of the tantrums
and, after that, no sweeter, obedient child ever existed.

V

Playing can-house music wasn't too healthy for a young man trying to find himself, so it's a good thing I knew Reggie and his music. Our family life in Indianapolis was dismal. We had moved into sad quarters. My father tried to make us a home. He went to a cheap furniture store and bought, on time, some of the worst furniture one could possibly imagine. Even at the age of fifteen, I saw the futility of his endeavors, but I said nothing.

Mother said, "Is it furniture or kindling?"

It was furniture made of the cheapest sticks of wood, highly varnished with a junky finish. But Mother had seen to it that her piano was there and that was all that mattered to us. We rattled away at four-handed noise.

I developed a lot of embarrassment about our situation. For instance, there was a pretty nineteen-year-old girl in the neighborhood. I saw her pass our house several times and admired her because she was petite and interesting looking. One day this girl knocked on our door and Mother invited her in. She introduced herself and said: "I'm a member of the West Side Welfare Group, a charitable organization. Could we help you people in any way?"

Mother froze. "Young woman, what are you talking about?"

"Oh, let's not be proud. You'll take a basket of groceries or clothes?" (Actually my father's pay check was delayed and we had been living for two days on Navy beans, cornmeal, and milk.)

Mother shut the door hard and turned to me. "*Never* tell Howard."

I began to feel women were a jinx to me, so I took to smoking a pipe that summer. Dad smoked a smelly old black briar pipe and played solitaire. In imitation of him, I got a pipe and sat around coughing and playing solitaire when I didn't have anything else to do. I worked at various small jobs—grocer's delivery boy or errand boy for the neighbors. Then, just as a change of pace, I had tonsilitis several miserable times. Oh, that hurt; to swallow was agony.

The worst of everything was that I didn't have a room of my own, just a narrow monk's cot in the dining room. Awake with my sore throat, I lay on the cot one time when a mouse came up to the bed and climbed up on my pillow. My tonsilitis was so bad I couldn't tell it to go away. It was a pretty low state when you couldn't tell a mouse to get off your pillow.

While I never found a tart with a heart of gold, not even gold-plated, I began to feel like somebody, playing can-house piano in the joints. I kept up my practice with Reggie Duval, who did more to shape my musical thinking at this time than anyone else. Reggie taught me to be honest with myself.

"Play your own style, Mr. Carmichael."

Reggie helped me because he knew I needed help, and he sensed my great appreciation for what he did for me. The things he could do with a piano were a standard by which I judged all piano work, including a lot of fancy masters.

I was running a cement mixer again, shoveling sand and cement into the bottomless steel gut of the thing twelve hours a night, but I worked on music somehow every day.

2

The worst work I ever did was in a slaughter house—a one-way gate for hundreds of thousands of steers, sheep, and swine. Kingan's Meat Packers needed help. I put on my corduroys and a pair of high-top boots—good tops but no soles—and lined up at seven in the morning with seventy-five other miserable job seekers. A big burly Italian in a fur-trimmed coat paraded up and down, like the Kaiser inspecting his troops. The Italian didn't look at me but only at my boots. With a quick jab of the finger, I was singled out for a job.

"Hokay—you gotta the job."

A blood-stained man took me through acres of smelly departments full of dreadful processes. We arrived down where the reeking walls of the plant dropped into the White River. A half-inch of ice-cold water covered the floor. The only windows were high up and nailed shut. I had a feeling that I didn't want my instructor to leave me. It was a forgotten dungeon, a hell hole full of death. The man took me to a metal trough through which dirty water flowed at a lively rate, and hanging from the ceiling over the trough was a half-inch water spout, also flowing at a good clip.

"Here they come," shouted the bloody ghoul.

In the trough several ghastly blobs of meat—looking like tortured babies—were headed our way. With an expert flip of the wrist, the man grabbed the first one in his hands.

"Watch *this*—it's easy."

In a flash, he jabbed the fatty hunk of obscenity up the water spout. There was a splashing as a putrid spray spattered our faces and hands. Then I noticed to my horror it was an entrail and the water was cleaning it of all refuse.

"That's all," the man said. "You take over. Get 'em all nice and clean."

"What *are* they?" I asked.

My teacher moved toward the door. "Them? Anybody knows a pig's ass when he sees it."

I kept the entrail cleaning job for three weeks. I had to quit because the motormen wouldn't let me ride home on the streetcar.

The leader of one of the neighborhood gangs was a lanky, big-mouthed, buck-toothed boy we called Butch. He had a sense of humor and a real hunger for music. My piano playing fascinated him when I managed to pick out by ear something that sounded like *Chong From Old Hongkong*, Butch's favorite. I found myself enjoying a gang popularity. From this came the decision we two ought to write our own songs. Why not?

This was my first serious attempt as a composer. Butch persuaded me to come to his house and we struggled for several hours without accomplishing a thing. I tried to create music. He tried to make up lyrics. But we just didn't have it in us.

"Give up?" said Butch.

"I think we better."

If I could have given Butch a few original notes I'm sure that he could have devised some good words. Butch was clever.

I tried to cultivate musical people. There was a harmonica player I knew. He was slightly older than the fellows in our gang but he would oblige us all with a fast concert now and then. We followed him as if he were a Pied Piper. He was able to play his tones as blues and that was always a thrill. He might well have been one of the first to "blue" a note.

An old piano solo, called *Operatic Nightmare*, originally composed and played by Felix Arndt, on a Victor record, was my favorite at this time. I would fall in love with new sounds in music the way some guys fall in love with women. Record players weren't too common then, and to hear the piano solo I found the only owner of a player: the neighborhood doctor.

He was hipped on music himself, so he didn't mind us intruding on his practice. He wasn't too successful a doctor.

"It's all belly aches anyway."

The record gang would gather in the doctor's office and between patients and seven-up card sessions I'd play the piano solo, one record over and over. Afterwards, I would juggle the tune in my mind until I got home and then pick it out all over again on the piano. This, and one or two other obscure records, would constitute an entire musical evening.

By the time 1917 came around we all knew we were not going to miss this fine noble war that was going on in Europe, and nobody but a few pro-Germans wanted to. We were infected with war fever. A U-boat sank a lot of big war orders just off the coast and the music turned from *Avalon* and *Dardanella* to

My Buddy and *I Found a Rose in No-Man's Land*. We hated the Kaiser, pitied the raped Belgians, cheered the Tommies in the newsreels, marching in mud to the tune *It's a Long Long Way to Tipperary*.

I saw how music inflated the wartime spirit, and the brass bands played and the big drums boomed and a million farm boys dreamed of being in a French barn with a cute farm girl wearing black silk stockings, whose entire vocabulary consisted of "Oo-la-la." The whole nation was singing: *Oh How I Hate To Get Up in The Morning, Someday I'm Going To Murder The Bugler, Katie, Beautiful Katie*, and *Mr. Zip With Your Hair Cut Just As Short As Mine*. George M. Cohan came up with *Over There*, and everybody sang *Smiles* and, in the beer gardens, a dirty song about a French girl.

It was the last of the romantic wars. Movie stars appeared to sell Liberty Bonds, and there was a huge wooden head of Hindenburg, and every bond buyer drove in a big fat nail. I joined in the fun when there was a parade, a block party, speakers to cheer. French officers in sky-blue uniforms, missing a leg or an arm, or an eye, came to encourage us to shout *The Yanks Are Coming!*

The farm boys and clerks put on the itchy, high-collared, pinch-hipped uniforms, and I decided soon I would, too. Trainloads of the recruits, red-faced, earnest, young, wide-eyed, went off to the training camps and thousands of them died there of sudden epidemic diseases. Black Jack Pershing's picture was everywhere and he *didn't* say "Lafayette we are here" but who cared?

Shipyard workers wore silk shirts, and the dust-brown Ford ambulances were blessed by the clergy before going overseas. Prices went up, there were bread riots—my mother had a hard time getting meat. The Swiss baker had his windows broken for being named Smertzheim; it was common knowledge he was a German spy and signaled the Kaiser from his roof every morning by hanging his underwear, in code, on the clothes line.

There were seductions, hasty marriages, back-seat romances,

the pledging of faith in the Allied cause, and Jack Dempsey posed in the shipyards wearing patent leather shoes, but he didn't enlist. It was a great war on the home front. And I wanted to get into it and away from my miserable jobs.

3

I worked and I was not cheerful. The corner drugstore gang looked with mocking disdain on the overcoat my mother had painstakingly made for me. Copied from a stylish belted model in a big downtown window.

"Well Hoagland, except for here and there, it's the same coat!"

I weighed myself. I studied the requirements for being accepted as a soldier and ate bananas and drank water until I was able to meet the minimum weight for my size. Something happened en route to the enlisting office, even though I stayed out of bathrooms.

"You don't weigh enough," said the recruiting doctor.

"I did this morning."

"We're not this desperate yet."

I went back to the cement mixer, the friendless days. Periodic trips—for weeks—to the recruiting office with my carefully hoarded weight continued. One day I made it. I was in the Army.

Hoagland Carmichael, Pvt. U.S. Army, November 10, 1918. I drilled in proud sweat for an hour in a dusty public school playground. One whole hour. The next day our sergeant called us together. "At ease, men. The war is over."

"What do we do?" I asked.

"Go home. Your names didn't go to H.Q."

The war over, I thought of Bloomington. I remembered fondly the kids I knew, the circuses coming to town, the flour sacks we collected from boarding houses and sold to the local grocer for a cent each under the impression he was a sucker.

I had been cheated out of my war. I'd go back to school. In my short military life I met a few soldiers who had been to Europe, and they talked of jazz now, right out in the open, not ashamed of it. They told me about the tremendous popularity of jazz in Europe during the war and what it was doing over there. I was excited and intrigued. They told me about the famous Negro, Jim Europe, who had a jazz band in the armed services in France. He was considered the king of jazz there. It was the beginning of jazz on a world scale. It was knockdown thrilling news to me. Those first European attempts, as I was able to tell when I heard some records, were not the kind of jazz that we were to develop later in this country. Often the first European jazz men just picked up the word *jazz* and gave ragtime a little tricky switch of some sort. It was good and as much of a tryout as they could have with their meager knowledge.

4

The post-war world came in with a bang of bad booze, flappers with bare legs, jangled morals, and wild weekends. Indiana University played Notre Dame in Indianapolis one of those weekends that fall, and I met some of the boys from home. The desire to return to Bloomington was building up in me to a crazy climax. Dad gave me four dollars to get down to Bloomington for a weekend for a long look around. On the train I met the mad, cheerful Bloomington High School basketball team. Seeing how happy and funny and chummy the fellows were, I was determined to get back to high school as soon as I could—any way but with a gun and a mask—and if I'd had the courage and the size I might even have used that way to get the cash to attend school.

When I returned to Indianapolis after a few days in heaven, I found work with an insurance actuary named Frank Haight. I had no specific training for anything but cement mixing, cleaning pigs' entrails, and roofing, but I was anxious to be a part of what I thought of as the better life. I was a willing and eager beaver. I soon could handle the "millionaire machine" (as we called the big calculator). I seldom made a mistake. There were people in the office who had gone to Michigan University. They were kind to me and I didn't understand why. They were north-side people, I was west-side, without their bathtubs and starched shirts and fingernail files. I was living in the Indiana post-frontier tradition where you took a bath a couple of times a week if you were finicky. My father took over the kitchen once in a while, bathing in the washtub. I used to admire his body; it was stout, sturdy, and sassy-looking. When I pressed my cheap clothes, the knees of the trousers were so full of a sweaty stiffness that regardless of how hard I tried to bang a crease in them, in five minutes the bags were just as prominent as before.

"Hoagland, you look like you tie blown-up bags on your knees."

"Now, Mom, don't you kid me."

"I'll sew you a good pair."

"No, Mom. They still kid me about the overcoat you made."

Styles were *sharpy* or Joe College. Pants were narrow and deep cuffed. Jackets were tight, often belted, shirts striped, or Princeton sloppy with button-down collars, shoes narrow and pointed, wide-brimmed flip down hats (gang type) for sharpies, pushed up flat tops for college types. A molting fur coat—finished off the proper body styling. The office staff—all but me—were college fashion conscious, adding gray double-breasted vests and thin gold watch chains. The wristwatch had not completely taken over yet. One of the men in the office asked me: "Are you a consumptive, Hoagy?"

When I got home that night I asked my mother, "Am I a consumptive?"

"No, of course not."

"Do I look like one?"

"Don't be silly. You were always peaked looking like."

I looked in the mirror and said to myself: I do look like a consumptive. I was white, sallow, thin-faced, and weighed 110 pounds, aged eighteen years old. But my hair was always well-groomed; I wore a silk stocking cap to bed to mold my pompadour.

It was ridiculous thinking I was sick. I was rangy, wiry, all lean muscle. I could have taken any of my Indianapolis fast-moving acquaintances out to the railroad track and raced them to the horizon till they dropped dead, and I'd still be going. But I felt unattractive, unpopular, and untalented. It all added up to a bad case of insecurity, and a session on a sporting house piano could often cut the blues. The new music I liked was best in the dives, in the poorer kind of clubs. I remember the blues singers, the early shouters of the songs. They didn't sing the blues in the rich places, in the smart roadhouses or clubs. They played black-and-tan joints, the smoky little places, the broken-down clubs, the ratty vaudeville houses failing to fight off the full-length movies. It was a time and an era—post-war—before people knew the blues were art, and it was a hard living and a lonely thing, the jazzmen told me.

The gang and I found all the places to hear it. It was best late at night when the lights were so low you couldn't see the peeling wall paint or the scars on the waiters, and the plumbing had settled down to a gurgle. The front tables were pretty well filled and the joint smelled of bootleg booze and face powder and happy sweat. The band wasn't tired any more, the drum-skins were shiny, and the piano player was beginning to bend lower over the eighty-eight keys. Into the yellow mist of a spotlight and smoke would come a black girl in purple face powder. Maybe no longer young, big in the butt in a dress dry-cleaned too often. After the introduction, she opened her mouth and if she had gold in her dentistry it showed. Once she started singing the blues, nothing mattered to me—smoke, cold, cheap liquor, the rent money, or the job.

There wasn't a lot of good blues singing around yet, but you could catch a batch of blurred notes from the colored church choirs, and they would make me tingle. The best for me were the seventh and the flatted third. I tried them on our golden oak piano. Mom was intrigued and I went into something like ecstasy. Now, I often wonder why the white man's musical imagination hadn't made these discoveries long before. But everything looks easy after somebody shows us how to do it.

W. C. Handy was already copyrighting a lot of the popular stuff. Within his limits, Handy did a good job. He took what he heard, wrote it down, and what might have been lost and forgotten remained real and solid, like *Yellow Dog Blues* and *St. Louis Blues*. And just around the corner were Louie Armstrong, Bunk Johnson, Jelly Roll Morton, and King Oliver, all driven out of New Orleans by the closing of the sporting houses.

5

The more I heard the more I wanted to try it. I sensed it was more than just the player blowing certain notes in certain remembered ways, more than changing and improvising as he went along. Often he was trying for much more, but he couldn't have put it into fancy words. Jazz is after all an abstract art, and so the results the player got were abstract, but based on the world as he knew it, suffered and dreamed it could be.

> I'm goin' to lay my head
> On some lonesome railroad iron
> An' let the 2:19 train
> Satisfy my mind.

It had for him, and for me, a poetry that made us laugh or cry, and when he was a genius it gave us ecstasy. Only I hadn't met a jazz genius yet and I hadn't figured it all out the way I put it down here now.

I saw jazz as a unique skill; it could introduce me to the sublime when its feet were still tapping out a can-house beat. The totality of feeling that came of a brass horn was amazing. Maybe, I thought, it was because jazz carried no long words, culture, or phony intellectuals' patter in the playing; so that, like all primitive sound, it was an emotion in most ways beyond taking apart and examining.

I was like a secret drunk about it, who sobered up every day to go to work. And the work I could get got meaner in the post-war years as the times began to roar and shake with a madness that had as its philosophy, "Die young and leave a beautiful body."

As I improvised with those wonderful flatted tones, I honestly believed that the great urge to hit them often and hard was helping bring this kind of music into focus. I began playing the pure and flatted note together to add something; to make a surging emotion stronger than in the old way. I called my style "sock time," and when I played *Sister Kate* in this way the place would rock. I didn't think of it as a style and a time coming together, but rather as an expression of a boy making new sounds to please something he couldn't express with words, even to himself.

VI

Oh, some of those jobs I had! That slaughter house foreman had picked me out of a large line of applicants because I was the only one wearing rubber boots in that filthy, sick-making place. I also worked at the Diamond Belt Company, where they made chains for bicycles and machines. I was just one small number of a large set in a big, inhuman factory. We did things according to ritual as sacred as a priest's gestures—we ate at certain times, loafed at a certain time in the toilet, performed our operations mechanically. The real assembly line blues.

I was earning eighteen dollars a week and this contribution to the family keep was keenly appreciated.

"We can get the piano tuned, Hoagland."

I told myself the world held more for me than the life-destroying routine of an ordinary laborer. But where the hell was an escape hatch? I never really felt I was a part of the scene except in the new low-life music. Fancy cats like Noel Coward could write something called *Twentieth Century Blues*, but they never had the real swing.

I felt I had the feel for the new music, but mine was a conglomerate existence; piano keys popping up and down at night, and in the day battery plates that came at you one every eight seconds to be inspected, bicycle chains that came at you every ten seconds for some reason I've forgotten.

Even the insurance job was monotonous. The figure combinations came marching at me a column at a time. I punched, pulled, totaled; punched, pulled, totaled all day long. And they came back in my nightmares: 1,432,040,60.01.

6,000,346.04.

Plus.

Minus.

The pork chop, fried chicken, watermelon, minstrel show myth in burnt cork was disappearing and a true native art was being born. The journey up for jazz had just begun, and not yet fully charted. A jazzman once told me, "Lots of folk, Hoagy, still can't see for lookin' how groovy a simple thing can become. And maybe soon some day it can be true when the money and easy times come in."

Easy times were a long time coming. Took a long time growing but when they were ready, the music was something the world saw for its worth.

Besides jazz, I retreated into the past, into memories of my boyhood, of all the kids I had known and what we had done. The quarry holes where we used to swim in frog eggs among old shoes and rusting tin cans. I remembered the neighbors who resented our smoking corn silk in their privies or when we dumped the outhouses over with a bang on wild yelling Halloweens.

I always remembered very well, and that was before Ernest Hemingway said: "We all had a girl—and her name is Nostalgia."

2

In January of 1919, having painfully scraped together ten dollars, I went back to Bloomington to re-enter high school. I had found out that the drifting migratory worker, the uneducated man had little chance in a mixed-up postwar world. It was a difficult and painful decision to make. I had to continue to earn money to pay my way, to go to high school with younger boys and girls. Supersensitive and wary as I was, I felt like a misfit, but also one with the secret gift, the touch of art. Grandma Robison gave me a room, a bed, a clean towel and my breakfast.

I got to know the musical pros in town. Hank Wells, who

played a hot fiddle in the Crescent Theatre pit with Hube Hanna's orchestra.

"What other town but Bloomington, Hoag, would have a five-piece band with a ten-reel movie?"

I admitted, "Not many, Hank."

Hank played the first hot fiddle I ever heard, maybe the first hot fiddle *ever* heard. Joe Venuti became famous later, sawing it off hot and lowdown, but perhaps Hank did it first. Hank's fiddling showed me that popular music could have more motion than we had used. He played a lot of piano too, great chords in a clean style. What I learned from him and Reggie Duval and Hube Hanna helped me push forward to the great adventure I was being launched on.

The Crescent Theatre held romance for me. The object of my affections usually sat two rows away. I was again taut with the inner agony of love. I never learned to avoid the trap. Like the moon calf that the writers of the 1920's were to put into their novels, I was the shy worshipper at a respectable distance of animated pink girl flesh.

She was certainly unobtainable for me. She was the University campus queen, Kate Cameron: a college prom trotter of fame, a flapper of flappers, unaware of a skinny, 110-pound roughneck trying to re-enter high school. We sat through the same show often—but apart.

The early fast-paced movies were exciting. Hube's orchestra tootling in the pit kept us in constant turmoil, we wise ones ever expectant of the moment when Hube would let go a gob of chewing tobacco juice into the open piano, a true artist's signal I found out for fast business with his right hand.

Hank Wells was three years my senior and a Scotsman of a good clan. He was serious, wide-eyed, slack-mouthed, lean-jawed, and charming as a trained bear. Come the cry of "Let's have a Coke," and someone was sure to say, "I'll buy Hank's."

Hank was the center of a personal cult. He played long and well and hard at the piano, head to one side, working the ivory.

When he had the yen to visit his Beta fraternity rooms, the gang usually followed. Then there was Gump Carter, always on hand, padding along, with his feet set apart at fifty-five degrees, partly bald, his mouth screwed into a nervous distortion in anticipation of hearing Hank do *Poor Pauline* again.

Gump had had a bad case of scarlet fever at the age of six and rumor was that he lost considerably more than his hair. Everyone liked Gump, and the Sunday music sessions were not complete without him. He organized more jam sessions than anyone else I know.

Gump's weakness was also my friend Kate, the college queen —he had a hard time keeping track of her whereabouts, in spite of his ability to show up, as she claimed, in three places at once.

"Have you seen Kate?" became an expression among the boys, meaning everything from "How are you?" or "To hell with it." From the Beta rooms we usually trekked to the Greek Candy Kitchen on the square. In the absence of a piano, someone dug up a nickel to start the pre-juke box music machine. We frequently ended up above Neeld's Hardware Store in the new rooms of Kappa Alpha Phi, the high school fraternity. A game of Five Hundred was always in full swing there, or Ed East was teaching the boys the new Kappa song he had written. I hung over the piano to catch a risqué lyric of some song Hank was swinging and playing:

Underneath the sheltering palms,
Oh, honey, wait for me.

"Come on, everybody in on the second chorus." And we'd bray away like hound dogs wormed on whiskey and black pepper. It was a singing, music-making students' world and I wallowed in it. I was hungry for friends and warm sounds.

Sunday nights the gang was behind the Observatory shooting craps or in the Kappa rooms until the early hours of the morning, playing cards, and quoting Kipling's "Hank of hair and a bone," and arguing about women. Then I staggered home to bed dog-tired, and Grandma Robison had the usual piece of apple pie set out for me. Nights were full of windy tossing of tree boughs outside my window.

3

My money melted away as if printed on snow flakes. I was broke and sitting in the Kappa hall, racking my poor brains. Someone said, "Come on, Hoag, play something."

I didn't feel like it. I had just come from making another luck-less tour of all the restaurants in search of a job.

"Not in the mood."

"Come on, Hoag. Try *Pretty Little Baby*. Hilas here wants to get his drums out."

"His drums?" I stared at the punk.

Hilas was the son of Mr. Steinmetz, the tailor. It never occurred to me he was interested in music. But there he was, looking like an asthmatic carp, dragging a set of drums in through the door, setting them up by the piano. I sat down and started playing.

"All right Hilas, beat the skins."

There were more important things on my mind than playing piano so the tailor's boy could practice on his drums, but he wasn't bad and he could get a lot better. The years in Indianapolis had not been in vain. I now had a steady beat in my left hand.

"Try and roll with the chords. Beat it out just a little ahead, Hilas."

He smiled through his fright sweat and his fat fingers twirled the sticks. I felt music surge up in me and I began to accent the upbeat, Reggie's trick. Hilas hit his drums. Soon I felt in key with their rhythm. Gone were the worries.

"Hilas, you're a sweetheart."

Gone the thoughts of a job. I had never played with drums before and had no personal conception of the surging lift they gave. They were like a mind-projecting machine, a perfect machine that with magic placed my fingers on keys that I had never hit before. I *felt* jazz; I was improvising like Reggie and it was coming *right*. Suit right, note right. Everybody gathered around and Kappa President Bob Strong said, "Hey let's throw a dance tonight. I'll give you guys five bucks apiece if we take in that much."

"We'll take it!" I shouted.

Five bucks! A fortune. The boys began to call the fraternity houses and spread the good word.

That night the new team of Hilas and Hoag walked into the twenty-by-forty upstairs raw pine hall over the hardware store. There were twenty earnest couples waiting, chewing their gum, inspecting their shoes, snapping their fingers. I knew I could play *one* piece with perfect confidence. A one-step.

I kept walking, my heart in my mouth, and sat down on the stool. My hands were spread out on the keyboard. I took a deep sucking breath and hit the keys. Hilas banged the drums. The building began to echo and couples began to swim across the dance floor in each other's arms. After five choruses, Hilas gave me the high sign to shut off with an ear-splitting crash of the cymbals and a clatter on the Chinese block. I was blowing like a harpooned whale, afraid to look up. Bobbed hair, lipsticked faces, two-lined mustaches, vasolined hair, spit curls, all made a montage of images before me.

"Great going!"

There was applause, what I took for thunderous applause, and more couples jammed the floor. College couples from the Student Building dance, high school kids arriving after the picture show. We were stealing crowds from all over town, even emptying the back seats of cars.

"Who's the kid on the piano?"

"That's not ragtime."

We went into a new number, me faking like mad. In the end, they had to turn couples away—at a buck a throw—and there was no way of ending the dance.

The pots and pans in the hardware store below clanked and rattled as I kept the piano keys warm. I remember lots of people, handshakes and hellos. I was helloed stiff. Voices yelled for water, beer, gin. People were hot and wet. I was a smiling physical wreck bent over the piano. By twelve o'clock I could hardly drag myself out of the hall on my rubber legs. I was pooped but happy. I was somebody now on the campus. All I had to do was finish high school. And I had earned five dollars. I would have to make more to get an education, but all night I dreamed of dancing feet.

4

I wasn't much of a student but high school was just for me a way-station to bigger things; the college campus was calling—and college piano waited—and meanwhile, I could begin to understand the Indiana soil, the limestone, and the underground water that causes maples to grow so big and beautiful. I was still goofy and poetic. There were trees three feet or more in diameter. They shot straight up, barren of branches for some fifty feet, then spread out into a huge umbrella of limbs and foliage like a green peacock's tail. Large beech trees shaded the Indiana University campus in my day and I wanted to grow tall as the trees—musically.

There were no walks, just natural paths winding among the trees, and they led to a street that bordered the east campus called Sorority Row. Quartets and early ragtime bands serenaded the girls at night, and everybody read or at least talked about *This Side of Paradise.*

The low stone wall bordering the campus on the south was the "spooning wall," usually occupied by quiet couples late at night who had stopped off there on their way from the Book Nook or a picture show.

To the north of the campus, bounding Dunn's Meadow and the old athletic fields, ran the Jordan River. On Indiana Avenue stood the Book Nook, a randy temple smelling of socks, wet slickers, vanilla flavoring, face powder, and unread books. Its dim lights, its scarred walls, its marked-up booths, unsteady tables, made campus history. It was for us King Arthur's Round Table, a wailing wall, a fortune telling tent. It tried to be a book store. It had grown and been added to recklessly until by the time I was a senior in high school it seated a hundred or so Coke-guzzling, book-annoyed, bug-eyed college students. New tunes were heard and praised or thumbed down, lengthy discussions on sex, drama, sport, money, and motor cars were started and never quite finished. The first steps of the toddle, the shimmy, and the strut were taken and fitted to the new rhythms. Dates were made and mad hopes born.

After that Kappa Alpha Phi dance I, too, hung out in the Book Nook for Cokes and coffee, and the tense, high-pitched enjoyment of just living. It was a step up for me. My high school bunch patronized the Candy Kitchen, but the Book Nook was a real honest-to-God college hangout for cave-type footballers, hair-oiled Don Juans—already in the John Held, Jr., styles. Batty and Bruce De Marcus made the scene. I had known them as tough little redheaded kids who fought each other bloody over a Daisy air rifle. They were back in Bloomington as saxophone players, and they were men of a limited but exciting world.

"Play, Hoag." Someone pushed me to the piano.

"Well—"

"Play."

I played for Batty and he played saxophone for me. When we finished, Batty was calling me dirty names and running his big freckled hands through my uncut hair.

"Oh you skinny bastard—*where* did you get that left hand—and *those* ideas!"

"I guess you've heard the stuff before."

"Never thought I'd hear it coming from you."

"Know any more, Batty?"

"Listen to these—and no clinkers."

What notes came from that horn—fast arpeggios and all of them tongued. Batty played an entire chorus of *Aunt Mammy's Jubilee* on one breath. His face grew Chinese-red and he gasped for air like a landed trout as he hit the last note. I loved him. Batty of the big hands, the red hair; the impulsive, talkative guy who two years later was as much a part of the New York scene as Wilson Mizner or Paul Whiteman. Later reports of him said, "He's the Four Hundred's choice over Rudy Weidoff and he carried it off with a farm boy charm. Why if he was walking up Broadway, toward the El Mirador Cafe, with his sax under his arm, and wanted to take a pee, Batty would stop a cab and ride two blocks to the Astor Hotel to do it."

The crowd in the Book Nook liked the music and we received two bids to play dances that night as a combo. The band just grew like Topsy, quickly to five pieces and had a fantastic local popularity. I was able to support myself and pay my school expenses.

I got a little fancy. I refused Grandma's offer of board and ate there only when I was too hungry to resist. I felt as Jonah must have felt when he spit in the whale's eye and said, "You can't hold me. *Nothing* can hold me."

VII

After we formed the band and started playing our dance music, I was pretty much on my own. I played for the same fraternities Mother had played for years before, and frequently in the same hall above the Monroe County Bank where as a kid I had stretched out across two chairs, dazed by noise and heat, and gone to sleep waiting for her to finish playing.

I was as interested in hearing good music as making it, and soon I was a kind of booker as well as a band leader, beating MCA into the racket. From then until I graduated from college, I invited bands to Bloomington, big bands who had the gift.

The high school fraternity dance of 1919 was planned to be an important affair. We had heard of a hot Negro band down in Louisville, and I signed them unseen and unheard. We put in three feverish days draping the new City Hall with gay banners, printing ornate programs, and talking of the coming of Louie Jordan's Band. (This was not the Louis Jordan from Arkansas who had a popular band in the thirties.)

I made big time in another way. I had the dream date of my life. Kate Cameron sensed a grand shindig that night and, not to miss it, she accepted a bid from me and had me dizzy with male pride.

There was a sense of expectancy when the big night arrived and Jordan's men, in fairly clean starched shirts and almost pressed suits, climbed up on the orchestra stand. We listened to the introductory crescendo from the little black piano player and our eyes went out on stems.

"Oh, this is *it!*"

The little fellow continued to test the action of the piano. He grinned, and hit a few chords of *Fate*, a masterpiece of minors. We laughed aloud and I forgot all about the soft yielding promise of Kate showing her rolled stockings under naked knees.

Jordan's men broke into *Russian Rag* as a grand march. But nobody marched. We did a wild shuffle of moaning pleasure. They changed the rhythm to a fast fox trot. The day of judgment was upon us.

I shouted: "I'm a Congo medicine man!"

Kate and I whirled and wilted to the floor. Someone said Hilas Steinmetz had fainted dead away. It was a breakdown, an insane dancing madness brought on by music—new, disjointed, unorganized music, full of screaming blue notes and a solid beat. We pioneers of it all broke down. I behaved to give the impression that I was unbalanced. And I think I was. Kate went home with a football player.

Jazz maniacs were being born and I was one of them. There were legions of us from New Orleans to Chicago *and* Bloomington was right in the middle of everything. Alleged by number counters to be the exact center of national population at that time. Louie and the boys played themselves out and the night seemed glowing with the discovery of something new and soul shattering. I went to my bed near dawn, feeling like all twelve disciples of a new godhead. I shivered as I remembered that band and its sounds.

It was never the music of nice comfortable well-bred people. It was the hungry notes of the disinherited, the enslaved and the ignorant. It was the meanness with a bare knife, it was the man in a cell, it was the cheap grab of diseased love, it was cold and rainy and it was steamboat steam and rivers in flood and mud every place (I was really keyed up). Sometimes it was the cakewalk and the breath of animal odors of the circus; it was brassy parades marching to bury a lodge brother with a ragtime dirge, *Didn't He Ramble*. It had the surface of a folk art—of what I wanted: simplicity and fun, as the rattle of early milk wagons made sounds in my hot head.

Reggie had trained me well. I understood. Blue music is antiphonal: singing a melody in antiphonal phrases while the instrumental skill is as busy as a fiddler's elbow weaving the music. The trumpet takes to the tremolo which shakes hell out of the timbre and tampers with the pitch. You can play it open or with a mute of corncob, hat, or hand—and it goes from the real high notes to a deep growl, getting dirty as it takes on the low-down variations. The notes count and the two that are the real blue ones are the flatted seventh and third. An extended blue scale is something to hear. Yes, I thought as I turned over near dawn, I'm on the road at last.

The blues I had heard were almost always in song form, usually a solo. The shouting blues were based on the hell-fire preaching styles of the churches, but used for joyful music.

2

Then I guess I slept, because when I opened my eyes the sun was high in the maples in the yard and the boss rooster had finished calling the hens to kneel.

I was not yet fulfilled, but I was anointed. I may have been a student, but I was never what you could call a scholar. There was so much life boiling around outside the classrooms that I didn't want to crack the books to see how it had been in the now dead past. There was more history being made around me than I could consume. Between math and music, math lost, and the contest between history and high notes left history behind.

"Hoag, you playing tonight?"

My high school studies suffered. Instead of doing my homework at night, I was out with the band making a living. I suffered with the fear I would not graduate. I wanted to go to Indiana University and that took good grades. In June when it was time to pass out the diplomas I was not among those who got one. It was a great disappointment but no surprise. I had flunked two studies, one of which was English History. The teachers urged me to make up the work during the summer months.

"If you do you can have your diploma in the fall, in time to enter college."

"I'll try, sir."

But the band had looked forward to their summer earnings, and I wasn't in good banking standing myself. We got a steady job at a movie theatre and that took up so much time study seemed something in another country. I made a visit to Indianapolis and brought my books along and laid them on the old gate-legged table.

"Mom," I pleaded, "you help me with these lessons. I'll never make it if you don't."

"Where do we start, Hoagland?"

"My teachers have given me a bunch of assignments."

My mother said firmly, "I didn't raise any dumb children. You'll study."

"I have to mail this teacher the assignments all summer."

"Well, I've a lot of postage stamps saved up. I could use a little English history myself. Who was the king who chopped off all his wives' heads?"

I said I didn't know and we looked it up. I set aside two hours a day for school work. When I had completed them I mailed them to the teacher. This went on all of a long hot summer, with new assignments coming to plague me every few weeks and to prove I did have a brain. He was a nice man, my teacher, and I'm quite sure he knew that a keen knowledge of English history would never mean a thing to me, so I passed and received a diploma.

I was close to tears when I held the bit of fancy printed paper that stated that one Hoagland Howard Carmichael had graduated from Bloomington High School, and could call himself a half-educated man. I spun Grandma Robison around, kissed her cheeks, and shouted, "I made it, I made it, easy as a second chorus."

"By the skin of your teeth, and you don't look like no professor to me. Go mow the lawn, and don't cut down the rose bushes."

But I could see Ma had a lot of pride in me, almost an awe; we weren't a family who had had time to pile up much education in the last hundred years. We were too busy. Education and degrees are very common today, but forty years ago we still remembered that Abe Lincoln didn't have more than a few weeks education, and any older musician could tell you no jazz man worth his salt admitted to any educating at all. Wearing shoes, using the cuspidor, and changing his socks once a week was civilization to him. Those of us who could read a little music hid the fact from our fellow maniacs. Playing perfectly by ear was something as fine as wildcatting a well or discovering a new continent. Life was simpler and harder for us Dan'l Boones of the jazz age.

3

The year 1920 is an easy time to go back to, because it was one of the happiest times of my life and I never feel too far away from it. In September I enrolled and moved into the Kappa Sigma house. I made many friends there. There was Wilbur from Huntington; Jack who was a roughneck from Terre Haute; Keller, the South Bend Dutchman with a big nose; there were Pink Cadou and Louie Mitchener and Stu Gorrell from Bremen. Louie was the handsomest man of us, particularly when we dressed him up in a borrowed tuxedo.

We were smart aleck and eager, popular with the upperclassmen, happy except when the grades came through, and we tried to uphold the daffy social prestige of our house on the campus. Music was not the dominating factor among our crowd. Fun was.

We called ourselves "Friends and Sitters." We'd sit in front of the fireplace for bull sessions. "Go to work" meant "grab a chair, boy, and toast your shins." Once old Pink hit the chair after lunch, he was a goner for his one o'clock class.

And the noise. The noise that never quite leaves your head if you have lived in a house along with thirty odd and exuberant guys. And the smells . . . flat beer and acrid ashy air drifting toward you as you cling to a last few moments' sleep after a bull session that kept you all awake the night before. The odor of wet basketball shoes and old catchers' mitts. The smell of that particular hair lotion Louie doused on his head and which came from the steaming bathroom . . .

And the talk. The talk of classes and lasses, and pass the molasses . . .

"Get your ass out of bed, Hogwash!"

You scramble from the covers and fight for a chance at one of three washbasins. Lousy breakfast, Spanish class . . . more classes. A chance to stand too close to that cute little dame on the steps . . . lunch on creamed chip beef and potatoes.

Announcement: There'll be a meeting of the freshmen in the card room immediately after lunch.

"What have we done now?"

"Shoot me, I dunno."

"You guys have got to watch your table manners. And tomorrow this house is gonna be cleaned *right*. It looks like the inside of a tornado. Unnastand?"

A dull science class . . . back to the house under strict orders: "You have to study. It's got to be quiet around here."

Five o'clock. White shirt for dinner . . . borrow a guy's tie . . . string beans and round steak.

"What does that cook try for, anyway? Can't she just *cook* meat instead of *tanning* it?"

"When you gonna pay me that six bits, fella? I gotta heavy date and I'm going to need it."

"Ten-thirty! Get your ass in bed, Rhinie."

The wonderful weekends. Housework all done. Football practice, the Theta front porch . . . the Book Nook . . . the phone ringing and the resultant rush to make a date.

The Tri-Delt hop. Benny Benson singing *Cuban Moon*. Hurry and get your date home before twelve-thirty. Back to the Book Nook. Somebody has a pint. "Play the piano for us, Hoagy." Dwight Van Osdale reaching to the big yellow moon for the top notes of *Love Me and the World Is Mine*.

Four years with the friends I had wanted so desperately, and found so satisfying. The bands and dances, the crises, and the music that kept coming out. And then the night Harry Hostetter ran nearly a mile to get closer to hear it because he had hunted it all over the world, then found it in Bloomington.

Jordan's band continued to play at local dances and sometimes they could be prevailed upon—by the use of cash—to stay over and play a Sunday afternoon session in the Book Nook. The motto of all listeners was, "Shake it and break it and hang it on the wall!"

These were epic jam sessions I never forgot. Roof raisers. But me and my little band didn't absorb Jordan's playing exclusively. We were young, feisty, and impressionable. We soaked up musical atmosphere here and there, an impression from a stone-age recording, an occasional hep trick from someone's style, and frequently a whole arrangement from a fancy band. What this sounded like when it came out of our band was personal and, I suppose, still raw.

It was the great time of experimentation in jazz, with only enough precedents to stimulate individual and original exploration but not enough nailed down examples to set any definite patterns as rigid rules. Everyone was holding on tight on his own.

"You hear Oliver?"

"He sure does it good."

"There was a piano player called Jelly Roll—what he does to a piano!"

"They play a real horn in Chi."

"Where can we steal some styles?"

"It's all free and easy, if you have an ear."

The jazz patterns we heard in one band would be picked up and expanded into new flights of fancy by other musicians the next night. The first rumble of the Roaring Twenties was upon us, and our heads were filled with the crazy new sounds. If I could take you back in time.

Anyhow, let me take you by the hand and lead you into the Book Nook on an average afternoon. That little gink over there flogging the piano—that's me. The one with the long nose and the exerted red face. The large freckled youth with the saxophone, the one making those long blue notes, that's Batty De Marcus. The high cheekboned unshaved youth slumped in a booth, that's a fellow called "Monk" Moenkhaus. He's composing a poem, and perhaps we hear Monk's weird coyote-howl laugh even above our efforts.

"Hiwahoo! Yahoo! What rhymes with purple?"

"Katie's drawers."

Observe the natives in poses of bored indifference—a fashionable state of mind: the males in greased hair, long sideburns, tight jackets, bell-bottomed pants. The flappers in knee skirts above large open overshoes, no girdles, often no underwear. They are seated in booths. Pete Costas, the proprietor, is punctuating his English with Greek epithets because Klondike Tucker, the Negro chef, has balled up an order.

"Gol damn it—is easy—hom wit eggs—hom wit hot cake—that boy is no Grik short order sport."

Howard "Wad" Allen is curved into a seat across from Monk, and the thing he toys with, fingering it sensuously, is a piece of lemon meringue pie. He loves to pat a lemon meringue pie—though blueberry will serve in a pinch.

Wad came to Indiana University in the fall of 1921, from Washington, Indiana, and he brought with him an abundance of easy self-confidence, a cheap mail-order violin, the praise of his parents, and the prayers of his music tutor. "Don't ever tell who taught you."

He had earned his college entrance money giving violin lessons to a big class of pupils in Washington. "Boy, it was the cat's pyjamas hearing all those little murders scraping catgut all together. Nearly busted my eardrums."

The violin had saved Wad's first year in the University by making twelve dollars a week playing motion picture music. Wad's roommate bought a saxophone on which he was given to slap-tonguing arpeggios. Wad, open-mouthed, heard the brass call and his own aspirations as a concert violinist withered away. He bought a saxophone. "I mean, I couldn't let that jelly bean make *all* the noise."

William E. "Monk" Moenkhaus was a professor's son. Crossing the Atlantic on cattle boats, he had made several trips to Switzerland and Germany. "Once you've seen one Alp, you've seen 'em all!" He walked with a slight limp which, according to Monk, was the result of a dreadfully exciting accident he suffered while climbing the Matterhorn in a storm. A lie, of course, but we enjoyed believing it.

"Lost two guides and a brandy-carrying dog."

Monk's face was big as a clock dial and bony; out of it stared watery gray eyes. The long hands that dangled at his sides wore blue fingernails trimmed in dark mourning. He made straight A's in a bored sort of way. "Only peasants take pleasure in good marks." As his writings progressed, he became the founder and chief spokesman of a campus cult which he named the Bent Eagles. ("We owe the Indians something—let it be avant-garde prose.") Through his Dada and surrealistic nonsensical writings, he became a campus character in the eyes of most people. And to some, a fabulous literary figure in the mood of Ezra Pound.

Monk had other accomplishments. He could put an eight ball into the side pocket with dirty pool skill and his choice of invective, thrown at the balls that failed to drop, were masterpieces later to be printed by Henry Miller. More important, Monk had studied classical music both at home and abroad and his attacks on the defenseless piano and cello were applauded at faculty functions, high school recitals, and sometimes by his college fraternity brothers, the Phi Gams. But these classical instruments were destined to be shoved aside in favor of a battered bass horn when the roots of jazz took hold in Bloomington. Why he never played in my orchestras I can't remember except maybe I couldn't stand to watch him blow the thing. He attacked it as a lover would a long-lost mistress, and he played as if he were to be taken out in ten minutes to face a firing squad.

The Bent Eagles became a screwball extracurricular campus organization with headquarters in the Book Nook. Pete Costas still owns a printed "Commencement Program." Pete is listed in this lampoon as President of the Book Nook Faculty, and

Hoagland Carmichael, D.D. (Doctor of Discord), Prof. of Cacophony.

I got hit by grapefruit rinds hurled at me when my music grew too sedate for other ears.

"Hey, now!" I dodged the rinds and stopped playing. "Monk is going to read his creation!"

There was a moment of quiet despair. "Oh no!" Monk rose calmly: "This is for minds keyed to vistas beyond the horizons of so-called rational thought."

"Sit down, you educated ape!"

> "Blooters, thou knowest no Heaven.
> Blooters, thou knowest only us.
> Bugs, men, tarts and fowls—
> They are the Children of Heaven. The end."

All Bent Eagles put their fingers to their mouths and whistled like idiots—which we were.

Not daunted by the whoops Monk read another:

> "If castor oil removes a boil
> And Oscar rows a goat
> Don't use your feet on shredded wheat
> Inhale it through a boat."

There were wild yells of pain. We shrieked appreciation. "Better than that vet, Longfellow!" The voice of a non-Bent Eagle asked plaintively, "What does it mean?"

Monk beat his brow. "This poor churl doesn't know what those immortal lines convey."

"It means just what it says," Wad Allen said, tossing a pie to the floor upside down, just to hear the sound. "Just *exactly* what it says."

Monk sighed, "Any of you Philistines want to go out of here on the back of your neck?"

I was trying to interrupt Monk long enough to say something about Jordan's band, but Monk wouldn't listen and Wad Allen came in then. He didn't listen either because he had a piece of paper in his hand and he wanted to read from it. It was another work from the pen of Monk. Wad read it to us aloud. As he read it we rocked with the silent glee that bound us together because we loved each other.

Thanksgiving Comes But Once a Dozen

Scene:

Somewhere between a large hotel. Perhaps there is a fire. People are snowing themselves under and the heavens are threatened with lard. In the background are firemen selling small pears.

Enter:

Women's Compound Tonsil Union singing:
"On glands and wheels the bakers roar,
As Harper's chickens, four by four,
Leap across the bathroom floor.
Amen."
(Cheers by Mrs. Baker)

First W.C.T.U.

"Friends, cannons and Thursday!"
(Louder cheers by Mrs. Baker who is affectionately called Old Aunt Cancer in her home town of West Hawkins, Nebraska)

Second W.C.T.U.

"I am from Roaring Pork, Idaho. I favor neither beer near the keg, near beer the keg, nor keg near beer."
(Old Aunt Cancer loses control and has an attack of chetherweg)

Third W.C.T.U.

(Unable to locate mouth and is speechless)

The End

I was high. I walked over to the piano. What I played we called *The Death of a Hog*. Wad Allen chanted an impromptu lyric. Monk screamed his delight. The Greeks who owned the Book Nook hovered unhappily in the background and curious on-lookers straggled out. We had the place to ourselves and we gave in to the dirge and to the piano and our own hysterical delight.

4

The Nook was our club—Moenkhaus, Wad Allen, Harry Hostetter, and myself used it for bull sessions. Harry was on my side now, musically speaking, watching me and listening to every note. I was his protégé and he wanted me to be good. We talked of things we were puzzled about. We confessed bewilderment and doubts and should a girl neck first date out? Are raccoon coats permitted on non-college males? Does gin taste better when doctored with home-brewed beer? Who is greater—Babe Ruth or President Harding? We also wondered where we were going.

Monk said, "Let's go paint signs on tin lizzies."

"Let's jam a bit."

"You're all so ignorant," said Monk, who was reading a broad named Virginia Woolf.

I protested. "Not ignorant about the music."

Buddy Bolden put a hat over the bell of his horn to get fuzzy effects and Freddie Keppard, another Creole, who had brought his band to the Columbia Theater in New York about 1915, showed them how to use a mute. They liked their music more in keeping with their climate though, slow and raspy.

"I hear they put Buddy in an asylum," Wad said. "I hope with all my heart that they didn't take his horn away from him."

"I'm wondering," I said, "what Buddy Bolden had in his brain when he blew the introduction to what we now call *Tiger Rag?*"

Monk yawned. "Who cares? I'm going to die any day now." (He did die. Just a year before Bix and the same year Buddy Bolden did). "I'm ready for bed—and every bed is prepared to be a death bed."

Back on the University of Indiana campus, we faced incongruous times. A fat cat member of the state legislature introduced a bill providing a fine and imprisonment for any female who wore on the streets "skirts higher than three inches above the ankle." The international news we ignored, all about German reparations, the Dawes Plan, and U.S. Marines pulling out of the

Dominican Republic. While a few of us early jazz enthusiasts were doodling and weaving our own daffy pattern across dance floors, larger segments of the population sat spellbound beneath the shadows on a movie screen. Clara Bow could bring a lump to your throat with the magic of her hips and eyes.

All around us snooks, members of the night-sheeted Ku Klux Klan were rising by the hundreds of thousands—and they were more active in Indiana than in any other state. The big indoor game was mah-jongg; even the campus cats played it. The new music, the steady beat of jazz spread. But the restlessness caused changes: Illicit liquor flowed faster, isolated gangsters ran many cities as personal empires. And women, in spite of legislators and clerical lament, were still shortening dresses, hair, and their reputations. And driving me slightly goofy with desire.

We were big-eyed with wanting, with making fun. A mixture of girls' names, old cars, unpolished shoes. A merging of youth with old trees, rain on sidewalks, and the smell of seasons. We got our kicks from the scrape of couples on a dance floor, the sound of music late at night across water reflecting a moon low enough to bite. Untested as we were, ignorant in many ways of the adult world (not yet called square), we did not brood too often, but tried to crowd life and get change from it. I liked to laugh and know I was part of a group, daffy to some, but it was *my* group, rich with the sense of belonging and also precious because I knew it couldn't last. There was a wide wide world out there, with jobs to be found and work to be done that fitted, or didn't fit, our moods. Being young, we knew it couldn't bend and push us around the way it had our fathers. If we worried about the things to come in private, in public we played the clown.

TWO

"The Little Stars Climb"

VIII

It was not always kicks and laughs; it was sometimes sadness. One Christmas we played Newcastle, Indiana. Our college band was at its peak and we were very full of our music and of ourselves. It got around to Christmas—the third Christmas for my last college band. "Carmichael's Syringe Orchestra," we called it.

"Alas," Wad Allen says, "a herd of elephants are singing Christmas carols below our window."

None of us laugh as we listen.

We have just played a dance. It is two o'clock in the morning and Wad has just come in. Somebody pulls the sliding doors in the dingy hotel room exposing an even dingier room, drab and cold.

There on a little table is a Christmas tree, dilapidated and maimed. One forlorn candle burning at the top of its scraggly branches. We stand looking at this little scrub and I finally muster all my courage to speak in an exaggeratedly deep voice.

"Well, well, look what we have here! Something for little Waddie Allen—'cause he's been a good little boy. And here's a surprise for Artie Baker. . . ."

A potato grater for Wad. A piece of rope for Art Baker. Someone gets a funnel. It is too much for us. No one yells an inanity. No one speaks. We look at the tree and the single candle shimmers and flickers and is reflected in the tears that stand, suddenly, in our eyes. We stand there, six little children of jazz, brave in long pants, and then the candle sputters out and we are afraid.

After a moment someone says something and we laugh. A little laugh. The band, the college band—one for all and all for one—and it wasn't corny.

It was the beginning of what F. Scott Fitzgerald is supposed to have named "The Jazz Age." Maybe he did, or only borrowed the title from someone in a speak-easy over after-dinner coffee spiked with grappo of a very high potency. He was a fancy hell-raiser whom I met from time to time, and like so many, he burned the candle at both ends.

Prohibition had been put over, but people didn't stop drinking. They were just served it in teacups. Monk—the Dada poet—saw the change in music, in sex, in art, and in drinking. He said to me: "The Jazz Age? A thing or a group gets a label stuck on it, Hoagy, and you can't pull it off. Someone once called something the Holy Roman Empire, and historians prove it wasn't Roman, or holy, or an empire any longer. But that didn't matter; the name stuck. Just so they'll talk of the Jazz Age."

"Could be," I said.

Monk was right. In the next few years we pioneers saw jazz every place and blamed for everything; the wail of a saxophone was the sound of doom to a lot of fat cats. An artist named John Held, Jr., drew the jazz-flapper: long long legs, cropped shingled hair, a cigarette in one hand, liquor flask in the other. Her sheik was apple-headed, his hair buttered down tightly. He wore wide-bottom trousers, a racoon coat, a crumpled little hat pushed up in front, drove a Stutz Bearcat or a tin lizzie and played or danced to jazz a lot. Freud was the high priest of the avant-garde salons where all the young folk drank and jazzed it away, and went to Paris or died young.

"Or both," Monk once said. "Most writers who record the events of the Jazz Age really know nothing of the real jazz. They mostly stick to the Ritz."

2

We barnstormed and slept in buses, ate road-house food, met the early jazz giants. But we didn't write about it, so it went into history all ass-backwards.

We saw jazz, already in the dives and moving into the speak-easies, set the tone and color of the country. We all dreamed of super jazz bands. Jazz didn't change the morals of the early twenties. But it furnished the music, I noticed, to a change in manners and sexual ideas. Women wore less and wore it in a slipping, careless way on the dance floors. Every girl wore silk stockings—and many rolled them beneath the knees so that every sitting-down showed the American female thigh, nude and lush, anywhere from kneecap to buttocks. ("You just know she wears them," said the ads.)

There was more lipstick, and one wondered at its color. Hair was still cut shorter, hung close to the skull; perfume was poured on—and not only among the factory girls and salesgirls—but on the housewives, the Main Streeters in Sinclair Lewis' best-seller, the society queens, and the wives of local bankers. Jazz was seen as the music of the rising sense of revolt.

While we played jazz, aging males acted parts in road-house weekends, crossroad flappers became chain smokers. Cigarettes were also for ladies now (even the jazzman's reefers), but of course not as much in public as in private or at parties. The protesting stomach showed that you got enough to drink at college dances, tired feet that you could do the dance steps. Charleston, Black Bottom, all the new stomps. Mixed drinking was the thing. Drinking out of a flask by necessity. Jazz dance hall cloakroom drinking by young girls in their teens and their dates.

"Got a jolt?"

"White mule." (Pure alcohol.)

"Down the hatch. *Ow!*" (Pause and shiver.) "Boy, that's *good!*"

"Who's your sugar?"

"She's the bee's knees."

"The turtle's tonsils."

"Baby doll, you're a sport."

"Boop-boop-a-doop."

"Drag the body on the dance floor."

"You're the cat's kittens."

"Is zat so?"

"Banana oil."

"Horse feathers."

The intimate talk didn't shock the smart folk. One was surprised how far we had come from Chic Sales' whiz-bang humor. Those words in James Joyce's smuggled-in texts or Bessie Smith's records—the low-down ones—were all soon collectors' items.

If I was part of some of this it was as a young man feeling his oats—and if I had something that kept me away from a lot of the most vicious part of it, it was because I had a fixation of my own, the piano.

"Hoagland, must you play so much?"

"Have I been playing a lot?"

"Don't you know? It's like a trance."

And it was. I was really hooked.

I kept exploring the piano and learning. The tolerance and understanding of our neighbors was amazing; living next to someone who hammered on the piano at all hours and all keys, hammered out barbaric music, often badly, groping for new tones and scales. Kindly patient neighbors suffered unprotesting (usually) while the little monster searched the piano keys.

3

I was creative, too. I aspired to write songs even before I entered high school. Every minute I could I banged away, hunting chords on the old upright; there are no sounds more irritating than unfound music.

We lived then in a double house, connected to our neighbor by a not so soundproof wall. With its two upstairs windows, one on each side of a bay, the house looked as if it were winking or raising its eyebrows when the blinds were raised in wonder at all the noise. We lived there for several months, with tenants coming and going in the other side of the house, but with no real complaints. "Loud little fella, isn't he?"

Then a man who worked at night moved in. He arrived home

at six o'clock in the morning and went to bed at seven, to sleep he thought. I got up about that time, ate my breakfast, and then practiced loud chords until time to leave for school.

After several mornings of this sawmill routine, the poor wretch could stand it no longer. Sleepless, eyes swollen, he came over and told my mother, "Ma'am, I'm dyin'. I got to get some sleep and would you please tell that kid to stop his banging on the piano. I drive the night express to Chicago. I'll kill two hundred people if I fall asleep in the engine cab!"

My mother apologized. "We're sorry to bother you. But Hoagland's practice lasts only a few minutes each morning and I would under no circumstances tell him to quit playing."

"Why, ma'am?"

"He has some talent for composing and it's important to encourage him."

"It's a matter of life and death!"

"I suggest, mister, it would be wise to move to another place. I have no intention of curbing the boy."

He left in a huff to hunt a moving man.

"Hoagland, play *that* part again."

"It's loud."

"We're free Americans. Play it."

4

The only place I was silent was in Bucktown among the Negroes. I liked what I heard. Their banjos and jugs and cigarbox fiddle music did a lot to inject me deeper into jazz. Negroes and the hill-whites and the fever-shaking crackers and the rivermen in their shanty-boats produced *Barbara Allen, Froggie Went A-Courtin'*, and *Casey Jones*. They knew them all, and more.

I liked best *Frankie and Albert* which led to the more famous *Frankie and Johnny* or *Lily and Frankie Baker*. Also *Ole Master Had A Yalla Gal* and *Mr. Boll Weevil*.

"That white boy—he all ears!"

Frankie and Albert had a lot of grandchildren.

Rubber-tired carriage
Kansas City hack
Took poor Albert to the cemetery
And forgot to bring 'im back.

Oh, he was my man,
But he done me wrong!

Me and the Negroes picked up the mood. The kids sang as they played hide-and-seek and stickball and tag.

All hid?
All hid,
    Five ten fifteen twenty
Is all hid?

Way down yonder
By the devil's town
Devil knocked my daddy down
    Is all hid?

The Negroes were often pious. The church laments that led to the blues had the most feeling and tenderness, and I'd sit listening in their whitewashed shack churches that smelled of laundry soap and old wood:

I wonder as I wander out under the sky
How Jesus, our Savior, did come for to die
For poor orn'ry people like you and like I
I wonder as I wander out under the sky.

It got me more than white church music. No one really knows who sang them first, but the old rotting rafters shook as everybody clapped out:

You got to cross that lonesome valley
You got to cross hit by yourself,
There hain't no one goin' to cross hit for you
You got to cross hit by yourself.

Bucktown may not have been respectable from our viewpoint, but I found it human and full of the same emotions, pities, cruelties as the upper layers of society. I didn't find it amusing when a white neighbor said, "Where ah come from, big plantation folk —we had nigrahs to burn."

It wasn't all sacred music. The Negroes worked hard for poor pay. They were exploited, so they turned to rum and pleasuring, and that music was often sad and scary, too.

> Way down in Boogie Alley
> Ain't nothin' but skulls and bones
> An' when I get drunk
> Blues goin' to take me home.

The first blues singers were powerful gals. Gertrude Ma Rainey, they told me, was the best. Born in Columbus, Georgia, around 1886. Her folks were Negro minstrel people who trouped the country. When only fifteen, she married Will Pa Rainey and went out with him in the Rabbit Foot Minstrels singing the blues. Sang the blues in rain or shine, in tent shows and joints, in camps and on the stage. A Negro vaudeville circuit made her famous and sometimes she got paid. Ma was short and she was heavy, and she was black. Ma found a girl named Bessie Smith in Tennessee, and helped her get on, Bucktown said.

For years Ma sang the blues. Her recordings were primitive things and only hinted at her putting over a blues number. They were made for the Negro trade by an obsolete process, sung into a large horn. Later I heard some of them in Bucktown, and she sang it somber, simple, and mellow, her vibrato easy and broad. Ma took the rocking rhythm and made it big.

I wasn't doing any better as a student, but listening to unrespectable stuff in a Negro shack, a man can get an education by just being ignorant.

> Cat man cat man
> Stay away from my door
> At night.
> Prowlin' round my back door
> When I'm gone
> You know that ain't right.

I wasn't dumb—the sensual content hit me at first. But I already knew as much as the bees and flowers.

I was still hunting my great love and was in fear that I would find her, settle down, and become a Babbitt (mock hero of the new best seller). It didn't stop me eyeing the girls. Thinking back, what a lousy lover I was! Quick as a rabbit and no fun at all for the girls. I suspect most of us were, and a good thing, too; fewer unwed mothers and fewer home-wreckers. I couldn't have wrecked a home.

5

We didn't live the fancy College Humor life. The hangovers in the Ritz, the near misses on the Princeton highways, the puking in gold-fixtured bathrooms, the crazy *crazy* weekends at Amherst, Yale, and Rutgers. That was written later by fancy novelists who never came to Indiana. Our girls were trying to make he-men of us but we were still hicky kids.

Every girl I knew wanted to own long strands of pearls in a hangman's knot and borrow the college boys' pull-over sweaters of fuzzy wool, to which were pinned Greek letter frat pins; the more the merrier. Flat-chested girls were the rule, with no shape visible from arm pits to thighs; the mammary glands had not yet become pin-up art.

Ball bearing hips, jello haunches free of girdles or even underwear. Soft felt styles and the first of the shoddy, shiny rayons. Seated on their spines, legs in the air, in the Stutz Bearcats or the high-nosed Packards, wrapped in school colors at games, kicking the lock step in hotel rooms and country clubs, while the band played *I'll Get By If I Have You* and *As Time Goes By.*

> Close the doors!
> They're comin' through the windows.
> Close the windows!
> They're comin' through the doors.

These were the girls in our lives but not for me, not for life, anyhow.

"Hoagland," I told myself, "take a girl who'll settle down and make a home, and have a couple of kids, and sew with her fingers instead of beating out the half-notes. A girl like Dorothy . . ."

I was thinking of Dorothy Kelly, that first love of mine back in high school days. But my thoughts were drawn back less to a particular, almost forgotten girl than to the feeling Dorothy had first called up within me. I had met her two years before this period of restlessness of which I speak.

It was when I re-entered Bloomington High way back in '19— and I felt old. Older than the little girls with pigtails and shy provocative smiles. Hilas sat beside me in study hall.

"Psst! Who's that bunch of sweetness across the table?"

"Dorothy Kelly."

"How old is she?"

"Fifteen."

"Jeez! Cute as the devil."

"She asked who you were."

"Really, does she 'go' for me?"

"She just wondered. Send her a note and see."

In a moment I shot a note across the table: "Hello, Hilas says you're some kid—and I bet you are. Meet me in the hall, baby."

She read the note with studied indifference. I liked the way she turned her chin up. I decided to give her a play.

Hilas slipped a note to me.

"Hilas said you were nice, but I bet you're not. I won't meet you in the hall."

I waited for her on the stairs after school. I almost remember the pattern of the gingham plaid she wore. I do remember slim graceful legs sheathed in white cotton stockings. I remember that the stockings didn't wrinkle.

"You know who I am, don't you?"

"Oh yes, Mr. Fresh-guy."

"Yeah! Well, I wouldn't mind having a date with you."

"Well, I *would*."

"I'd like to get acquainted."

"Mother doesn't allow me to have dates with anyone but Tony."

"But . . . Tony's just a *kid*."

"Yes. That's the reason."

It was nearly a week before she would let me come to her house to see her. A week of watching her in classes, keeping her in sight in the crowded halls—hearing about Tony taking her out in a car. Then, one day, she let me come to her house.

"I heard you play, last night. I was at the dance."

"Tony took you, didn't he?"

"Um . . . I love the way you play. You and Hilas."

"Thanks. I don't know much about music."

"Play . . . play for me."

"What?"

The next thing I can remember, there was a song, the first tune, I suppose, that I was conscious of composing. Sometimes I think I've forgotten it, only to find that I can still play it. There aren't any words to it, but it runs along lightly, merrily, a thread of feeling holding it together.

Dorothy sat beside me and her cheeks turned a little pink.

"Why, that's lovely. Did you really make it up for me?"

Afterwards we sat on the davenport and held hands. She let me kiss her once. I ran out of the house, not knowing why, but I was back in a few minutes, talking quietly with her through a bedroom screen. And then, I walked away and looked at her little frame house as if I'd built it with my own hands.

I was in love. Swiftly, surely, eternally. It was as beautiful as the first flatted fifth I had found and for me it was a lasting thing. I never completely got over it. Six years later she married Art Baker, my trumpet player.

6

What was I like in my teens? Earning my way, trying to get through high school, wanting to go to college? Not sure yet that my music was everything, I often watched the local red-necked lawyers on the courthouse steps getting their two-toned shoes shined. They would light up their stogies, slap each other on the back, and then go into court to take opposite sides for and against some poor victim. Why not be a lawyer, I often thought. Smoke good cigars, have a fat, laughing face, get my paws manicured by the peroxide blonde with the wet open mouth at the hotel, flash a diamond Elk's head stickpin, be a big shot in ward politics.

"Poverty puts no gravy on your corn meal mush," Ma Robison used to say.

The lawyer's profession was a lure for a poor boy in shabby clothes hurrying through life with no brass rings for free rides on the merry-go-round. Dad had suggested law; maybe it was time to please him with this.

I was still lean, still small, but I wasn't as rabbity as I had been. I had real friends and I had music. As to looks, I wasn't Milton Sills or Francis X. Bushman, actors that fluttered female hearts at the movies, but I was keeping my head a little higher and had a deeper interest in things outside myself. There were two young Hoags: the public piano player, and the kid making dreams. All my life I've been trying to merge the two. Just when I think that at last they overlap each other, with no edges showing, one of them gets up and runs.

At college, I made a lot of dreams, but there was also the public life, the campus life, the frat house existence, the after-hours over cokes and hamburgers. There were long sessions at the Book Nook piano, and I've the photograph to prove it, me in a long oversized green slicker and a sphinx-club knitted cap on my head, showing the edge of a high country haircut in back.

Always there was a sense of nature in the midst of these buildings in which we ate, slept, studied, courted, danced, and pranked. A world without trees was unthinkable. We met under their shadows, we dated there, carved bark with penknives, leaned against them, stole rides on kids' swings. In season we saw our trees molt, go bare, come back in bud, turn green, then gold and red. The best smell on earth could be a dusk with a parasol of stars coming out and people burning raked leaves, the pungent smoke escaping from the darting red-orange flames. That's all, just leaves burning and night falling to earth and getting into your bones. You couldn't explain it, but it was one of those moments.

We would get restless and break out, just ride the country roads, sing and slap at each other, and go out to bray at the hunters' moon. It was a communion of young people that we never shared with our elders.

IX

I don't know about genius, but I've had a lot to do with talent —and I've been struck by a fact: the middle west producing all those musical mutations in the twentieth century. In the farmlands among the Indiana-Iowa corn, and from the cow-pasture universities, there sprouted a beardless priesthood of jazz players and jazz composers. Instead of buttermilk and Blackstone, we were nurtured on bathtub gin and rhythm.

The professors in thick glasses can't account for the phenomenon, this mystic midwest response to jungle beat and plantation chant. The explanations I have heard are more ingenious than convincing. I never succeeded in getting a satisfactory answer. It just happened, like a thunder cloud. It may sound sentimental to say that young men caught fire in a quest for beauty, that they dedicated themselves to its realization, starving and striving, laughing, dreaming, and dying. So it's sentimental, but I think it's true. I became aware of what jazz means to those of us who felt it profoundly—a glow of tonal perfection in harmonies and beats that had exaltation in it. The soggy, esoteric piddling of the pundits never impressed me much. They were always telling us *why* and *how* we did it, and we knew very well we didn't do it that way, or for their reasons.

My own involvement is harder to put in order or, rather, harder for me to define. I had a drive that I call my Hoosier heritage, and the desire to make something of my life, something solid and respectable. Yet I was usually in conflict with that dreamer inside me.

My band kept busy playing for the local movie house, but

most of the first summer I frittered away hanging around other bands—in Indianapolis, Chicago, the lake shore resorts.

I returned to the I.U. campus musically rejuvenated. When autumn came I had to start thinking about a career. Some people said I should study law and I had been thinking of it. "When everybody starves, a lawyer is eatin' high on the hog."

Could I become an Oliver Wendell Holmes and sit on the Supreme Court, or a big corporation attorney with a battery of Harvard law clerks and a yacht anchored in the East River? I felt more like Huck Finn, wanting to play hot music like Louis Armstrong, write blues like Handy or Clarence Williams, be part poolroom loafer and sit in the shadows of jam sessions, listening.

After I met George Johnson and saw how the jazz life was, I decided for one time to try to be respectable, to study for the bar. I had lost most of the band anyway. The boys I had lined up ran out on me to join the campus competitor.

"Hoagy, this guy can read music."

"I can't match that, fellas."

Four of us went to Boston that fall to see the Indiana-Harvard game. With ten dollars between us, borrowed from one of the more warm-blooded professors, I, as the smallest, was buried under the pile of luggage. I stayed there until we reached Cleveland the next morning.

The porter spotted me and I had to win his confidence by buying him his breakfast and telling him I knew all his relatives in Bucktown. He managed to conceal me from the conductor by standing me behind the toilet door. "Just yo' keep flushin' that crapper!" Later I was locked in a linen compartment, trying to look like a towel.

Our spirits were high, and for a gag the team put me in a big music store window in Boston. I played the piano and was billed as "The Shipwrecked Dog-Faced Boy Wonder. Speaks no tongue, plays any sound by ear. Do Not Feed. Will Drink *Anything*."

2

Indiana lost the game in a grey, driving rain, and we rode home with long faces and sore tails. Somebody else had to ride in the john.

I attended big games all over the country, from Ivy League to cornbelt silo teams. There was never anything like the football crowds of the twenties and the wild weekends that followed. The college boys and girls in their strange clothes, muffled in moth-eaten furs, with bowler hats, carrying banners and blankets and lots of bathtub booze. At Harvard the students rode in collections of the most fascinating cars ever made, the Stutzes and the Jordans, the old-style Packards, and the snotty Pierce-Arrows, the air-sucking Franklins and the snazzy crouch of the few import jobs, whose hoods were closed not by hooks, but by a broad leather belt. *That* was class. In Indiana, we never had much better than a Ford car and bailing wire repairs.

We drove wildly with primitive brakes. The roads were still farm trails, service stations had signs reading *Free Air,* and comfort stations offered corn husks or old mail order catalogues. If nothing else served, we'd pile into the flivvers of the lucky owners, tin sides decorated by banal wit: *Four Cylinders, Six Girls; Don't Say No, Say Maybe; Nobody Ever Died for Wabash;* and certain erotic mottos written in an easy to make out number code.

Sometimes I helped around the house when they caught me. The old Armstrong upright was getting out of tune and so with the help of my sisters and a couple of neighbor kids I took it apart on our front porch, cleaned and washed the hammers and keys, dusted out the box and soundboard, put it back together and then tuned it all in one afternoon. It sounded fine.

We read about the wild Long Island girls with flailing arms, bobbed hair, and willing for anything. The golden flask, the contraceptive, the sacred old school colors, the removable rear seat, the blinding headaches were standard for a big eastern football weekend. Sudden death on ill-banked highways, blindness from poisonous wood alcohol—these were some of the things that produced these sleazy titles, *Flaming Youth* and *Dancing Daughters*.

But Indiana U. and Purdue were both state schools, and had to split school funds voted by back-country farmers who didn't hold with fancy living. To get new dorms and classrooms was like pulling teeth. We students had to sign personal pledges to get a gym built. When we got a football stadium, the concrete was so poor it crumpled away in just one year. But we did have good teachers, and you could get a fine education.

3

Monk, muttering about Montmartre, the Left Bank, the Latin Quarter, was composing an epic.

Monk and I and Harry Hostetter were sitting in my old jalopy —a beat-up Ford—when he handed us the poem. "I am writing under the non de plume of Wolfgang Beethoven Bunkhaus."

"I get it all right," I said. "It's a jazz poem."

Harry asked me, "How'd you meet George Johnson?"

"He was visiting somebody in Indianapolis. And right away we were crazy in the same way. We went walking down a street and he doodled and gesticulated with his hands as though he were playing and he emphasized the up-beat. I went nuts with excitement and we both nearly walked into the side of a car."

Monk said, "What about the poem?"

"Later I got hold of a saxophone for him. He doodles like Batty, but he has a jerk in there every once in a while on the up-beats."

"So what?"

"It makes me weak, thinking about a whole band playing that rhythm," I said.

"A lot of things make you weak," Monk said. "Now this poem—"

"He ducks his head down to one side when he doodles, and

when he plays. He only stresses the first and third beats of the measure, but man, he rides you along."

"Why don't you go on up and hear them play?" Harry asked.

"I'm going. Took a job. Lake Manitou. I was glad to get the offer."

Monk swung his legs out of the car and leaned back in the seat. "Good, are they?"

"Yeah, although they're not so jazz crazy as some of us."

"Show me how you sock it." Monk was interested.

I began to shake and shout: "Doodle-loodle, la-de-addle—it's the way George accents the down-beat then the up-beat with your fist in your palm."

Monk doodled along with me; his fist hit his palm with the same sort of joyous accent that I loved.

"Makes you feel good," he said. "Now about the poem." But we just walked away. To hell with poems.

I had a law course on my mind and I kept kidding myself jazz was low-down and not for a full career. My resources, aside from my music, were limited. I was fully aware of this. And my more serious self could be objective about it. We talked a lot about it.

"It's a low life. Look at their women." I said. "Traipsing around all over the country, one-night stands, the same old shop talk, same old speaks. Meeting in dance halls, falling in love with the music, they said, not the guys, the horns they blow."

I wanted a girl to settle down and make a home, and have a couple of kids, sew with her fingers instead of beating her tootsies on a ballroom floor. A girl like Dorothy. I was thinking a lot about Dorothy Kelly.

At the Friars Inn, I found George Johnson and Vic Moore, a drummer, at a table. The place smelled just right—funky, run-down, sinister, and dusty. Leon Rappolo, the clarinet player, was wiggling into action in his seat. He started *Sensation Rag*. It was the doodle-style George had taught me. Then George Brunies, the trombonist, picked it up and blasted his notes jerkily, with penetrating brassy tones. The notes surprised me at unexpected times and in unexpected places. They went right down through my gizzard and made my feet vibrate. George bounced in his seat like a trained seal, watching my reaction. I was biting on my tongue and looking very serious and idiotic.

Vic Moore laughed like an idiot and drummed the tabletop with his hands. "I'm modern now."

He was a demented monkey, as the band moved from tune to tune.

"*Farewell Blues*," George said.

"*Panama*," Vic said. "Jig tunes from New Orleans."

"There's a kid out at Northwestern comes down and sits in with them every night, named Murray—Don Murray. We all sit in once in a while."

I said, "Just for looks they're the dopiest-looking bunch I ever saw."

"They hit the weed."

"Weed?" I lifted one eyebrow.

"Marijuana, tea, muggles, muta, reefer. They call it lots of things."

"What does it do?"

"Things."

"Habit-forming?"

"No. Only a little."

I pounded on the table. "Let's get some. . . ."

A slight, extremely young kid in a belted pile coat, with cracked patent leather shoes, had just come in.

"Who's that?"

"Bix Beiderbecke."

Mr. Stanley was about to meet Doctor Livingston.

The Carmichaels and the Campbells picnicking near Bloomington, Indiana, at the turn of the century. I'm the runt just right of center.

My mother and father, Lida and Howard
Carmichael, with my sister Georgia and
myself, 1905.

Mother with my sisters Martha, Joanne, and Georgia, just before Joanne died in 1918.

Ma Robison and the "Little Old Lady" quilt she made.

Mother in 1944, when she was named Indiana "Mother of the Year."

X

Bix came over to our table, his eyes bugging in their sockets. "Hi, boys."

George said, "Hoagy, meet Bix Beiderbecke. Bix, Hoagy Carmichael."

"Hi," Bix said through a slight set of lips, a small mouth. He didn't pay much attention to our introduction. His eyes and silly little mouth fascinated me. He said, "See you 'round."

When he had gone, George leaned over to me. "Ought to hear that kid play. He's got ideas, but his lip is weak."

"Where's he from?" He was fascinating in a grotesque way.

"Davenport, Iowa. Going to Lake Forest Academy. Comes to town every night to listen to jazz bands. Nuts about Ravel and Debussy's stuff."

"Sounds like a goof-off to me," I said honestly.

"The kid's got an ear. He can tell you the pitch of a belch! Listen, what's with you, Hoagy?"

"Nothing. Looking for something hep."

"How about Palm Beach? Vic's family live down there."

"They have palm trees, Vic?"

"Big bastards," Vic said. "They drop coconuts on yo' head, right split yo' goddamn skull."

Vic smiled, overdoing the Dixie accent and the old Southern grin of hospitality as he winked at George. I felt they were closing a trap on me, but a Florida trap sounded cozy.

"What will we do there?" I asked, already half in the box.

"We'll make music for private parties."

"Swimming in the wintertime."

"Bix is going to join us."

"I have doubts, Vic, as to your ability as a band manager."

"A chance to play Chicago jazz with us boys, you'll toss it away?" So, being weak but eager, I agreed to meet them on the Florida train in Indianapolis in a few days. Mom and Dad were not pleased at my news.

"Quitting school, Hoagland?"

"Well, just for a teeny bit."

"Off to Florida to play that jazz? What about Law School?"

"It will still be here when I get back."

Grandma Robison joined in and shook her head. "Remember the boy who came back to Bloomington from Indianapolis to finish off his education?"

"I remember."

"That was Hoagland Carmichael wanting to be somebody. Wanting to be steady and solid. It isn't hard to be like other people, Hoagland, if you want to be."

"But this trip will help pay school expenses. I can go back to school later. I'll have money in the sock."

"The Carmichaels never had the common sense of us Robisons."

It was grandma's final argument, comparing blood lines. I put my arms around her—she was dear to me, and good to me—but my demon was pulling me in two directions again. "Don't feel so bad about it, Ma. I've got to have music. Besides common sense keeps you in a rut. The world is going places, and I'd like to go along."

"You've got a band at school. You going to run out on them?"

"I'll be back."

"You'd shoot anyone who did that to you."

"I'm trying to make something of myself."

"You can't be a lawyer playing jazz in Florida. I suppose you're trying to outrun your father's record for moving around?"

That hurt and I shut my mouth. I was beginning to understand my father's frantic discontent. I was on that train to Florida, wheels clicking over the rails, the steam engine tearing into the night.

2

We slept through Georgia in our seats; lying-down sleep was for the rich. As we pulled out of Jacksonville for the last dash down the coast we were out on the back platform among the cinders and the soot, singing *Chicago* and *Panama* to the station agent. George and I had never breathed ocean air before and we felt great.

Vic said, "Beats the cold damp air in Indiana."

"Sure does, man."

"Do-doodle addle paddle . . ."

Blue skies, tall green growths, the twist of foam-topped surf on yellow sand, the warm air.

Our first impression of Palm Beach, acquired in the sticky throbbing night, was disappointing. The dark leaning forms of palm trees, bone-white roads, the smell of sun-tormented lawns resting at night, the barking of frogs from behind walled gardens, all was strange. Vic's family was glassy-eyed in their greeting, but game.

The sun came up howling, and the sky was the perfect blue of a stage set. The air was clean, polite with a hint of tropical promise, and the white and pink villas spelled money—lots of money. We threw on our clothes and rushed outdoors.

We kept right on running all the time, trying to do everything. We saw people riding around in wheel chairs and I thought they were sick. We rented bicycles to move faster and see more. It was so wonderful we didn't try to get playing jobs for ten days, and then only with a shrug because we were broke.

A private party was our first gig. It was such a fancy place that I could see what God would do *if* he had money.

There was an ornate long and busy bar with everything from beer to absinthe. The tanned figures of the girls and the luxurious house made me think of the life of a sultan. It made our music zing. We had six or eight tunes down pat, and we had rehearsed just a little. Our hostess—she owned every other pineapple in the world or an auto factory, I forget now—liked our music and wrote us out checks for twenty dollars each. The music didn't get over too well. These people were used to polite club music. Our style was a little too advanced.

3

The president of one of the larger public utility companies hired us for a shindig. He gave parties in Palm Beach that were replicas of Nero's Rome. We played. The vintage champagne flowed as though he had an artesian well.

It was so Scott Fitzgerald and Jay Gatsby, life copying art. Eastern accents. The white-flanneled handsome men and jeweled women—the eager polite drinking, the ring of refined laughter and crystal glasses—it all was just as the novelists wrote it down. At evening, the dinner jackets showed and the barman rattled his silver cocktail shaker as if part of our combo.

The guest list included Billie Burke, Flo Ziegfeld, Irving Berlin, and others of comparable fame or notoriety. Berlin listened to our music, but the dark lean poker face never showed if he liked us or not.

Vic said, "That's Irving?"

George nodded. "Two hundred hit tunes."

"And he can't play piano good at all."

Vic said, "That's class. Money-making class."

I impressed one of the younger Wanamakers with *Nola* and *Canadian Capers*, piano solo stuff—and with the winking eyes of a beautiful Follies girl and a generous helping of champagne, I impressed *myself*.

This, I felt, is the new Hoagy Carmichael, getting fifty dollars the date. No longer the shy kid who used to get into the movies free because his mother played picture-show music, no longer making a buck a week ushering at Bloomington's Grand Theatre, or hustling pool to pick up a quarter at Tom Huff's Poolroom.

"Take a solo, Hoagy!"

Did I ever run a cement mixer in Indianapolis twelve hours a night?

"Enough diamonds at the party, George, to pave my Grandmother Robison's kitchen, wall to wall."

The party warmed up. My hands were good, beating out *Canadian Capers* and a Follies girl was draped over my shoulder, and maybe Irving was listening. I finished and took up a hollow-stemmed champagne glass. "That was music," said Mr. Berlin.

"I guess so, Mr. Berlin."

People asked the great man to play his new song *Lady of the Evening*. Berlin fingered out the song with a feathery and uncertain feel of the ivories, but with lots of charm.

Vic, George, and I looked and listened. Vic said, "As a piano player he stinks."

"Hoagy," said George, "if anyone who plays that feeble can write that good, you can write a song, too."

I said maybe I'd try a song sometime. But I had a date with the Follies girl, so not tonight.

"Wait till Bix gets here. We'll really blow up a storm."

"I bet he doesn't show."

The twenties Florida boom was only just starting: the rich, the tourists, the suckers, the con men, madams, card sharks, interior decorators, nut-bread doctors, gold-diggers, Chicago mob men (fish belly white), retired chain store kings, newly-rich stock speculators, all were beginning to fill Florida.

What a time for my conscience to begin to bother me!

The wild, crazy season wore to a close and Bix never arrived. I was sad about that. They had told me he was so great. But our band was a success in its way. We played a jazz the rich crackers couldn't understand. A local long-underwear band in gold lamé jackets with an electric light in their banjo was more prosperous than we were, and worked more. We felt only pity for these dismal squares, even when they silver-plated their derby hats.

It was for the best that Bix didn't come down. If he had, I would have stayed with the band and would never have finished college.

The season ground to a stop at Palm Beach. Vic and George

wanted to get back to Chicago and get a band organized. "We'll call it the Wolverines."

"What kind of name is that?" I asked.

Vic said, "The kind of name dopes ask, 'What kind of name is that?'"

George, the practical one, said as he lowered his four-dollar Panama hat over his brow to keep the lime-white sun from his eyes, "We need traveling loot."

We made getaway money in Monticello, a small town in Florida, booking ourselves as "The Country's Foremost Chicago Jazz Band."

We stayed at a friend of Vic's and they had an eighteen-year-old daughter whose beauty outshone anything you could imagine in a southern belle. I was stunned and she liked me. The next night she was to play the lead in a high school play and, of course, I was to be there. It was agonizing. She and the play were so bad that I was in hysterics, but with the family near me I could not let go those gales of laughter that crowded my insides. A few did escape at the wrong moments, of course, and I was embarrassed. The next morning on the train north, some of those Indiana girls still looked good to me.

4

Having traveled now, I was aware times were changing with the rush of a bullet. Some people I knew were fermenting mash, cutting hair tonic, recooking extracts. All this gave the gangsters, the bootleggers, an idea—and then an empire. Gangs spread out, contacted smuggler's ships rolling on a leeshore twelve miles out, or on the Canadian lakes. Jazz men went to work in the speakeasies. Cargoes of whiskey came ashore in the murky lake coves by fast cabin cruisers. I didn't protest; no one did much.

Even in a college town I saw the young quit their jobs to drive trucks guarded by imported mobsmen armed with Thompson submachine guns. Some of my pals quit school to pilot the beer cargoes. Highjackers stopped cargoes at interurban boule-vards even in Indianapolis.

The fancier speak-easies felt the need for a jazz piano. I was an easy ear for anyone who had come up from New Orleans and could talk about jazz to me. I could picture it: the walls dirty and unpainted, the brick-faced houses on Rampart and Canal Streets dividing the sheep from the goats.

If I was indifferent to the bootleggers, I was certainly in-terested in the roots of jazz. There was a man once in New Or-leans called Buddy Bolden, they told me, big and black, a hulk of a man. Drinking and cutting, he ran a barbershop and printed juicy gossip in his own newspaper. He organized a ragtime band. Ragtime was what the white folks called popular music, but Buddy and his boys turned it into something new and jazzy.

I heard about the old New Orleans places, the Eagle Saloon, the Masonic Hall, the music corner of Perdido and Rampart, lonely nights on Bourbon Street, the Church of St. Louis where the horse of General Jackson prances on its hind legs and the General sits, doffed hat held high, beyond him the river. The sidewalk place that sold coffee and doughnuts to the boys who went there, bleary-eyed and shaky after a night of playing. The odor of the river and the street full of sun. I could almost taste and feel it. Later, when I went there, it was just as they told of it.

What drove it all north was that in 1917, Storyville closed down and the speak-easies were in the need of music. So jazzmen spread out, moving north, east, and west; drifting, following the rivers and roads looking for a buck, a freebe, a place to play their music. The riverboats, that had seen good living and the fancy sporting women, were turning into cheap excursion steam-ers and showboats. *The Capitol, St. Paul, Sidney,* and what re-mained of the big river fleets carried jazzmen up to St. Louis, Memphis, Cairo, and Davenport. Some turned up in Chicago asking for a job or a handout.

When they hit our town, as some strays did, I'd listen to them play, listen to them talk. To me it was like hearing of Gettysburg from someone who had been there. They spoke of tooting into the Red River and the St. Joe, down the Delta, past Algiers Point, into the Gulf, and along the bayous choked with river flowers and 'gator snouts.

Eating and loving, they said, riding on the rivers with orchestras, steam calliopes, and forming bands with names new to me then: Louis Armstrong played in the river bands, and Fate Marable organized them out of St. Louis. Good men like Pop Foster, Baby Dodds, Johnny St. Cyr, all played jazz as often as they could. They carried a hot trumpet and a sweet trumpet, and played twelve numbers every three hours; two of these numbers were usually the wildest jazz there was.

The jazzmen had drifted into Chicago early, I heard. In 1915 Sugar Johnnie and Roy Palmer and Larry Duke were doing jazz type vaudeville in Chicago. A year or so later they were playing the DeLuxe Cafe on the South Side with such people as Lil Hardin, the non-New Orleans jazz pianist. Wellman Breaux Braud, bass, and Ram Hall, drums. From 1912 to 1917, Freddie Keppard's Original Creole Band, I discovered, had played cross-country. A lot of little bands were playing in the Negro section. In June 1915, the first important white jazz band came to Chicago: the Tom Brown Band from New Orleans opened at the Lamb's Cafe. Ray Lopéz, Gus Mueller, Arnold Loyocano, Will Lambert made up the band, with Brown himself at the trombone.

They had a grand sign put up, I was told: BROWN'S DIXIE-LAND JAZZ BAND, DIRECT FROM NEW ORLEANS. I wondered how one got into the ranks of the pioneers.

As I was to find out, accident was as good a way as any. And the ability to keep from eating too often.

XI

So by accident or destiny—take your pick—I entered the stream of jazz history through the Wolverines. I didn't know it was history. I was looking for a place to play my music, and there were certain tunes buzzing in my head and asking to be let out.

Bix was already a name among jazz musicians, but it was not until the formation of the Wolverines that his remarkable talent was put on wax. The story of Bix is partly the history of the Wolverines. It was one of the first and probably the most famous of the Chicago School jazz groups. It was the band that later first recorded a Hoagy Carmichael composition, which made it important to me.

The Wolverines were organized in Chicago in the spring of 1923. The personnel of the band was: Dick Voynow, piano; Bobby Gillette, banjo; Vic Moore, drums; Min Leibrook, bass; George Johnson, tenor sax; Jimmy Hartwell, clarinet; Bix Beiderbecke, cornet; Al Gandee, trombone. Leibrook and Gandee joined the band in Cincinnati. Ole Vangsness was the original drummer when the band played at the Stockton Club in Hamilton, Ohio. Vic Moore was called in from the "Ten Foot Bored" in Chicago when Ole quit and this group opened at Doyles Dance Hall in Cincinnati after the Stockton Club job blew up in a wild melee on New Year's Eve, 1923.

After Florida, life for me had calmed down only for a little while. In the early summer, my friend Batty De Marcus got a lot of new phonograph records he had made. They were popular in after-dark spots. He told me stories of the musicians in New

York, and I pictured America as one big night club. Gene and Dudley Fosdick, sharp supper club players, had come out with Batty, and I met them all in Ed East's music shop.

Batty said, "Play them Reg Duval's *One-Step*—that's Hoagy's hot specialty."

"If you can stand it," I said.

I was eager to show my stuff. Then I switched to *Chicago* and then to a slow rendition of *Panama*. Batty called me dirty names again and ran his big freckled hands through my hair.

"Why you s.o.b., that's damn good!"

I played *Sister Kate*, socking black and white notes together (such as E flat and D natural) with the third and little fingers of my right hand. This created a screwy, discordant sock-time that always shivered my spine. Gene Fosdick made silly noises (which were his signs of approval) and went into a spasm of uncontrolled laughter.

I was happy that the boys liked it. We carried on until Ed East had to throw us out.

Two nights later I received a long distance call from Batty at Liberty, Indiana. "Come on down, you stud possum, immediately —for a serenade at Oxford College."

"It's 9:30, Batty."

"Catch the 10:15 train and come sober."

I boarded the train for a two and a half hour ride. I had decided I had lost my cotton-picking mind, as the saying goes.

Oxford, Ohio, was a pretty town. Cy Milders, the campus crooner, was waiting for me in a truck with a piano ready to go. Girls' dormitories fairly cluttered the place, and the game was to visit all of them with truck and band. Batty was in great form, and Cy's voice rang out like a bell full of gold coins. Dudley Fosdick took a chorus on the mellophone. I had never heard hot music played on such an instrument. The bell of the horn nearly touched the truck floor and gave out a guttural tone that was like the barbarians at the gates of Rome. Gene romped on his soprano saxophone, the high notes piercing the night air. The supper club boys were in the new spirit of things. We finished with sweet music, and the college girls went back to bed to dream dreams college girls dream. The truck was smoking. We were dried out.

Gene Fosdick, now my buddy, decided, "We gotta go to Chicago and team up on a job."

"Mainly I can't wait to see George again and to hear the Chicago music. Maybe Bix will turn up."

2

Once off the train in Chicago, we found George Johnson, Bix Beiderbecke, and Vic Moore in a hotel room, all primed for a big night. Bix, sleepy-eyed, said, "We got the mixings."

"A couple of quarts of gin and a package of muggles. It's enough to start," said Gene.

We went to the Lincoln Gardens, a southside black and tan place. King Oliver's Band was there. This was the solid real jazz. Louis Armstrong played second trumpet for Oliver. His white teeth showed when Bix gave him the high-sign.

Bix said, "That's my boy."

Louis' wife, Lil, was playing piano and she could, too. There was a bass fiddle and clarinet, a regular jazz combo. As I sat down, I lit my first muggle as Louis and King Oliver broke into the introductory part of *Bugle Call Rag*. Everything was chaos at our table. We smoked and gulped our terrible drinks. Bix was on his feet, his eyes popping out of his head.

Louis was taking a hot chorus. Gene had a mild spasm, finally overturning the table and sliding off his chair in a fit of stupor, muttering to himself in his own strange style.

The joint stank of body musk, bootleg booze, excited people, platform sweat. I couldn't see well, but I was feeling all over, "Why isn't everyone in the world here to hear this?"

Gene said, "Because they're outside it."

The muggles took effect, making my body feel as light as my Ma's biscuits. I ran to the piano and played *Royal Garden Blues* with the band.

Music meant more than flesh just then. I had never heard the tune before, but full of smoke, I somehow couldn't miss a note of it. The muggles had carried me off into another world. I was floating high around the room in a whirlpool of jazz. The rest of the night I have no memory of.

Around noon next day, I woke up, a living corpse. George showed us no mercy and told us to get dates and come to the S.A.E. house at Northwestern to hear the band he and Bix were with.

"It's the Wolverines."

Gene and I staggered in, crashing the S.A.E. house as if we owned the place. I didn't want to dance; I froze to a spot in front of the band when they started off with *Tiger Rag*. Bix looked down at me and winked; he fascinated me. He never used words much to express his feeling, just grimaces. The band sounded even better to me than the New Orleans Rhythm Kings. The rhythm was stronger and the licks that George, Bix, and Jimmy Hartwell played were so precise and musical. Bix's breaks were not as wild as Louis Armstrong's, but they were hot, and he selected each note with musical care. Bix's playing dumbfounded me and the band was more than I could believe. From his expressions I could see Bix took delight in seeing what he could do to me. When the session ended he said, "Hoagy, you got it real bad."

"I sure do, Bix. I sure do."

3

In Chicago, a new facet of jazz in the hands of white boys was bringing new sounds and ideas into the music. They didn't find it easy. There were places in Chicago where we unemployed jazz players hung out, our heads pushed into upturned coat collars, horns in battered cases, neckties knotted wrong, and our tailoring sharp but worn. We stood on the sidewalk in the sun and talked about the music. We ate hastily and not much in the little tired places where the food was cheap and the dark coffee could be sat over a long time. We came out chewing a free toothpick, the hunger still on us. We hunted work in some gangster road house or hoped to tear off a recording for some fly-by-night company. Mostly we just stood and waited. We were, for better or worse, the men who made the new sounds. There were never enough jobs and too many new kids who thought the world was waiting for the sunrise of their talents. Like myself. I couldn't live, I felt, if I were not part of this, way in.

Chicago style came out of a lot of this standing around, of kids and old-timers talking it over and trying it on. Black and white. It was a real school, a real style, and should be judged for what it did best, not for what it didn't do and often didn't try to do. I was jumpy about it; always in the back of my mind was that damn college course, and the thought that maybe I'd end up only a lawyer after all.

The Chicago school didn't come from hearing Louis, or King Oliver, or Bix alone. It came from a stronger mixture of Dixieland and New Orleans, and through the twenties, Chicago school was a mixture of both. Muggsy Spanier and the Bucktown Five did some good things in it and recorded their best in *Mobile Blues, Everybody Loves My Baby*, and others. The tempo was very fast, but the feel of the rhythmic beat was fine.

When the Rhythm Kings disbanded and pure Dixieland left Chicago, Chicago style pretty much held the field. Louis Armstrong was still recording classical jazz with his Hot Five and other combinations. Jelly Roll Morton was recording his Red Hot Peppers.

Chicago style was true to jazz and goes right back to 1922 when five kids at Chicago's Austin High School got up a band of sorts. They were Bud Freeman, Frank Teschemaker, Jim Lannigan, Jimmy and Dick McPartland. They drifted into The Wolverine group. Soon they were to begin recording the first of the new style.

They had more novelty. Moving away from the usual rhythmic jazz beat, they did *China Boy, Nobody's Sweetheart, Bug-*

Frog Blues and others in their own way. They used a heavy beat and it got hot and high. Chicago style had a trade-mark, breaking its beat up into successive patterns. They used the riff in their own method, not what it became in swing. Maybe the solos were show-off but they were good Lake Michigan style. The harmonized sections were arranged and the technical facility was amazing. Teschemaker's clarinet, I remember, was wildly rhapsodic, played out of tune in dissonance and quarter-tones. Tesch played free-for-all, trying to develop it into a modern music. It didn't go too far, but there was nothing to prevent a genius taking the style into true jazz greatness.

Wingy Manoffe, Sid Catlett, and Frank Melrose played it. Pee Wee Russell took over when Teschemaker was killed in an auto accident (death by Detroit tin was a new menace). Pee Wee's spit and growl tones drove the purists into a frenzy. The later style could best be heard in sides like *Barrel House Stomp* and *Tillie's Breakdown*. It was a good attempt to show that all white jazz was not just an off-shoot of Dixieland, note for note. We never overlooked what was new and always tried to learn something. The original sitting-in stuff had been a collection of serious jazzmen taking it over and trying it out, but the public jam sessions often were exhibits of wild bouts of sounds.

It fit the towns it came from; it played earnestly the way it felt.

Chicago didn't give me a job, and so when Gene Fosdick got a gig at the South Shore Hotel, Lake Wawassee, I went out, too, on the Fourth of July night—in a glow of fireworks. We opened with *Runnin' Wild* without any rehearsal. The band was a miracle of sound and fury and making everything do.

At the end of that number, I was forced to get air to cool off. It was fifteen minutes before we could get ourselves to play another number. We knew that we were good, but the Wawassee crowd didn't think so. The dopey vacationers preferred the stock orchestrations at Ross Franklin's Waco. The lake crowd was one big loyal family, and Ross was Papa. We didn't stand a chance, so we packed to leave.

Gene said, "They like marshmallow music."

Before we left, Jean Goldkette came down to the lake from Detroit to see Gene Fosdick about joining the band at the Greystone ballroom. The band was just fair.

A few weeks later, Don Murray showed up at the Greystone ballroom in a turned-up collegiate hat and a rotting raccoon coat. The kid sat in for a number and he panicked the boys. This was the beginning of a great Goldkette band that would have knocked Paul Whiteman's records off the table if the younger generation had had anything to do with it. But they didn't pay the bills or have the cash. Gene Fosdick wasn't very impressed with the offer and had a hankering to get back to New York. Goldkette gave me a once over.

"Maybe you're a comer."

"How about a job?"

"Not yet."

This didn't butter any wheat cakes, and when Tommy Bassett wired for me to come to Lake Keuka, New York, for the balance of the summer, I was on my way before dark, just in case I owed anyone any money.

4

George Johnson followed me to Hammondsport, New York, in an old jalopy he had picked up someplace. We had a tough time trying to sell Chicago jazz to the Ithaca boys. Especially tough and deaf were the rich wine merchants who lived in the hills around the beautiful lake. The wine cellars were large, and we spent most of the hot afternoon in them recovering from the night before. We were invited to make some tests of wine for an old red-nosed wine presser. He took us deep into his cellar.

"You taste with the back of the mouth—don't swallow too soon."

"Don't wo ry, we know."

We tested everything from champagne body to aged wines. We found each keg better than the one before.

"You swallow *too* fast."

"*Very* good."

When our work was done, we had to be assisted out of the place on our rubber legs. Good stuff had a kick, too, I found out.

I was, as usual, low on fees for my return to school. I thought it would be wise to take back a case of real champagne to make traveling expenses. I found out twelve quarts in a suitcase weighed almost as much as I did. It was hard getting it on and off a train. The eight o'clock Hudson tubes ride to Manhattan Transfer was a nightmare. I had the feeling everybody in New York knew I was toting booze. I didn't let anyone handle the suitcase for fear of breakage.

Seated on the Pennsylvania train for Indianapolis, I was relieved. It was easy after all, I felt. I got off the train at Pittsburgh to grab a Coke. When I returned, the train was just gone with *all* my baggage. I wired Columbus, Ohio, in panic to have my baggage transferred to the following train. I boarded it with a feeling I would end up in jail.

I gave a five dollar bill to the porter: "Pick up my suitcases tomorrow morning at seven o'clock."

"Sure will, suh."

I woke after a night of hot and cold sweats and reached gingerly under my berth. The battered suitcases were there, and hadn't been tampered with. The porter said, "You sure travel heavy, white boy. I done near rupture myself."

"School books," I explained.

The champagne brought me a hundred dollars more than it cost, which was enough to pay my law school tuition and my first month's fraternity house bill. I could have bought that porter a truss and still made money.

XII

The college world of study and shim-me-sha-wabble of the early twenties that I now submerged myself in was like nothing that had gone before in American education. The staid and somber schools of the East were set in the classic past, just beginning to stir from their Latin and Greek, and glance with interest to new ideas. An Indiana college was still callow, warm, set in a farm tradition, and practical. One had to come from it fit for a career, able to get a job, and help support the fields of the Republic with taxes.

The snobs, some of the rich, and the deeper students went East to the hallowed halls of learning. Those that stayed were mostly fun and, like myself, often worried about lasting the course.

The buildings were old, the ivy crumby with insects and the woodwork full of small animal life. Sanitation was there, but in only fair repair. But I wasn't too particular in that direction. I was bathing more often, but not becoming a fanatic about it, and my clothes were natty—the best in my price range. I liked to look well-groomed, unlike most musicians. I cut my own hair a lot—I disliked the germ cultures most barbershops were; I cut my own hair to this day. We still wore garters, vests, and underwear. BVD's were the popular next-to-the-skin items and we wore undershirts, too; the loss of that garment didn't come till a decade or so later when Clark Gable exposed himself without it. Most of us had a pair of pyjamas—which lasted the whole season with only one or two washings.

Our rooms were sties, and the habit of collecting street signs, outhouse doors, broken tennis rackets, oars, and moose horns as wall decor was the mode. The day Wad Allen staggered in with a full-sized cigar store Indian was like the discovery of an unknown El Greco.

"Got it," Wad panted, planting the wooden Apache among us. "Got it just ahead of a posse and a real live bloodhound."

The student who would hang up a reproduction of a modern painting would have been suspected of purple vices and illusions of gender.

2

In the spring of 1923, as a big wheel on the campus (there was a shortage of wheels that season), I booked the Wolverines at Indiana University for several dance dates. The Wolverines were popular with young people. They didn't bother with waltzes or sweet arrangements. Other bands were playing stock orchestrations or special arrangements of sweet numbers. Contrary to the general impression, the Wolverines were not strictly a jam band. They had arrangements, even though the actual parts weren't written out. Bix and Voynow worked out the arrangements at the piano and the boys learned their parts by ear.

"Give it to me once more?"

"Going long hair?"

"I'll get it next time."

Bix and I were becoming friendly and I could see the tragic note deep in him. He had a kind of despair about him, even then.

But the discovery of the magic of the Wolverines was like a new star flashing into the heavens. I remember the lawn of the Pi Phi house at Indiana University in the gathering darkness, the golden lights just going on, and what was I doing? I was doing a jig. I saw that Harry Hostetter was dancing also—both of us dancing to an orchestra packed into the back of a two-ton truck playing a midnight serenade on Sorority Row.

The windows and porches were filled with faces as a cornet solo cut out.

I said, "That's the Wolverines. That's a *band!*"

Harry could only moan and agree.

When they finished playing *Farewell Blues,* Harry and I could just stand there and look at each other.

He had been away in the Navy. After we greeted each other, we stood on the grass as he talked of music in far places and how much he had missed dance music.

"I hadn't heard much jazz except for a few records, then today I heard your band. It was good, but it didn't turn me inside out. But tonight . . . walking home from Tom Huff's Poolroom and *that* cornet sounding out . . . I started running toward that sound like someone who had just had a saint's vision.

"*That* was Bix, Bix Beiderbecke." And *I* did a little raving.

It was dark and cold, but we didn't want to part.

I said, "Just four notes, he didn't blow them he hit them . . . the tone, the richness . . ."

I lost the words I wanted to say.

"Whatever it was, he ruined me."

That's what the Wolverines and Bix, with four notes, could do to one young American in the early twenties.

3

One reason for the band's popularity among us that year was that it drew a lot of sturdy supporters from Indiana University wherever it played within fifty miles of the school. My Collegians band had educated the students to an appreciation of hot music and many became jibbering fanatics.

When the Wolverines played for us the evening ended with the dancers massed around the bandstand listening with interest as the boys took their choruses, yelling and stomping their feet in appreciation.

"Go it, Bix! Send it!"

The band enjoyed what they were doing. They never tired and often after a backbreaking, lungbusting evening, a group would get off in a corner of a joint or a room someplace and jam until daylight. Sandwiches and bottles all around, the bear-pit smell growing stronger, the one naked electric light hanging in the ceiling picking up players and listeners.

I began to understand Bix at least as much as anyone could. Bix was a fine extemporaneous artist. He could play a counter harmony to a waltz melody (with someone playing the lead) that was as exciting as *Copenhagen* to my now experienced ear.

I tried to explain Bix to the gang. Trying to put Bix together for them—and myself—so that they would see and hear and feel him the way I did. It was no good, like the telling of a vivid, personal dream, knowing that it wasn't making sense to anyone else: the emotion couldn't be transmitted too clearly.

"He was a little punk," I explained, "who ran to the piano when he was three and played a tune all the way through on the white keys, the only ones he could see from where he stood, and he didn't make a mistake."

"Sure, Hoagy, sure."

It was best just to hear Bix, sloppy, souped up; he'd look around him, always the enigma.

What was he really like, forgetting the legends, the novels, the bad movies based on his life?

In Harlem, in Hollywood, in the Chicago South Side, in the Le Jazz Hot joints in Paris where the dicty folk come to listen to his records, they still talk of Bix Beiderbecke.

4

The legends aren't very true but they have been growing and I'd like to put down some facts.

Leon Bix (not short for Bismarck as some claim) Beiderbecke was born on March 10, 1903, in Davenport, Iowa. His folks had made their money in coal, but they had culture besides, and all loved music. His sister played fine piano. His mother had studied piano and pipe organ and when ten years old, had won a medal at it. His grandfather led German-American music in Davenport, and his grandmother's father played a church organ in Europe. It was in his genes, like the color of his eyes. He was an earnest, watching, listening child—always alert.

Bix never was much of a sight-reader, but he wasn't as ignorant as some legends said. He took lessons on the piano from a Professor Grade. When only three, Bix could play the melody of the Second Hungarian Rhapsody. On the cornet he never took a lesson in his life. He never played it right, some said, just grand. He was surprised once to find he was not playing it in the same key as the piano. He couldn't read cornet parts well and struggled along with violin parts which he found easier reading. He loved the third valve on the horn—everybody else used the first two keys most. It was all wrong according to the teachers, but he got a good flow into his horn chords. He liked the cornet, its full mellow charm, maybe because it was close to the human voice. It had just the sting he wanted and he stayed with it. It tongued easy and one simple mute was enough. Bix didn't put much mute in his legato styling and his round tones were mellow, not brassy—and so full as to blow you out of the place. Vibrato was a dirty word to Bix.

Bix did plenty of playing alone, often to a record on the family Victrola. King Oliver, Louis Armstrong, Bix knew their recordings as a kid. LaRocca, too, and Emmett Hardy, Paul Mares, Fate Marable and Johnny Dunn. Early and soon he couldn't resist it.

Bix was close to his mother. She remembers him in his teens playing his cornet to LaRocca's recording of *Tiger Rag*. From Oliver and Louis came the off-scale tonality. The river boats all carried the new music by then and hit Davenport. There was Hardy, a white hornman on the Strekfus line boats; the *Capitol* had bands with Oliver and Louis in them.

Bix loved the real old blues and adored the phrasing of Bessie Smith and Ma Rainey. He was a jumpy kid with a horn; a thousand kids must be like him every place even today, thinking of what they want to say and copying ways of saying it. So he went on listening to the press-roll on snarls, the newer jumps of the short riffs, and even the rinky-dink bands that played jitney stops around the town. Bix played it all and learned a lot, and then they sent him away to school.

Bix had two years in the Davenport High School, then in 1921 was put into Lake Forest Academy on the North Shore of Chicago. New Orleans and Dixieland music was just hitting Chicago and Bix played in the school band, first on the piano and then as a star on the cornet. Hating to study, he didn't get good marks, and was already a drinking schoolboy, like U.S. Grant. He drank gin, played music, and was amiable. They kicked him out of the school and instead of going home, he hung around Chicago, did a few nights gigging, and waited for the Wolverines to start in business. He sort of knew his destiny and never did much to change it.

The Wolverines, bright-eyed and bushy-tailed, opened at the Stockton Club, a dive near Hamilton, Ohio. They were popular, always a mob around Bix, Bix and his horn.

5

Some said, including me, that the Wolverines were the best white jazz band in the country with compliments to the Original Dixieland Jazz Band and the New Orleans Rhythm Kings. Their playing was leading to Chicago style, and they vo-do-de-o-doed maybe a bit too much, but it was all right to the early cats.

Their playing sort of took the style away from the Rhythm Kings, rode it a bit higher in quality and arrangements and, I thought, developed the most drive of any band in the world of that time. Hearing them today on old recordings, with all their scratchy faults, no Dixieland group, even of recent years, quite comes near to what the boys had. Even such important figures as Bud Freeman, Pee Wee Russell, and Charlie Teagarden, among many fine combo men when playing as a group, lacked just a little something in all-over sound and beat compared to the Wolverines at their top.

Bix had manners and looked clean-cut even when seedy. He always tried to keep his stubborn hair slicked neatly back. The girls liked Bix, and while this mother thing may have held him back, by 1927 to my surprise, he was digging up dates in various places the band was playing. I even caught him dancing in a hotel ballroom in Indianapolis, when he was touring with Paul Whiteman's band. He looked like a man who enjoyed a girl, and enjoyed dancing, too. Years later, after he was dead, I got a letter from the Indianapolis girl he had been dating, and she said, in part: "There will never be another Bix Beiderbecke, always the same—sweet, kind, affectionate. I was about the only one Bix had dates with at that time, although at parties the girls really swarmed around him. The girls were crazy about him, but Bix seemed to live in a world of his own, and that world was music. As many dates as I had with Bix, and as close as we felt toward each other, etc., if there happened to be a piano around somewhere it was not long until Bix would be sitting at the piano. . . ."

He was the star of the Wolverines. They didn't play much of a repertoire but in time added a dozen good tunes. Because they couldn't read music, except for two men, they didn't add much to their list of numbers, but played it over and over again for those who liked it, maybe ten choruses at a time.

It was a tough go for real jazz players because the big bands were coming soon to cater to sweet tastes, people dancing the Charleston and Lindy Hop as respectably as they could, and even trying soon the Black Bottom and Big Apple. Bix played lake boats and hung around sessions jamming New Orleans style. When he rattled around with the jazz crowd sitting in dives, he always carried in his pocket the iron mouthpiece of his cornet, taking it out and fingering it while he listened to others playing. It was always handy if someone asked him to sit in, and he didn't have his own horn.

"Don't miser that bottle, pour."

He was not a show off—just a good listener.

For a year he played in Frank Trumbauer's band at the Arcadia Ballroom, St. Louis. He was pulling down good money— a hundred dollars a week—and he held on to it pretty good. He was a saver. His tuxedo trousers had gone shiny and were giving out and I doubt if he had more than one pair of shoes. But he never let the customers down if the mood was on him. He was— to use a worn-out but true phrase—a sweet soul.

It was in St. Louis that he went daffy over modern music—the new concert stuff, new to him anyway; Ravel, Debussy, Mac-Dowell, and Stravinsky. This was where he got the whole-tone scales and the whole-tone chords he was to work into his stuff. He had a recording of *The Firebird Suite* which he wore out in no time.

Later he went into Jean Goldkette's Orchestra, and we at school through *The Indiana U College* newspaper voted him in 1926 the greatest "dirty" trumpet player in jazz circles. They put quotes around "dirty" as if not sure what the word meant.

Goldkette's Band was a hot and sweet pop band, mostly hot. They hit the Blue Lantern at Hudson Lake, and Bix played cornet, piano, and, a few times, the drums. But it was a high-priced band and when bookings got tough, Bix went over to Whiteman. When Bix got sick from drinking too much, Whiteman took care of him and sent him home for a rest cure with pay.

6

I'm getting a little ahead of the story but it gives a picture of the man. Bix got rather fat and there weren't many moments when he was feeling in key with the world. But he could still play the horn. When the band played Los Angeles, Whiteman used Bix only in the hot group with Trumbauer, Bill Rank, and the Rhythm Boys.

Bix used to start his journey to the end of the night after the places closed and he'd latch on to anybody who felt they could keep up with him—the brothers Dorsey, Ben Pollack, Joe Sullivan—at white dives or Negro places with just enough air to breathe, a piano, and a place to stash the bottle. Bix was getting two hundred a week and extras from the wonderful recordings he made with Frank Trumbauer's band for the Okeh label.

By the end of the twenties, Bix was on the way down—not yet on the skids, but the good time and the big time was behind him. He didn't like radio dates. Radio meant twenty numbers in an hour, six of them usually new, and the tricky arrangements were tough for a man who was never much of a reader. The pressure, the tension, didn't help his frayed nerves and the whiskey moved in for good. Lots of it. He was our golden boy —doomed to an untimely end.

But to get back to the early Bix when I first knew him.

My college band was fooling around one day with bits and pieces of music when Bix joined us. He had come to Bloomington with the Wolverines on a date I had booked for them in competition with my own band.

"Got your horn?"

"Sure."

"Mind putting it together?"

"No."

At the crucial moment Bix played a break of four notes, so perfect in outline, so spacious and exhilarating, so true-toned and resounding, that I collapsed on a sofa, exhausted with pleasure and excitement.

The trouble with telling the Bix story is that the legend and the myth have become so hard set into the history of jazz that the truth has to elbow its way past things that never were, or didn't happen the way they were told. There has been a novel inspired by Bix and a movie made of it. *Young Man With A Horn* was a good novel and the movie of it (in which I played the part of "Smoke") was a good adaptation of the book. But its success was tempered by the mistaken belief of the critics that it was supposed to be the story of Bix's life.

He was Bix, the real Bix, not the wild-drinking madman of legend. He was neat, he was kind, he was low-keyed. He drank, but not in the *Lost Weekend* kind of drama; his drinking made him thoughtful, and the mood was always of man searching, not howling. At this writing I know there are two books being written about him and the confusion may well be adjusted.

It is his gentleness that is lost in the legends, his ability to charm, to hold friends, to make one feel that it was still possible to know and need—and be known and needed by—another human being.

XIII

I led two lives: a surface existence at college classes, and an almost underground one as a jazz revolutionary.

I became the owner of a car we all called "The Open Job." It was a 1915 Ford that had served some hard years as a delivery truck. It had been stripped down until there was nothing left but the chassis, a high front seat. A boxlike affair had been nailed on behind. It still smelled of sheep dip, steer manure, and chicken crates. The crank had the kick of a maud mule, and bailing wire was about all the repair tools needed. The fenders were gone and so was the hood. "The Open Job" was one of the first stripped down college cars in the middle west. I never allowed her unlovely sides to be marred by any wisecracks, and I kept the oil level up so she responded gratefully every time I flipped the crank by breaking into a bone-shaking roar. As she had a large crack in the motor block, I never put in water for short trips.

Most mornings during the winter I'd have to brush six or eight inches of snow off the motor before I cranked her up, yet she always started and I'd sail down Indiana Avenue on my way to an eight o'clock class in a cloud of blue smoke.

On a particularly cold morning, I'd jump to one side after cranking her because she'd be frozen in gear and would come at me in a running start like a bull charging. Once I missed her as she went grinding by. I just stood there and watched my beloved crate go down the driveway under a full head of power and head toward the campus. A passing idiot saw "The Open Job" go by without a hand at the tiller and he did a bronco-busting act to get at the wheel and save her from an untimely end, wearing out his elbows and knees in the process.

"You oughta hold on to her," he said.

"I try, mister. Thanks."

"Noisy little thing, ain't she?"

"Give you a lift?"

He shook his head. "Never in my life."

2

It was a time of real love affairs between people and their cars. We knew more about them than people know today, and we could operate on them like a brain surgeon. Also, people kept cars for years—like faithful dogs they were attached to.

I took better care of that "Open Job" than of myself. Once I drove to Indianapolis to visit the folks. They were living on Neal Avenue. Mother was impressed. "Hoagland, it sounds so good and loud."

My father said, "It sounds like a sick egg beater. How you doing, Hoagy?"

"I'm attending classes."

Mother sighed. "Attorney at Law."

I didn't feel like explaining that that title was in doubt.

At the end of the street was a machine shop. The car was ailing and the machinist there told me to bring it in, borrow his tools, and work on it there. I gratefully accepted the offer and proceeded to tear the old body and innards apart bolt by bolt, nut by nut. I reground the cylinders, put in new rings, reseated the valves and cleaned and reassembled the entire motor and chassis, and it started. The garage man was impressed. "How'd you do it?"

"I don't know. I just played it by ear."

Dad had doubts, but Mother felt I was on my way to *some* greatness. We played two-handed piano and I taught her a lot of jazz chords that she began to knock around like an old jazz buff.

"You don't think it's too late for me, Hoagland?"

"Listen, you could give even Bix a bad time on the eighty-eight."

I went back to school aware I had four people cheering for me. I wished *I* knew where I was really going.

My campus capers and my band interfered with my studies, but my academic efforts were serious and brain battering and of some consequence. That other side of me, the one that had been taught that security was synonymous with solidity, kept plugging away at the law course—too erratically to be called doggedly, but I showed some progress. Yet I had to admit, as I cracked a volume of Blackstone, or Holmes on Torts, that the band came first.

Paul V. McNutt, one of the Betas who during the late teens helped push Hube Hanna into a flurry of right-hand octaves in chronistic runs, was my prof in Equity and was also dean of the school before he became prominent in politics, governor of Indiana, runner-up as presidential timber, etc.

Paul was clever as an instructor. He had the faculty of scanning his notes from right to left with a broad sweep of the head and eyes as though he was trying to recall his vast store of knowledge. I was highly impressed until one day I discovered every word he said lying face up on his desk. A wonderful man and roommate of Wendell Willkie, also a near great. I got a B in Mr. McNutt's class, I'll have you know.

Life among trees and umber fall fields—wood smoke, steaks sizzling, *hard* cider from a mug, and girls—all dolls under candle light. Outside, a day dying in sunset. The stone-age cars full of soft and ardent bodies, all alive and kicking. Years I shall never forget with friends I wanted so desperately and found so satisfying. I relished it all. The bands, the dances, the crises, the occasional studies, and the music that kept coming out of me. All I devoutly hoped for most during those years was that I would keep on growing. I was still lean and small; even the shadow of a football player snubbed me.

We lived hard, played hard. When some conscientious historian gets around to writing a definitive history of jazz, the chapter on Indiana's contribution will be of some value. The whole state was one big stomping ground for jazz enthusiasts and the crossroads stopover for every jazz musician who had something hot to display. The Wolverines got their start in Indiana. We hosted Don Redman, McKinney's Cotton Pickers, and the great Jean Goldkette band. Charlie Davis' band was in the hub of music around South Bend. Charlie Preble, the trombone player with Davis, wrote about those days in *Tempo* magazine: "Incredible as it may seem, the Wolverines were tremendously popular around Indianapolis. Remember that at this time Louie Panico, who introduced the wow-wow trumpet, was at the height of his fame. But here was an organization playing music that was two years ahead of the times and drawing capacity business. They were in the groove on every number and the swing of that band has never been bettered by any white band since. . . . The band's staunchest supporters were recruited from Indiana University. Hoagy Carmichael had educated those students to an appreciation of hot music that was really remarkable."

3

My own bands at this time lacked any considerable musicianship and certainly any finesse. We had the feel for the new movement and occasionally the boys in the band would interpret it right and we would get hot. We were not consistent and still lacked something. I was an individualist at the piano. It was difficult for the other boys to simulate and coordinate their efforts with my antics. We were not basic. We were experimenting. We found and lost the beat along the way sometimes. We played popular but I injected sock-time, ensemble phrasing, and some of Ted Lewis' style into our effects.

Ted's recordings were something special in the early twenties. For all his clowning, he was not too far back in the race for getting jazz properly before the public. His muted trumpet and trombone could keep us glued to the early Victrola—glued close, for the low phonetic recording mixture then didn't give the music full value. The vocalist recorded at the same horn as the band, which didn't help.

Somewheres, then, or later, we tried them all.

We wanted to do something important. Make it mean more, get it across. It was a time of "getting it across," of "socking it home."

"Boy, if we could only record."

"We will, some day."

"When?"

"When you get all those clinkers out of that horn."

The birthplace of recorded jazz was a rambling brick building on the bank of the Whitewater River gorge on the edge of downtown Richmond in Indiana. The factory was the home plant of the Starr Piano Company and tucked away in one unused corner was the tiny phonograph recording studio that the firm called its Gennett Records division. It was primitive, simple, and effective. And truly a pioneer.

British-born, John Lumsden Gennett founded the piano company before the Civil War, the first west of the Alleghenies. Henry Gennett, son of the founder, had charge when the firm decided to make talking machines. Success led to record-making and trouble. The new venture found Gennett in litigation. Victor brought suit for alleged infringement upon the patent on a record-cutting stylus. Gennett won the case in the U.S. Supreme Court after a long fight and the victory made the instrument public domain.

The firm began to expand. Just after the First World War, annual production was 15,000 pianos, 35,000 spring-driven phonographs, and more than 3 million records recorded in their Gennett studios.

Vines now obscure the Gennett trademarks on the old brick buildings, but some of the master discs of the rarer jazz gems may some day be re-pressed. During the depression, many of them were sold for the copper they contained.

Many early jazzmen remember the rambling brick plant on the bank of the Whitewater River gorge at the west edge of downtown Richmond, Indiana. The Starr Piano Company tucked away the tiny phonograph recording studio in one corner of their factory.

The studio was primitive, the room wasn't soundproof, and just outside was a railroad spur with switch engines puffing away noisily. Yet this obscure recording studio in a small Indiana city saw a history-making parade of musicians. They made the name of the Hoosier Gennetts one of the greatest names in recorded music and the gold-lettered Gennett label is one to collect.

Gennett began recording in 1916, and so by accident Richmond, which is near Chicago, became the birthplace of recorded jazz.

The First World War had ended when King Oliver and his band came upon Gennett. The Creole Jazz Band. Gennett allowed them to play some New Orleans style music for a test record. Among the bandsmen was Louis Armstrong. They played *Dipper Mouth Blues* and the Creole Jazz Band made the first recording of a jazz session to be released to the public.

It didn't take the nation by storm, but it was a famous beginning. None of us knew we were making jazz or recording history. It was a job, and a chance to put down something on wax.

Among the now famous names who recorded jazz classics in Richmond were Duke Ellington, Fletcher Henderson, Wingy Manone, Jelly Roll Morton, Husk O'Hare, Guy Lombardo, Bix (of course), and others. A side line were items of Americana also waxed at Gennett: William Jennings Bryan's "Cross of Gold" oration; sacred music by Homer Rodeheaver and Gypsy Smith; songs by Cliff (Ukelele Ike) Edwards and others. They ran from physical culture exercises to Ku Klux Klan speeches.

But by the early 1930's, the depression slowed Gennett's recording business. The Gennett label disappeared, and is seen now only among collections of rare records. Gennett remained in the record-making business, making millions of records annually. But all copies of master discs were recorded in studios elsewhere. They are sold under the labels of a dozen other recording firms.

Few of the great early jazz recordings survive. We lost, gave away, or broke our copies. And others wore out from constant replaying till the grooves were smooth highways. Yet in whatever shape found they are the only echoes of our lost lives.

4

Joseph Oliver (before being crowned "King"), born in 1885, grew up on Dryades Street in New Orleans. It was a big step up for jazz. Buddy Bolden was high and Bunk Johnson was setting the cornet style. Joe Oliver, as a kid, played in a colored kids' band. When he was fifteen the boys' brass band went on tour, going by steamboat to Baton Rouge. It was a tough time for touring bands and there were knife and bottle fights. Joe came home with a knife scar over one eye. Other jobs were hard to get, so he became a butler.

Joe played his horn in the servants' rooms, very mute, and not letting out. He also—in time off—played in bands; the white folk didn't mind and let him train a boy to take his place when Joe had to play. He tried out with the Eagle Band but they said he was loud and bad. The Eagles didn't worry over written-down music, and Joe Oliver had been too impressed by the written-down so he couldn't fly high with them. But then he got the idea of it. He played at funerals and he worked out a variation on the old hymn *Sing On* that nobody wanted to miss when they got buried. Joe worked hard and listened to Bunk Johnson play and he worked out that stomp of his own, *Dipper Mouth*, and that was his trademark. Everybody used to shout out for Joe: "Give us *Dipper Mouth!*"

"Just hold and I will!"

Joe crossed Canal Street, and joined Manuel Perez's *Onward Brass Band*. Joe really could blow and in no time he was playing in Storyville, his horn wide open. He played with the Aberdeen Brothers, in a dive corner of Bienville and Marais, with Big Eye Louie, Deedee Chandler, Dick Jones. Joe began to blow in B-flat and when he walked out of the dive into the street blowing that horn, the whole street stopped to listen.

"No one had ever done it like that before," they said.

"He's the king of the horn blowin'."

He blew so hard he poked one eye blind.

When the war closed Storyville in 1917 there was a lot of old New Orleans men who couldn't get work and among them was King Oliver. He went north and among the first public playing he did in Chicago was in the streets under the El trains in the Loop, playing tailgate trombone from a wagon to get people to buy Liberty Bonds. He was also indoors playing at two South Side joints. His Creole Jazz Band playing the *Royal Garden Blues* set his style. He was one of the sights of Chicago just like Al Capone and the Charleston contests.

King Oliver liked Chicago, but he didn't change much. He remained a horn player from the south, a big feeder, eating his big plate of hominy, and now that he could afford it, a half dozen hamburgers and a quart of milk, his idea of lunch.

At Dreamland, he organized a new band and did something daring, he got a woman, Lil Hardin, to play the piano. She came to Chicago from Memphis to go on studying music in the Fiske University style. But somehow she got crossed up with jazz, and she stayed with it. I remember her, dark and earnest, really giving the keys a workout.

The band played every night till 1:00, then packed up the stuff and moved seven blocks down to the Pekin Cafe, to go on from there. The Pekin was always exciting, full of spenders, tarts, bootleggers, and killers. The reek of new alcohol gave it a flavor. The golden years of popularity were whizzing by for King Oliver. The band went on tour and came back, and King had Louis Armstrong come up from New Orleans to play with him.

They played at the new done-over Gardens, that tall, thin building with scrolls of stone cut into its façade, its balconies looking down on Thirty-First Street. Nobody used much written-down music, just a few marked up sheets with the titles torn off ("So no cotton mouth kin steal the stuff"). All us white boys were coming in and borrowing from King Oliver. The Dixieland boys at Friar's Inn had helped themselves to *Jazzin' Baby Blues,*

playing it under a title as *Tin Roof Blues*. Joe and Louis went on
with their duets, and everybody got involved in improvisations.
That was when they began to make records for Gennett. At the
studio they moved Joe and Louis twenty feet back from the
recording horn.

"To keep from wrecking the joint."

Louis, damp handed, did his first record solo, *Chimes Blues*, and
the handkerchief trade-mark of his was born. They made some
other records and the band broke up. Joe Oliver was slipping.
He was running into hard luck. He took it in his stride.

The Defender carried an ad in 1924, the year George Gershwin
was working on *Rhapsody in Blue*.

"*At Liberty:* The celebrated King Oliver's Jazz Band—8 men
playing 15 instruments. Open for engagements in or out of
Chicago. Joseph Oliver, 3033 South State Street, Chicago."

5

No takers. The Gardens burned down on Christmas Eve, just
when Joe was getting together a new band to open there, still
billed as "the world's greatest jazz cornetist."

Joe got into the music publishing field. "Office hours, two to
four every afternoon." Joe was writing down all the things in
his head, putting down what he remembered, things of his own
when jazz grew up. He and Lil Hardin arranged them and got a
copyright and published some of it. They did a fine job and
saved a lot of what was best in King Oliver's music, what made
it so original and important.

Joe sent out letters: "I am at leisure should you . . . have anything to offer I would highly appreciate any favor you render.
Respectfully yours, Joseph Oliver."

Joe went East to play two weeks at the Savoy Ballroom in
Harlem. After that he played around, but turned down the Cotton Club when he found out a lot of music was being played
below scale in New York. He didn't play that way. "I ain't no
Joe Below." Things got worse and he was down to one-night

stands in Brooklyn, Newark, Asbury Park. But Joe was as good as ever.

Joe tried tours and the band got stranded, dead broke, in whistle-stops. He settled down in Huntington, West Virgina, owned a bus and for four years played around in the country. Then a frost split the motor block and after Joe fixed the motor, the bus was wrecked. Greedy lawyers hounded him over the accident. Then the big one hit. He had no money to take care of himself and his teeth came out.

"A horn man with no teeth, he ain't no horn man at all. Good store teeth cost money."

To finish his story, he had high blood pressure and doctors cost money and he didn't have any. He wrote his sister: "Should anything happen to me, will you want my body? Let me know because I won't last forever and the longer I go, the worse I'll get unless I take treatments."

There was nobody to save Joe Oliver. "Don't think I'm afraid because I wrote what I did. I am trying to live nearer to the Lord than ever before. . . . Goodnight, dear."

Two months later he was dead. His sister spent her rent money to bring the body to Woodlawn. But there was nothing left over to buy a gravestone; it's still the unmarked grave of a king.

If they ever erect that stone I'd like to suggest the words to be carved on it. They were shouted by someone just before the last wonderful chorus of *Dipper Mouth Blues:*

"Oh, play that thing!"

XIV

To get back to those first jazz recordings for Gennett. A few months after Oliver did *Dipper Mouth Blues*, now a collectors' item, the Wolverines made their first records, with Bix Beiderbecke and his cornet. And one of the first recordings was a composition by Hoagy Carmichael. It came about this way. . . .

It was the spring of 1924, and it seemed the moon was always out; the air of those nights was for me full of sweet smells, an atmosphere soft and pale purple. The grass was greener, the moon was yellower. I was feeling no pain. Even the bootleg likker didn't bother me. I'd take a drink of whiskey with Bix that tasted like kerosene in my mouth and like a blowtorch going down.

"Best I ever tasted."

"Have another, Hoagy. Turn the record over."

The Wolverines were in town for a dance on the campus (one of ten dances I had booked for them). Bix and I were lying in front of the fraternity house phonograph, early in the morning. We were playing Stravinsky's *Fire Bird*. I remember our talk.

"Wonderful. Another slug?" Bix said.

"What's wonderful?"

"Music. Busts you wide open."

"Sure. Whiskey, too."

"Guy used to be a lawyer," Bix said.

"Who?" I asked, feeling guilty about my law courses.

"Stravinsky."

"Rimsky-Korsakov touted him off the law."

We passed the jug.

"Touted him offa the torts, huh?"

"I dunno who he slept with."

"Torts."

"Turn the record over."

There was a long silence. "Why don't you write music, Hoagy?" Bix asked, rolling his head around to face me.

"You're the one that writes music. When you put a horn up to your mouth, you write music."

"Write music, Hoagy," Bix said again, as if he hadn't heard me.

"You do yours different every time."

"I like it different. Like Rimsky-Korsakov. He heard this Stravinsky cat and told him to give up the law. . . ."

"We already said that," I said. "Stravinsky study law?"

"Sure. Young guy like you. He studied law, then Rimsy—ah, hell, you know who I mean—he told him to write music. So he wrote this. The fags dance to it."

"Dance?"

Bix got up clumsy, half-loaded, and did an entrechat. He fell down and lay where he fell, moaning softly. I turned the record over.

"Ballet, they call it," he said.

"Sure is," I said.

We lay there and listened. The music filled us both, I sensed, with terrible longing, dreadful urges, wonderful desires. Coupled with white mule liquor, it was strangely moving. It made us very close and it made us lonely, too, but with a feeling of release, a feeling of elation and ecstasy. You don't forget such a mood. They only come a few times in a lifetime.

The record came to a stop. A long silence and I was afraid to speak, afraid I'd break the mood. I can still see Bix lying there, the music still echoing in his head and me knowing it.

"Bix, I'm trying to be a composer."

"Who's teaching you?" Bix asked, rolling his head on the floor so he could look at me with his half-hooded eyes.

"Everybody."

"That's nobody, Hoagy."

I said, "Everybody is teaching me to be a composer. Every time I see a pretty dame I learn more how to be a composer. Every time I hear a Bucktown dance I learn how to be a composer. I'm dizzy."

"Nothing wrong with you," Bix said, "except you're drunk."

"You, too."

"Never said I wasn't."

Of all my meetings with Bix, this one is clearest—I remember every word we said—and every drink we took. It was like a mutual confessional.

"Funny little horn you blow," I said. "I'm gonna play me a horn. You try to blow it all out, Bix, you try. . . ."

2

I woke up in the Kappa Sig house, my head still echoing with Stravinsky's *Fire Bird*, my mouth still filled with the kerosene-taste of white mule. Who is that guy in the other bed sleeping in his underwear? It was Bix. A pale blond galoot needing a shave, sleeping in his tattered underwear with his funny little mouth open, smelling like a distillery, his crumpled clothes piled on the dirty rug, the hole showing in the sole of his right shoe.

"Bix," I said, gummy mouthed.

"Go away." He opened one eye.

"Get up. We gotta get going."

"Lemme have your razor, Hoagy."

"Wash your face," I said. "Sorry I haven't a fresh blade."

"Where are my shoes?"

It wasn't easy to coordinate our fingers and limbs.

"You dressing?" I asked him, shaking smoke from my head.

"I'm trying."

We were earnest as we mumbled and fumbled in our hangovers and dressed with uncertain hands.

Slowly, half-buttoned, we walked downstairs, holding the rail, and out into the sunlight. All at once it was fine. My flivver, "The Open Job," was waiting. I had to start her.

"Get up there, Bix, and yank the spark down and ease up the gas when she catches."

"Okay."

Bix sat idly behind the wheel, twiddling the spark lever. I got to the crank, kneed it in, pulled out the wire loop of the choke with my left hand and gave her a quarter turn. "The Open Job" roared to life; I leaped to the controls before she died. We sailed down the street, steering poorly.

The spring air, soft and cool, was in motion, blowing the fumes from our heads. It blew away the hang-over and drunk talk, the music, the inside secrets we tried to put into words. Drunks talk too much.

We went chugging down Indiana Avenue, our minds personally unoccupied, aware we were alive, surveying casually the small-town Sunday morning. People coming from church, smugly pious in their righteousness, dressed in their best, at peace with a world Bix and I never knew. Happy contented people.

3

We got to the Book Nook. Monk, the Dada poet lolling out front, was watching the scene. Monk looked at us and drawled, "Look at these guys riding around with their kidneys."

For an instant we saw ourselves as Monk saw us, then we put the vision from our minds and wandered into the Book Nook. Monk sat down limply and started talking about Teapot Dome, the dead Harding, the oil gangs. Monk was, I saw, as indignant over the theft of oil from the government as the people walking home from church. *Why didn't I care more?*

Coolidge was president, business was sound, things were all right (with a few notable exceptions). Gradually the talk got to the things we *really* cared about.

"What are you going to do this summer?" Monk asked Bix.

"I think we got a job in Indianapolis."

"Whereabouts?" I asked.

"The Casino Gardens."

"A good place."

"Play something on the piano, Bix," Monk asked.

"Just a little," Bix said, and he went over and sat down. He didn't seem to play well or with any sureness of touch, even if the notes were coming out right. He was fingering something of Ravel's. He could play only part of it. His fingers—small for his size—were stiff and they seemed to go the wrong way, like a cat stretching a slow paw to find a note that wasn't there. Chords I'd never heard, little odd-shaped chords that shouldn't be played on a piano. They were interesting even if they did make me squirmy. Then I saw that was the way they were written. When the melody escaped him he improvised stuff as good and always with a delayed beat with the left hand that made me squirm even more, for fear that he was going to miss it. It was beautiful and I was a bit jealous.

I said, "I want to play a horn. Bix can play the piano, maybe I can play a horn."

"Oh shut up."

But I insisted. That night I got a horn. I played it. I played it badly, all right. I blew my lip to a shred, blew fraternity brothers right out of the house at practice time. They took to hiding the cornet in a chandelier. It didn't stop me. The University *Daily Student* recorded the end of this period, using the name Wad Allen had stuck on me:

SCIENCE CURBS HOGWASH McCORKLE'S CORNET

In two minutes the sucking of California lemons achieved the end that forty deafened men failed to accomplish in a period of several weeks. Hogwash's cornet is banished.

Hogwash was puffing his cornet, his eyes and cheeks were bulged and his massive body was writhing to the rhythms of the horrible musical blurbs emanating from the muzzle of the instrument.

At that point six scientifically-minded youths filed into the room silently and stood in solemn and sinister poses. Hogwash McCorkle raised his eyes and continued blowing. Then—at a signal—the six produced lemons and sucked them. Hogwash's jaws began to ache and his lips puckered. A faint wheeze was all that came from the horn.

A stock of lemons was kept in the fraternity house and I would have to drive into the country in "The Open Job" to practice in the shade of a defenseless tree. I carried the horn around with me like a baby, at night put it to sleep in its cradle case, an old faded-green velvet box. My ambition knew no bounds. I even tried to push it on my own band.

"No, Hoagy, we need you at the piano."

"No guts, none of you."

"That's right."

Our band played the Senior Siwash, the last dance of the year on the campus. I took the cornet along. It was a shambles. I had difficulty collecting the money for the engagement. The other members of the band turned mean so I gave up the horn. But I was not convinced. I still think the cornet was my instrument. All I needed was practice. But I turned to composing.

"That's better," said Monk. "Composing is rather a silent thing."

"I'm never going to listen to your poems again."

"Yes you are, Hogwash."

It was Wad Allen sneaking up behind me.

"Monk just did this pretty little play for the Vagabond and we beg of you to face the East and utter not a sound while I sic a chicken on it."

Wad read:

Culps Down Feltment, Or Whose Color Is Your Sweater Now?

Scene: The Mississippi. It is evening and there is a feeling of football in the river. Three old men are seated on a nervous horse.

First Old Man:

I am an old man, now. For many years I have been coming through the weather. I own a garage.

Second Old Man:
    That reminds me of Minnie.
Third Old Man:
    Whose horse? What Minnie?
(First old man falls off horse and drowns. He goes down spelling sapolio—horse becomes ambitious and looks like violin)

Act II

Scene: Market in Hthvp, Siberia. Two old men and nervous horse are measuring pears.
Enter: Four-story building followed by several smaller stories. Man leaps from window of building and lands on nervous horse. Horse dies.
Man: (Whose real name is Hollis Twelvecakle alias Horace Dozennoises, but better known in his home town as Leah Q. Peters) Did I hear you guys talking about Minnie?
Second Old Man:
    Whose Minnie? What talking?
(Third Old Man dies of enthusiasm)
Second Old Man:
    When Minnie was nine years old she got an option on a deep chicken.
Twelvecakle (sobbing on pears):
    Whose chicken? What Minnie?

The End

Later I read the play to Bix. In response he uttered the only inanity he could think of at the moment. "I am not a swan," he said, which was to become a byword between us in the years to come.

4

Since I had heard Berlin in Palm Beach I had been a composer. The only trouble was I hadn't composed. So I decided to compose something. The way Da Vinci did Mona Lisa—I hope—to get it off his mind.

I went into the Book Nook and sat down at the piano. I got up, scratched, and ran my fingers through my hair. I sat down and played Zez Confrey's *Kitten on the Keys* to loosen up. I had learned it from a record. Then I doodled aimlessly for a while. I went over and drank a Coke. I got kind of excited and went back to the piano, determined to bring this thing to a head.

The Wolverines were coming down for the weekend to play a dance. I would compose a piece for them.

I said to the counterman, "Here it is the beautiful spring. Awful good time of the year to write music."

"Sure is."

"You think so?"

"Well, I ain't no piano player so maybe I don't know."

He was no help and I went back to the keys. I got a phrase and played it and played it again. Again and again and again. I was emptying the Book Nook. The students, after profane pleas that I play something else someplace else, were leaving in droves.

Finally their pleas prevailed. They drove me out to the street. I made my way back to the Kappa Sig house and started on the cigarette-scarred piano to drive my fraternity brothers crazy. Before supper I had it! Well, I had *something*. I wondered how Mozart or Bach or Stephen Foster knew they had a live one.

The Wolverines arrived in town. I played it for them, proud as a farm wife throwing twins.

"It's got four breaks," said Wad.

"Call it *Free Wheeling*, Hoagy."

One of the Wolverines (I don't remember who) said, "We'll record it for Gennett."

They got out their instruments and two of the band memorized it.

"Here, use this chord."

"Bix, remember this part."

"Okay, Jimmy, fake it for sixteen."

Jimmy Hartwell set his hands fingering in the air.

George Johnson kept nodding he was ready.

They went off with the music in their heads. Someone got me out of bed Saturday morning a week later and there was the record. I felt as flustered as a new bride. The Wolverines had gone to Gennett in Richmond during the week and recorded my composition under the title *Riverboat Shuffle*. I sobered up and experienced a strange detachment from it, maybe setting the pattern of my emotional responses to almost all the tunes that followed. Nothing.

I listened to it, silently, head down, eyes closed. Somehow there was no thrill there (I could have cried).

"It's a great arrangement," I said soberly. "Thanks, fellows."

George was proud of me, and beaming.

"That's all you feel?"

"I never listened to my own music before. I guess I don't know how to react, George." (That has been a major tragedy for me about a lot of things. I either don't react or I react too much.)

But I was a composer and that was a heavy load.

XV

Having become a composer I decided to travel. I went up to Indianapolis, and I strutted around a bit, my head full of unwritten music. I also took it easy. I was amazed at how easy it was to become a composer. All you have to do is sit in the Book Nook and write something, show it to the Wolverines, wait till the record comes out, sit on the front porch and something fancy would happen—or seem to happen.

In the meantime Dick Voynow had played the record for Irving Mills of the Mills Music Co., New York. One day I got a letter from Irving Mills, Music Publisher. I had never heard of the firm. It began in a very friendly way:

"Dear Hoagy: We have heard the Wolverines' record of *Riverboat Shuffle* and we wish to publish the piece. Enclosed is contract with Mills Music . . ." I didn't read any more; I grabbed the contract. Hoagland, the lawyer, didn't notice it had no promise to publish, only a line to pay royalties *if* they did publish. I was too happy to be legal. I dreamed about how I would spend the royalties. I had forgotten that it had taken twelve years of solid piano pounding, happy moments, hard ones, the sad times and the good ones, to produce one little tune. It was easy, I felt. I could do it again. A dozen times. A thousand times, but later.

Having written music, I felt I could do it again—but I was still in awe at the idea, and I didn't rush right into any new composing. I told myself, let the well fill up again. I made the rounds among my fellow musicians—fellow professionals.

The Casino Gardens was an open-air pavilion on the highest bank of the White River near the outskirts of Indianapolis. The dancing area was surrounded by gay, fluttering umbrellas; the moon always seemed closer with the floor open to the sky, sugared with tiny stars. The orchestra played on a tiered platform under dim lights. A most romantic place to a successful composer. I relished the smartly dressed boys and the white-clad girls in their summer dresses, their big hats: ever-changing patterns moving to the music under the big yellow moon. They danced because they loved to dance (and were the best dancers in the country), their young bodies gliding silently not to miss a wicked note or beat of the band.

I came to sit and listen to the Wolverines, their music coming to me slightly muffled but in all its glory. They were at their best playing low-down and rutty in the open air, and Bix would cock his head to one side and pop his eyes as he played. There would come a shower of notes of such beauty that the dancers would move back to their tables as though they were sleepwalking. It was a sin to dance to this sacred stuff. The music, the people, the night all had merged into that rare thing—a perfect moment.

As for me, I inhaled the streams of melody cutting the soft summer air and knew what true pleasure was.

Bix would hunt me up during intermission by way of taking a cigarette break. We would find a secluded room and a piano where we could doodle *Riverboat Shuffle* or *Copenhagen* without interference. I'd doodle the melody and Bix would pump the bass and imitate cymbal licks.

"That's it, Hoagy."

"Thanks, but it's the way you taught me."

Doodling—or noodling—was a favorite pastime of ours. Doodling was what the Four Mills Brothers introduced years later, and made into a fortune. Bix and I didn't think it was commercial. We didn't think. It interfered with our doodling and the sounds we made.

The disintegration of the great Wolverine band began late that summer. Vic Moore, with his walrus mustache, left the drums in favor of Vic Burton, who booked the band into Gary, Indiana, and later the Roseland Ballroom in New York, where they failed to draw crowds. Their failure in New York is one of the mysteries in jazz history. Maybe they were too early, too original, and not loud enough.

I heard Bix had jumped the band to join an outfit in Chicago, and Jimmy McPartland took his place in the Wolverines. He blew a great horn but the band was slated for extinction. As with the buffalo, time may have meant the Wolverines to pass.

2

In the fall of 1924, I was at the University to wrestle with more law courses—and re-collect a band of my own. I went back to school lighthearted, always a mistake. It was fine to be back. The old musical gang were all there and prepared to play.

"Just tell where and how."

The Indiana Theatre in Bloomington renewed our contract for another season. This job was a lot of fun. The students sat usually in the front rows, feeding and necking. If they thought the music poor they would shower the band with peanut shells and any other objects at hand. When the debris fell dangerously thick, the band would switch to a sure-fire arrangement of *Alabama Bound*. That would calm the critics.

In a few weeks the mid-term exams were on me like Frankenstein's monster. My grades were pretty middling. The flunk-out blues hummed through my mind as I stopped in the Book Nook one morning; the low-down mood lay on me thick as mule-hoof glue. Blue mood. Mac McCarthy, a contemporary, was having a morning spasm on the piano. It always amused me to watch him play. Mac's technique was the most ludicrous I'd ever heard. When he got hot he flapped his hands like chicken's wings and drooled slightly from the mouth, as if swallowing a shot of the white mule we got from the coal mining towns. The nerve and muscle reaction to potent white mule was amazing and fascinating to watch.

"Listen to this, boy."

He was going good. I stood and watched somberly as he gradually wore himself down to a nub.

"Take it, Hoagy," he said, heading for the spittoon.

I sat down, extending my arms in an imitation of Mac and started playing a hodgepodge of frustrated feelings all tumbling inside me. I struck a peculiar strain and carried it along carefully, as if it were a crate of eggs.

Mac caught it. "Do that again, boy," he said.

I looked up at him poker-faced.

He beat out a slow hesitant rhythm on top of the piano with the flat of his hand.

I was working as if in a trance. I changed the rhythm to a fox trot; then back to waltz time. Then back again. Class-time came and went. Lunch time came and went.

When I finally finished what I could of the main theme, I had seventeen measures.

"Only seventeen measures," I said in despair.

"I wasn't counting," Mac said.

"Go away. Haven't you any classes?" I was wringing wet and sucking air.

"I never heard of that one, Hoagy."

"Who has? Doesn't seem to make much sense."

I worked out an interlude, an odd chanting theme that had occurred to me as I played. Mac stood beside me, his rhythm beats on top of the piano spurring me on.

"Keep rolling, boy, keep rolling."

"To where?"

"Sounds good," Mac said. "You need an introduction."

"I guessed that."

I worked a while longer, alone except for Mac, some stray geeks coming and going around me. They knew I was crazy. When the introduction idea was ripe, I played through the whole thing from start to finish, hardly daring to breathe.

"What does it sound like, Mac?"

Mac's big foot stomped out the rhythm and he started drooling again, a sure sign of intense cerebration in his family. "Sounds like a whore chanting in church."

"Wrong—" I said. "More like a colored woman washing clothes. Big stack of dirty clothes . . ."

Mac nodded. "The dirty clothes blues."

"Something like that," I said.

Mac left—he had a girl. "Keep trying."

Ed East, a Bloomington boy who became known for his radio and motion picture acting, was first of all a piano player and composer. *Hello, Hoosier Town* was one of his songs, and once I asked him:

"How do you write songs, Ed?"

"I don't know," Ed told me. "I don't know."

And he was right. No one ever knows. You don't write melodies, you find them. They lie there on the keys waiting for you to find them. They have always been there. If you find the beginning of a good song, and if your fingers do not stray, the melody should come out of hiding in a short time.

Melodic patterns and sequences that go to make up a finished song are almost as firmly knit together as the molecular structure. One who has played and sung thousands of good melodies and who can let his heart sing and his fingers play with tempered emotion and without arbitrary direction may well be a composer. When you *know* you are on the right track, pound it out for all you are worth and shake up the emotions. This may help shake up the old piano to give you more.

I played the new music again and again, for hours. I could think of nothing else. I was bewitched and dog tired.

Harry Hostetter came in near dusk. I played it for him. He stood there and listened, his eyes half-closed, poker-faced.

"Once more," he said, "and stop shaking. It's good."

"Good or pretty good?"

"Both."

I played it again with fingers like dead eels. I hated *all* music, *all* composers.

"Hoagy," he said. "Maybe it ain't so bad."

"You're an encouraging bastard."

I went home and fell into bed, unwashed, unthinking, my mind dissolved.

3

Curt Hitch and his Happy Harmonists, the band from Evansville that played Wolverine style, came to town two weeks later to play a dance. They heard me play the tune.

Curt nodded. "Son, we're going to make some records for Gennett. Write another tune and we'll record both of them."

"Sure. What?"

"I need a fast one, a hotsy number."

"That's all you have to tell me?"

"That's all, composer."

So now I was composing on order. I might have been weak in the head, but I was a work horse when the creative enigma had me in a hammer lock.

I worked out another tune for Curt, the best I could to his specifications. I called the new tune *Boneyard Shuffle* as a sequel to *Riverboat Shuffle*. With these two tunes, we piled into my flivver, lit out for Richmond and the Gennett recording studios. I didn't feel too sure of myself. I was nervous in anticipation of my first recording. The studio was a dreary looking Rube Goldberg place with lily-shaped horns sticking oddly from the walls. It didn't have the effect of soothing me. Yet I knew it was a magic spot. Here one's efforts were given some sort of permanence—at least were put on wax.

I asked, "This is *all* we need?"

"Sure."

The horns sticking from the walls looked spooky and I was pretty upset by the time we were ready to make test records.

A voice said, "We'll do a playthrough."

We ran through the tune for the technician. Like everyone there, he picked *Boneyard Shuffle* as the best number.

I said, "*Boneyard* is just a hotsy-totsy number and everything has to be hot these days."

Curt said crisply, "At least we think so."

The technician pursed his mouth. "Me, I'm dubious about using the other tune at all. Its timing is twenty seconds too short."

"Never mind."

"Let's toss it out entirely."

I protested, "Just twenty seconds. Hell, the time it takes you to sneeze and light a butt. Twenty little beats of your lousy pulse." I acted as if my future hung on those twenty seconds.

The technician picked his nose. "Well, you guys are the music boys—what do we do?"

I made my face into a mask of despair and turned it in the direction of Curt.

"Hoagy will put in a piano solo," Curt told the technician.

I looked at him and felt my teeth chatter in my mouth. "I can't just do a piano solo part," I said.

"Sure you can."

"Not with you mugs standing around breathing down my neck."

Curt said, "Take ten minutes, boys, and go watch the choo choos outside."

They left tactfully and I stood staring at the piano. And I tried to think of a piano solo. It was drilling in solid rock with a pencil point. I thought of my family, my little sister's funeral, my mother playing hymns on the old golden oak. I thought of Monk, of Bix saying, "I am not a swan." Everything whirled past, but my fingers lay numb on the keys, and time was running out. Scared, worried, I hit the piano, thumping out notes.

Five minutes later I called the boys back in. "It's this or nothing."

The technician gave the signal—recording—and we began to cut the wax.

Harry Wright started his introduction on the clarinet. He stood there, blowing plaintive notes: young and new to this business. I saw he was shaky too—I wasn't alone in my buck fever! He could hardly hold the reed in his mouth. I don't know why you can't hear our knees knocking together on the record. Maybe they shook in rhythm to the music.

Fred Rollison on the cornet was taking it easy, saving his lip for the lead parts.

Suddenly it was time for the piano solo. I had banged out something while the boys were out, but would I be able to repeat it? My hands were damp as I hit the keys, getting into the start of it. The rest was just prolonged nerve reflexes—I wasn't having any part of it myself. And then it was over. I was entirely unconscious of anything I had played. We staggered through the last chorus. It was finished, done—buried.

I looked up. Someone said, "That does it."

The technician, obviously still unimpressed, said, "I'll play it back. You can hear it and make any changes."

We looked at him. "Make changes? How could we change it?"

"It's your record," he said.

Then we were hearing ourselves do the side. It all sounded oddly historic and far away. I tried to believe I was hearing *my* piece. It was difficult to believe that. The tune came real, then my piano solo began to fill the dismal little room. I didn't recognize a note of it as it ran its course. The record ended. There was a war whoop. "Whahoo. We did it!" We danced around the studio, berserk, arm in arm, howling like Apaches on the war path.

The record, we frankly thought, was terrific.

That was the mildest thing we said about it. Youth is rarely modest, and I was still shaking from the piano solo, so shouting was a fine release. A few years later, I built the piano solo into a song and Johnny Mercer wrote a lyric for it. We called it *Lazy Bones*.

We left the recording studio higher than kites. Harry Hostetter got a copy of the record, *Washboard Blues*, and wrapped it in an old shirt and laid it in my old car. A few days later he took it to a stone cutter and local poet in Bedford, Indiana, a man named Fred Callahan, a friend of Harry's.

"Fred, we need words to *this*."

"Got a lot of gravestones to shape."

"Come on friend—your customers are in no hurry."

"All right, I'll listen."

Fred played the record a few times. He laid down his chisel, looked pained, and took up a pen. He wrote a lyric about an old colored woman scrubbing clothes and named it *Washboard Blues*.

"What do you think, Harry?"

"A beautiful job."

That's how things were done in those days. And we had only delayed the customers' gravestones about twenty minutes.

4

I don't want to claim any virtues I don't have, and I don't think helping one's family is a virtue. I see it more as a duty, a very pleasant one. I had a strong feeling of obligation to family. Most of the money earned in my early days, running a cement mixer in Indianapolis, I contributed to the support of the family. In my college days I managed to send little gifts from time to time. In later years, it was easier to help more.

I had a kind of obsession to get the family things I was not able to get for myself as a boy, little luxuries I thought of. Once when I was attending a Kappa Sigma convention in Denver, I spent my last few dollars for an Indian rug that I knew would delight my mother. She looked at it and said: "I don't know—people may say we have Indian blood."

When my band was playing at a Lake Erie resort, I brought her a picture of Pygmalion and Galatea. I never knew just what my reason was for buying that particular picture, but my mother treasured it. "Galatea isn't a bad looker," she said, "if you like stone women, and *he* evidently did."

"It's just a legend."

"Well, talk starts from *some* facts."

Once I spent my last dollars on a hat for Grandpa Robison: it was his birthday and I felt I ought to bring him something.

Pa was getting along in years, but was spry enough to walk to church and back, except that his memory played tricks on him. I felt a new hat was something that he would like and use. His own hat was a beaten-up object of a nondescript color, originally black, I guessed, and rather flappy-doodle in a worn-out old age. On the frontier they used to call that style of hat a bee-hive. It was handy for lifting hot stove lids, brushing off a bench, and in a pinch could hold a couple of quarts of water if you finger-plugged the holes.

The new hat for Pa was a snazzy number, not too conspicuous, and of a gray English complexion, and for me just then, expensive. I waited until Sunday morning when Pa in his birthday best sallied out to church.

"Surprise, Pa." I pulled out the hat and set it on his brow at a jaunty angle.

He thanked me profusely. Ma brushed him off and I led him to a mirror for inspection. "Now take a look."

Pa looked at himself with obvious approval for some seconds. Then his mind began to wander. "Hoagland," he said, turning to me, "I look purty good this morning. Just right except for this gol-durned hat I got on. Remind me to get a new one."

5

In the winter of 1920, I took down with the flu. Dorothy Kelly, my high school sweetheart, came over to see me. Lying there in bed, my bones aching, I felt ashamed of being such a poor object, trying to cringe down into the bed to nothingness. I disliked Dorothy seeing me looking like that. She looked wonderful.

"Now cheer up, Hoagy—and stop frowning."

Her visit was a tonic, and in a couple of days I was up and soon away. Grandma Carmichael asked Dorothy to dinner.

"You mind, Hoagland?"

"No. A dinner for us to be topped off by your cherry pie?"

"If you want. Nice fine girl, Dorothy."

"I guess so."

It was a wonderful dinner, and Dorothy was laughing and lovely and I was in love again. Outside, it was a cold, blustery night but inside it was warm, a night of closeness and silly talk. When the Bloomington power plant failed (as it often did in the days of the utility sharper, Sam Insull) we stood two candles on the table.

Grandma kicked my Uncle Edwin under the table.

"Ouch!"

"I think we'll leave the young folk alone."

"Why? *Ouch!* Okay!"

And was I glad.

The candles on the table burned in the best china candlesticks; Dorothy, a picture to take your breath, grinned, "He takes a hint."

I carried the candlesticks to the piano and I played a little piece on Grandma Carmichael's old Chickering upright.

"This is for you and me, Dot."

"Just for us?"

"Nobody has ever heard it but us."

"Thank you, Hoagy."

"Hoagy!" What a nice sound! It was always "Hoag" before, but this was softer, more intimate. I kissed her for it and it was to remain my name ever after.

"Let's go for a ride."

We bundled up and went out into the crisp cold night. Dorothy climbed into "The Open Job." I turned the crank, expecting the usual explosion that the motor was alive and willing.

Nothing happened. I cranked again more frantically, almost dislocating my back. "The Open Job," faithful through the years, was dead as a doornail.

Dorothy laughed, "Oh, you and your broken down tin lizzie. Let's go back and you can play for me." Which I did. And I felt sorry for all the college couples out necking in the cold of their open cars. I was deeply in love. But as usual, I couldn't commit myself fully.

I did feel, though, that the old car had let me down, even if it had meant a cozy evening. There was no doubt the jalopy was getting old.

I sold "The Open Job" to two innocent freshmen, rosy-cheeked and with money. They promised her a good home, humane treatment. I got ten dollars for her and a tennis racket that needed restringing.

They had no luck with her. She finally rolled up to the curb in front of the dean's house and died—under a strange hand. They left her standing in a cold rain, inert, a relic of a lost time. I found her there the next day as I was hurrying alone to the Nook. Alone, cold, wet. Her radiator dented in hopeless shame. I patted her a couple of times, fingered her carburetor.

I said, "I'll take you home."

I adjusted gas and spark, I tugged her choke. In the still falling rain, I seized the crank. I gave her the old quarter turn. She roared into snorting life. I sold her again, for ten dollars, to Old Man Becovitz, the junk man.

It was easier to get rid of the car than the image of Dorothy. And so we continued to be sweethearts, not pledged, not sure of each other, but dazed by love and touched by passion. I was aware that there was lacking in me certain firm convictions as to just how much I would sacrifice for love, and what love could give me in return. It was, I suppose, a kind of weighing of the pros and cons, and that, in love, leads to nothing but trouble.

My secret self, the shy part that lived in the shadows of the public figure, never did make up its mind about things, but always let the other fellow carry the situation, *any* situation. I was healthy, sensual, normal in most respects, yet I was not honest in my relationship to a personal emotion that was very strong and should have been all giving.

It could all go back to my roving father, that ever-hunting, never-finding parent who terrorized our childhood by tearing up our roots so often. From then on I never seemed to be able to make any move without first taking two steps backward to see what it would, or could, do to my life. It's movement but not progress. I was unaware of the basic fixations I had gathered in my childhood, and I may be wrong in what I say about them, but it was years before I could mellow and relax, and give and take in the emotional wars between men and women without making sure that the escape hatches behind me were clear.

We are all stained by something penetrating in our past, and our reflexes master us at times when we would rather have lost our heads. I was, as a young man, a poor head-loser. Which didn't make me less of a misfit in the big, brassy world I had to live in. This is all just the long way round to saying I was a heel about Dorothy. Or can I claim I was too young to understand fully my developing feelings for women? But then who cares for a young boy's side of the story.

XVI

Near Christmas the family ties ached like old scar tissue. I was dependent on Mother for warmth and encouragement. I was beginning to understand Dad. I headed for Indianapolis to visit them and we tried to create a mood out of Dickens. Bix came to town and phoned me.

"Come down to Richmond with me—hear us make some records."

"Feel in the mood?"

"It's cake money, Hoagy."

I met him in my new Ford, a Christmas present to myself. Bix smiled. "You were one for fancy living."

"Just transportation."

"I'm doing some records for Gennett so let's go. But first stop around the corner here. I want to see someone."

"O.K."

I asked Bix, "Who's going to be with you on this date? The last one was a grand futzup."

"Going to record in slow-drag style."

"That's new."

"I've got some guys who can really go. Tommy Dorsey, Howdy Quicksell, Don Murray, Paul Mertz, and Tommy Gargano. They're going to drive down from Detroit and meet us. Stop here for a minute."

"What are you going to make?" I was impressed.

"Hell, I don't know. Just make some up, I guess."

"Bix, it sounds great."

"The guys are bringing three quarts."

I was having some misgivings. Bix was in high spirits, looking good, and kissing a pretty girl good-bye.

"For a start."

"What time is it?"

"Oh, three or four. We better get going." The need for sleeping never entered our heads. "Let's go over to the Ohio Theatre and jam a while."

"That will weaken you for recording."

"Just wind it up, Hoagy."

We got to the theatre after closing and took over the grand pianos in the pit. All alone in the empty place, we banged out chorus after chorus of *Royal Garden Blues*. Every interpretation was hotter than the one before. One of us would do the bass chords while the other ran hot licks. I played one-fingered versions of Bix's cornet passages. I think that pleased him. A few hours from dawn, Bix said, "Time to leave."

"If you say so."

We started for Richmond. A cold crisp night, the world rimmed in white frost. Around us the landscape slept and trees stood stark and strong. We were halfway to Richmond in the chilled dark morning, the hint of day growing slowly. We stopped.

Bix took out his horn. "It's just the most goddamnest wonderful time."

He cut loose with a blast to warn the day and to start the horizon stirring. My own horn, long unused, was lying in the back of the car. I got it out. Solemnly we exchanged A's.

A new car, a frosty crystal morning, smoke just beginning to curl like hat feathers from the farm houses, the dormant bush set in mirrors of roadside ice, and we two young men, the only two living things in sight.

It was not yet dawn and the world was still half in darkness. The horns felt cold in our hands and it took courage to put them to our lips. Some bird, lonely and cold, gave out with an awakening cry.

"*Way Down Yonder in New Orleans,*" Bix said.

"You hit one I know."

Bix was off. Clean wonderful streams of melody filled the dawn, ruffled the countryside, stirred the still night.

The trees and the ground grew clearer, the sky turning from black to sepia to pale green, toned in just right. I battled along to keep up a rhythmic lead while Bix laid it out. A wind drove autumn's dead leaves around us. Bix finished in one amazing blast of pyrotechnic improvisation. He took his horn away from his mouth slowly, as in a sleepwalker's dream.

"Hoagy," he said thoughtfully, deadly serious, "you weren't bad."

"Jesus, you think so?"

We drove on into the burnished day—and I knew it was another of those great moments to remember.

2

We got to the studio in the smoking weather, met the boys, and sat around a while exchanging stories. We all felt warm and intimate. The bottles got near sea level. Bix started doodling on his horn. He seemed to find a strain that suited him. By that time everybody took a hand in composing the melody and the true friendship of musicians began: with the music.

I have a photograph taken of the group that day. Bix is casual, leaning against the piano, his legs crossed; he's in half profile and looks young, a little boy grown up too soon. Tommy Dorsey is beside him, bespectacled, his trombone at his mouth. The rest are in various negligent poses, waiting for the damn camera man to get out of the way so we could get going before the edge left us.

"We're ready?" Bix said.

Everyone nodded. "Oh sure."

As far as I could see they didn't have any arrangement worked out. Or tune either. Yet when the technician came in and gave them the high sign, they nodded.

"Spin it, Sam."

"Any time you're ready."

Away they went, down into the lowest darkness of mood and music. Dorsey said in the break: "Call it *Davenport Blues* in honor of Bix's home town."

"Thanks, fellas."

It had been done in lazy jig style. As the dead bottles—empty— were racked up, the recording grew screwier and screwier. I smiled and tried to keep them company, glass by glass.

A high number was *Toddlin' Blues*. By the time it was finished, they were all having a little trouble staying in front of the horns. The effect to my willing ears was wonderful. They used the "I'se comin' " strain from *Ole Black Joe* and performed miracles with it. Bix just grinned and finished the last bottle. "Waste not, want not, Hoagy."

Driving back in a bone-chilling blizzard, Bix nearly froze to death in his sleep. I asked myself, where are you going, Hoagland? Hot jazz, hot trumpet, music, blues, stomps aren't for you as a career. The law is noble, the law is fat with rewards. That's where a man, a lawyer, finds security and position. That's how a fat cat gets into the exclusive country club and plays golf in the afternoon. And yet there was the story my father used to tell of Abe Lincoln seeing a roadside gravestone reading: "Here Lies A Lawyer and An Honest Man," and Abe asking, "Since when are they burying *two* men in *one* grave?"

3

Bix and the group had hexed me. Back at school, I'd no sooner crack a book than I'd think of the musty recording room, the smell of bad whiskey, the sounds recording on the turntable. I missed it, wanted it, shabby unknown as it still was.

Raining—a perfect night for studies, I'd say, but I just couldn't get started. I'd bolt, in my green slicker, an old felt hat pulled down in front. Outside, the storm, outlined in soot and sulphur, was passing to the east. Lightning still etched yellow cracks occasionally, over the tops of the big maples shaking in their moorings.

I was in a bad mood. On slick, empty streets I moved toward the door of the Book Nook. It was fairly crowded, people held captive indoors by the storm. Monk and Wad and other members of the Bent Eagles were in their customary places. The air was still electric, smelling of ozone and wet wool and mud and green growing things.

Inside, all eyes focused on me as I came in. I kept one hand thrust deep in my coat pocket. I was seized with an irresistible impulse to act out my mood, to go on a desperate, rasping, emotional binge. My eyes at hatbrim level glared, looked straight at Monk and then from one form to another. I leveled on one or two faces, then I shifted my glance back to Monk. The Dada poet just stared back.

"Hogwash has been eating bird seeds."

Somebody tried to laugh—thunder rolled—rain curtained the windows in silver floods. I wished I really had a gun. I was as batty as a creep but deep down it was wonderfully satisfying, macabre, and new.

"Don't move, anyone. I have a revolver!" I said. I tried to make the words come out in the hollow tones of a dry-mouthed killer.

Someone started to say, "Calm down and—"

Slowly I made a complete circuit of the booths, throwing a glassy stare at the occupants, never dropping my wide, mad grimace. There was a hush, a kind of frozen photograph of a fixed action. Finally, I walked to the counter. Stacks of heavy china dishes attracted me. Without looking, I reached out my hand and gently pushed a small stack. The dishes made a fearful racket as they smashed. The audience gasped for breath. I moved to the biggest stack. I pushed it close, closer to the thin edge of destruction. A couple entered—a flapper in wet fur—a jelly bean in wide pants—I wheeled around.

"SIT DOWN! AND—DON'T MOVE!"

They sat—quickly—without a word. Pete Costas, the Nook's owner, moved carefully in my direction, like a bull fighter testing a red cape. A motion of my hand in the coat pocket stopped him cold.

"Don't do it, Hoagy; they *very* expensive."

"Shut up."

I looked squarely into his eyes. I gave the dishes one more small perilous shove, just this side of disaster. The tension in me was awful and painful. I pushed my hat back, walked quickly toward the door. "I think I can go up and study now. Thank you." I left quickly. Banshee howls were audible from the Nook as I crossed Fourth Street to my room. Either I had a big hunk of ham in me, or I was really so disturbed that I had come near to a breakdown, I didn't know which.

I thought of poor Buddy Bolden—pappy of jazz—who had been locked up over eighteen years then in a Louisiana home for the insane, a staff barber, while all unknown to him, jazz came to full maturity.

It was a close call for me. Soon on the campus the story was spread that the Book Nook had been demolished the night before, singlehanded, by an unknown hoodlum. Town people, driving by in their cars, stopped to inspect the damage, and order a hamburger or a banana split.

Looking back, I think what nearly drove me insane was that I didn't know whether jazz was a passing fad and I was kidding myself, or whether it was so large and overwhelming that it might destroy me.

It comes down to this, I thought: any art form is as great as the people who come along and work on it. And jazz had been so for the few people who had played it—or who sang it or wrote it.

It's new, I reasoned, it's done a lot, and could have done more. Some of it is the work of a race and a people; it's the music of most of the lonely, the sad, the happy, and the hopeful. When the right people come along to take it someplace new, they will. Meanwhile, you can only wait. There must be a kid with a horn playing alone, dreaming of what he can do and maybe he'll be the big gun of jazz, or more likely he'll die in an alley of bad likker, freeze to death with nothing to show for it but some scars. Maybe some other kid besides me is mooning over a battered piano, hoping to get into a band and make enough money to survive. Maybe he'll play music that will grow with the years so that when he's mature, it will be the real jazz. So I didn't go insane, not just then anyway.

Some other jazz men have left records of their early reactions. Bunk Johnson remembers his mother saying, "Son, mama saw a cheap cornet and a new one and as you are doing so good I got to get it for you if you will be a good boy."

"Now I was that," he said, "and my dear mother got it for me."

And King Oliver wrote: "I only need one thing and that is clothes. I am not making enough money to buy clothes as I can't play any more. I get a little money for the use of my name and after I pay room rent and eat I don't have much left."

And here is how legends grew: "The first thing Bix did was go to the closet and pull out a pint of gin. Then we went to a Chinese restaurant," said George Wettling.

4

In the fall of 1925, I was peddling dance programs to help the educational kitty along. Mostly I was at the books: Torts and Contracts, Briefs and Pleadings—the Law, and through the Law, a fat life of a lawyer—in the future.

But spring threw me off the tracks again. The smell of spring and home-brew sidetracked me. I took to spending afternoons out at Granny Campbell's. Granny was an old Negro mammy who was as wrinkled as a prune. She had a sure touch; malt and hops and yeast merged, fermented and sizzled in the dark brown potent brew she dispensed to low-budget college groups.

"Man, it hit you just right—at the right price."

"It seems to percolate your insides, just as you said, Mrs. Campbell."

She'd grin and sing:

Nobody knows my name,
Nobody knows what I've done.
I'm good as any woman in town.

I'm no high yella
I'm a deep yella-brown.
I ain't gonna marry,
Ain't gonna settle down.

But Granny also had a misery; a misery or two. She'd sit in her old creaking rocker and ask to be handed her own bottle of beer. I drew up another rocker for myself.

"Mr. Hoagland, you a lawyer fella—I got myself arrested once for a makin' this brew, an' I want to ast you—you so biggity a-studyin' for the law—is makin' home-brew a *sin?*"

"Not to anybody on the campus that needs it."

I laughed, drank, and her way of phrasing was like a little tune. "Old rockin' chair's got me, cane by my side . . ." What was the note I needed? A tune, part of the tune was running through my head with the home-brew and the creak of the rocker.

I took on so much brew that on the way home I jumped into the new city reservoir with a couple of friends to cool off. I stuck my head up out of the water and saw my friends frolicking and splashing about.

"I got it!" I yelled. "The music!"

"Put a cork in it, Hoagy, or they'll jail us forever if they catch us."

"But I got the song—part of the song!"

"Let's get the hell out of here, or it will be ninety-nine years in the big house, *with* a song or without a song."

"Yes—we better run for it."

It was a serious offense to swim in the city reservoir. It was the first decent water Bloomington had ever had. We drove off—but didn't escape the law. We were jailed that night for reckless driving on Third Street on our way to Rose Hill Cemetery. Someone wanted to hunt four-leafed clover.

The desk sergeant asked me: "How do you spell your name?"

"C-a-r-Michael," I told him.

Pink said, "Wait until he comes to mine."

"Cadou," I said, turning around, "what are *you* doing here?"

"Don't you remember, Hoagy? I helped you drive negligently."

"I thought a guy named Pink was with me."

"Was that a *sin?*" Harry Hostetter asked as we strolled happily to our Lysol-smelling cells.

I lay on the thin frowzy blanket and wrote out the song—in my mind. Old Granny Campbell had oiled us well. When the sun rose over the campus, Tom Huff left his poolroom, came over the hill and bailed us out.

"You fellas oughten to drive when lushed. I got enough trouble running a pool hall."

"It hit us suddenly," I said.

"Oh that Granny Campbell—I hear she's a voodoo queen."

"Maybe," I said, wondering what was making me itch.

5

It had been a good year, with the usual few bad moments. A year now drawing to a close and my college days with it. A month after Christmas, barring accidents, I'd be a Bachelor of Latin Law. A full-grown college-bred male. No more jazz, no more swimming in the waterworks, no more homemade beer at Granny Campbell's. Adolescence would be safely in the past. However, the national and personal future looked rosy. Stu, a Kappa Sig brother in Florida, wanted me to come down and take a job offered me by a M. D. Carmichael (no relative) whom I had met during my Florida trip. ("You graduate and I'll take you on in my office.")

"Dear Hoagy," Stu wrote, "Miami, the Magic City of moola, hip flasks and dough, the land of palms, the whacky metropolis, is the unblemished nuts. Real estate is selling like a million dollars a spadeful, and living quarters are very seldom. Corn Flakes are thirty-five cents a bowl. Miami, the cockeyed wench, is wondering what it's all about, and so am I as we Charleston on the piano lids. It's warm and swimmy here, crazy as a laughing farm. You must come down. Not with a band. Night clubs are fouled full of wind-jammers and you wouldn't stand a chance. Acts are the rage; naked plucked dames and wobbly chorus gals that would be boo-ed off an armpit burlesque show are eating three times a day, getting fat.

"Land is selling above water and below. What a boom—a regular land rush. Everybody has their heads together dealing—even the suckers get rich. Come on down, Hoagy boy, and be a lawyer among the grapefruits and the 'gaters. I'll be standing on a corner waiting for you, smoking a dollar seegar. I look like an old man with egg on his fly and a green collar-button stain on his neck. I'll be picking my teeth with a kitchen match and reading a last week's newspaper about sex crimes up North. By the way, Hoagy, I'm crazy about the letter X. Say it eleven times; it sounds like a little boy scratching his behind with a piece of cocoanut shell.

"Hurry on down and be a real lawyer. Yours, Stu."

(One year out of college Stu was running the city desk of the *Miami Herald*.)

6

Being a stanch union man, Dad heard about the big double pay for overtime in Florida and it took him no time to get mother and my two sisters to heave ho. The pay was good but they had to live in a shack. No houses for rent. And no piano but, by God, Dad owned an automobile, the worst worn-out heap of tin shavings you ever saw. When I heard about this I was anxious to join them in the boom country and hang out a shingle: Hoagland H. Carmichael, Atty.

I would miss the campus life—if not the classes—miss the roar and the doing of four years' routine of being a college boy. I brought away not just banners and a tarnished silver mug or two, but an ache for a way of life that suited and sustained me.

I could have become the eternal college student, always on

campus in some little job, growing old and worn among new classes. Only my demon drove me. I would miss the band. I felt I could capture a little of it to take away with me. As a farewell gesture I arranged with Gennett to record two tunes with my band. Not for posterity, for me. (Monk asked, "What has posterity ever done for us?")

It was a bittersweet recording. I was pleased to be able to do it, even though I knew it was ending one phase of my life. I have always been prone to delay partings, leave warm ruts, discard old things for new.

It was Gennett's first use of new electric recording equipment and the sides were clear. It sounded great to us. Tears came to our eyes as we all listened to it, full-grown men sniffing back sobs for a last, last time. Every note was an individual thing, a part of the man who played it, and that man a friend. Then fate put her big foot in, and before we could get a single pressing, the master record was destroyed in some technical mix-up. Three years of musical sweat and friendship melted away into a blob of twisted copper. Carmichael's Syringe Orchestra down the drain.

I was leaving the next morning for Florida and felt sad and low at the record loss. Odd how a thing can be lost and still with you. I could hear it clearly. Wad never better on his saxophone, Chet Decker's inspiring rhythm on his drums, Billy Little over his head and yet pretty wonderful. I'd even see Art Baker's handsome face creased in concentration, his lip pressed into his horn, thinking of Bix, I was sure, as he pushed the little valves down. Harold George with the big horn and the bad heart. Wasn't anything wrong with his heart that day, nor the horn. Bridge Abrams' happy face bowing his fiddle like a demented octopus. And me, trying hard, a lot of piano I hoped to make come out right.

And at last I won a law degree. I had it—a Latin Bachelor, on stiff, fancy paper—just right to frame and hang on the wall while waiting for clients. I had made it: what could I do with it?

THREE

"When Stars Are Bright"

XVII

The world in which I came of age was only occasionally the world of jazz, of bootleg booze and postwar frenzy. It was a world of middle west conservatism, blanketed by many Victorian carry-overs. From what we read, we young people didn't feel that the old world could have been any more virtuous than the new—in spite of the chastity belt. Human nature being what it has always been, we smugly said, man must have indulged in as many vices then as he did now.

The average undergraduate of the 1920's wasn't a jazz man. He was a lot of other things; radio-bug, grind, drip, highbrow, muscle man, but he was rarely a jazz man. He read *Judge* and the old *Life* magazines for wit and, certainly, the mad "smart" world of *College Humor*. His favorite artists on the more progressive campuses were probably Jefferson Machamer, Russell Paterson, Milt Gross, Peter Arno. In my community it was John Held, Jr., an amazing draftsman with a keen eye to caricature who was able to catch in controlled form the frenzy of his flappers and campus philosophers. The undergraduate, if he talked of music at all, was likely to engage in some numb discussion of the relative merits of girl singers. He was considered one hell of an entertaining guy if he could do a reasonably accurate imitation of their *boo-boo-boo* style of crooning. A kid who could dance a bit, strum a uke, wind a victrola, was a music master.

The average co-ed was soon to be an admirer of crooning male vocalists and her party vocabulary was sprinkled with "keen" and "nifty" to describe the things she liked, or "vile" and "smelling to high heaven" for things she didn't. She rolled her stockings, took her chances on the back seats of strange cars, shingled her hair, and smoked cigarettes in a holder.

Male audiences at sports events were either cocooned in coonskin coats or those God-awful slickers that got stiff in cold weather. As I remember it, the lady folk had little or no style about them except perhaps a pompon pinned onto an imitation baby lamb jacket. No celebration of a grid-iron contest—win, lose, or draw—was a success unless everyone got a fragment of a goal post. I never went in for that sort of heraldry.

Looking back, it's amazing to me how many of the big fancy names of the arts we set aside for those we Hoosiers had a hankering for. Gene Stratton Porter ("Girl Of The Limberlost") beat out James Joyce on the campus, and we thought Booth Tarkington was the greatest of the American novelists. The wit we admired was of George Ade, a very funny man, whose ability to tell fables in slang of the day was more popular than any comic of today, even if less rewarding at the box office. None of us would think of starting the day without reading "Abe Martin" by Kin Hubbard; it added just the right philosopher's note to the morning. Hubbard, a much neglected humorist, would please today's ironic world in all its trouble. He appeared on the front page of the Indianapolis Star. I am tempted to quote him out of context, which would be unfair. Maybe I'll have a project of declining years: editing a book of his best sayings.

If all this made our campus appear rural, in many ways it was. We had our wisenheimers who knew all the arts, and also in personal relationships kissed and told. They were great talkers, but me, I didn't really believe all they told. We were not sissies and we all let fly with a wild oat. But there was always the feeling there was more shine and polish to sinning in the fancy Ivy League colleges.

I remember having Coke with a campus queen and getting on the subject of sex.

"Well, Hoagy," she got around to saying, "I think it's perfectly all right to go the limit with a boy you really like, because if you don't he gets all worked up, and kind of sick and jumpy.

So a girl is really just trying to make a more healthy country. . . ."

I wondered why I hadn't thought of that myself.

Our heroes of sports were Charlie Paddock, Nurmi, Dempsey,
Babe Ruth, Bobby Jones, and Tilden, and a greased channel
swimmer named Ederle. ("A gorilla can whip Jack Dempsey
with one hand tied behind his back," said Arthur Brisbane.) I
never quite understood whether Helen Wills (Miss Dead Pan)
was a headliner because of her tennis form or her physical form.
(When I played against her in the forties, I had to admit it was
her tennis.)

Paul Whiteman was at his peak, a big band with arrangements,
known as "schmaltz." He was a fat national institution and when
he and his Palais Royal Orchestra gave a concert at Aeolian Hall,
New York, assisted by George Gershwin, whom he commissioned
to compose *Rhapsody In Blue* for the event, presenting symphonic syncopation, the event nearly made a lady out of what
some people thought was jazz.

I heard the Whiteman-Gershwin concert at the Murat Theatre
in Indianapolis and I was greatly impressed. But oddly enough,
I also watched Rudolph Valentino do a dance or two to some
strange Spanish melodies the same year and I was more impressed.
The *Rhapsody In Blue* thing was not new to my ears but the sexy
music of the small group that accompanied Valentino had fire in
it. It was neither blues nor jazz and it added to my thinking—my
composing thinking, as you will see later. This might have helped
in my attempt to write the first American approach to the
rhumba.

2

After the Gennett Record bust session in Richmond, Carmichael's Syringe Orchestra looked itself over, shook hands all
around, shed a few tears and I was off for Florida by way of
Washington. Halfway through Ohio it rained that night and to
amuse myself I recited Monk's story about Silo McRunt to the
purr of the finest motor ever put in a Ford. It was relaxing.

SILO McRUNT, AGE THIRTEEN

Once upon a time, during an extra horse. Silo McRunt, age thirteen, tried to count up to his mother. His actions were noticed by his wet neighbor (a mere bacon fanner by trade) who had just defeated his breakfast. He rushed to the phone and called Vacant 780-W, which is the number of the Hard Lard Connecting Works. Frantically he described the situation to Mrs. Razzbushel, author of 'The Veto of Lard Harness,' or the 'Hard Varnish of Leto.' Mrs. Razzbushel had been suffering with bundles for three days, but she poured herself into the hearse and drove at neckbreaking speed to the scene of little McRunt, age thirteen, counting up to his mother.

She sped through the night like a damp sausage. She had a ham in her hand and the blisters on her feet sang like turkey in the twilight. Meanwhile, and unknown to her, an old man sat down in his grave.

II

We must return to the scene of little Silo McRunt, age thirteen, counting up to his mother.

'Have you ever stink like Bozo?' he cried, falling on his bargain. McRunt, of course, was what one would ordinarily McRunt. And, why not McRunt? Others had often McRunt. From the wooded hills and templed valleys came the soft sweet echo—'McRunt.' In the Northwest, the people adopted a slogan—'Fifty-four McRunt or forty.' Even in far-off Europe the feeling prevailed. Swarms of Germans filled the public squares singing, 'McRunt Uber Alles.' In local, Idaho, a man died near a gymnasium covered with McRunt. Even old horses sweat like McRunt.

The wet neighbor was confronted with a desperate situation. He stretched his ears for a sound of Mrs. Razzbushel. He was rewarded with his wife's belch, near the cistern. She belched again, nearer the cistern. 'Ain't gravy windy?' she chortled, and with a final blast she tiptoed into the cabbage.

McRunt had won.

Two days post diploma, in hillbilly country, I parked the car to eat a rancid lunch. The waitress said, "Passin' through?"

"That's right."

"Fer Florida?"

"I hope so."

A seedy-looking bum with a deputy's badge next to me on a stool asked, "Yo' got a license to conform with West Virginia laws?"

"What laws?"

"Pay fer yer vittles, come with me."

He took me before a dirty-faced, unshaved individual who allowed as how he was the justice of the peace.

I said, "I never heard of any special laws."

"I fine yo' sixteen dollars."

"Look here!" I said.

"Yo' got sixteen dollars?"

"He do," said the deputy, taking out my wallet for me and pulling out the sum. "I reckon half this is yourn, Judge."

It was divided right before my eyes. My academic knowledge of the law stood me in great stead. I knew enough to keep my mouth shut when being taken in chain gang country. I rushed out of West Virginia. A fool or a non-lawyer would have gotten sassy for justice and ended on a gang.

I stalled in a snowdrift just outside of Uniontown, Pennsylvania. A native said, "First time in history anyone got stalled by snow on the Lincoln Highway."

"I'm historic."

They pulled me out of a drift eight feet deep.

"Deepest drifts in years."

"I'm sure of it."

Snowbound in Pennsylvania I remembered parts of Monk's play: "The Building of the Wedding Hen." Enter: Balloon Ascension—rest of play performed in a small cave in Kokomo. Enter: Paperhangers shouting "Hen-diana, t-hen, Wiscons-hen, not-hen!" Third paperhanger: "Give these to mother." . . . Takes off trousers, dies. The end.

3

I got to Washington and found my old pal, Hank Wells, up to his navel in the business world. So deep it took us ten minutes to find a bottle, a piano, and have a jam session. I said firmly, "I put jazz behind me, forever, two days ago. I'm a shyster now."

"A man has to kind of wean himself," Hank said. "Taper off."

"I'll visit my music publisher."

I left Hank, and oddly, for a man bound for Florida, ended up in New York, to see Irving Mills about publishing *Washboard Blues*. The record business was booming and the sheet music market was ripe for picking. Tin Pan Alley I found to be a lot of dusty unswept rat holes.

Irving Mills offered me a job in his publishing house. "You could make records here and compose like a mink."

"Not me, Mr. Mills. New York doesn't look wholesome to me. No trees, no leisure. Faces I don't understand."

"That stuff—trees and leisure—it can kill you."

"I'll think about it. Goodbye."

A one-track mind have I and so a one in a million chance to do what I should have done went by the boards. I had a bigger boom than Florida in my right hand but took the left hand road.

That night before I left town, Batty De Marcus, George Murphy, and Johnny Johnson threw a party for me in the Club Mirador. Red Nichols was there to show me the eastern jazz style and to hear my new piano antics. George made me repeat the story about my job at Kingan's cleaning pigs' asses to bring the jam session to a close. I guess Red told that story one hundred times.

The twenties in New York City under a full head of steam moved ahead, with drunks and unemployed reporters and jazz-men playing the match game for drinks in the speaks on 59th Street, where a tenor banjo, with ukelele stringing, would be strummed, while the cop on the beat mooched a free bourbon and branch water. I liked the twenties at the end there, where it all came to a witch's boil. And I feared it, too. It was too rich for my country boy blood. Follies girls and Peter Arno faces on the yachts on Great South Bay, some jazzmen playing *Hold That*

Tiger on deck, and Templer roadsters, Packard and Jordon convertibles parked on the dock.

For the good listeners we played the right jazz; the squares could go hear Vincent Lopez play *Nola.* A drunk in the john next to me at Helen Morgan's was wearing a boutonniere of the Legion of Honor, and by his side, maybe, was the guy who killed Dot King or knew why Arnold Rothstein was really rubbed out. I didn't know—and what was more, I didn't much care. Hating violence, I read mostly the sport pages. The best things in life don't make headlines.

4

It was exciting to hear jazz in New York City, but I attempted to demonstrate what the boys in the sticks were doing.

"Listen, we're not that far back in the woods."

At one session where I was playing away, George Murphy, the actor, and then half of a small-time dance act, broke into gales of disrespectful laughter at the way I dressed. He didn't like my country tailoring.

"That coat," he said, "it's from the Joe College comic strips."

"Nothing wrong with the coat whatever," I said "It's coon-skin, maybe radical in design and tone, but it didn't cause a lifted eyebrow in Bloomington."

"But the sleeves, Hoagy, catch in the keys and make you skip a beat."

"Naw it just gives the hot lick a new twist."

By three o'clock we were exhausted, and George told us a funny story that we didn't laugh at so we knew we were worn out. That's when you catch on it's late and you're ready to fall down.

George was poor then—and a Democrat—but he was to get an MGM contract soon, and Louis B. Mayer would convert him to the true faith of the gold-plated Republican ranks.

George and the rest urged me to stay on in New York, "coat and all." But it was not for me.

"I'm going to Florida."

"Who ain't?"

I did four hundred miles the first day, five hundred the second. The washboard Georgia roads unjointed me. I had left hazy and hung over, but at last there was West Palm Beach. It was hardly recognizable. It had grown, it sure had, since 1922 when I last saw it. What had been a quiet resort town was now a mad frontier city in white linen suits and panama hats. Everyone was for himself, as if scheming to get his picture on the silver dollar. Prices were sky high. My friend, Cookie (Wilbur Cook) was already a lawyer; together, we moved into a dingy green basement apartment. True to his word, Mr. M. D. Carmichael, my patron, came through with the promised job, and I hung out my shingle:

Hoagland Carmichael, Esq. Att. at Law

Cookie was a fine hound-dog, bourbon, corn pone lawyer. My association with him rubbed some of his legal knowledge onto me. I got fifty dollars a month as a clerk, and anything extra I could pick up on my own, free to choose among mule-kicking cases, collecting bad debts, shotgun weddings, orange grove escrows, wife beating, fishing contracts, land assessments, incorporating of fine companies by men with earnest smiles and no assets. Things went along first-rate.

Music hardly entered my head. I played piano occasionally in a little cafe where we dined on soft-shelled crabs, turtle soup, swamp-raised steaks, feeling smug not to be one of the jazz hounds stranded in Palm Beach and Miami when the bubble burst. And it burst like the dam at Johnstown. Everything fell apart, screams rent the air, the years of the locust were upon Florida. It was great for lawyers. They feed on disasters—other peoples'.

Jimmy Hartwell and Taz Walters, two of the Wolverines, checked into town. Taz had joined our little band at Lake Manitou back in 1920 and sang like a bird. He was not only hunchbacked, he wore leg braces. We'd take him out to the golf course to watch us hit the ball. One day he threw away his braces, wobbled around until he was sick in the stomach, but in a week he had a five iron in his hands.

Taz had a pawn ticket and a tale of woe for me. "Jimmy hocked my watch to have professional show business photographs made of himself. He looks good; still my Ma gave me that watch for not smoking before I was twelve."

"Got a job?" I asked.

"Going to play a ten-day triangle cruise between West Palm Beach, Havana, and Miami. Things will be all right."

I felt a twinge of envy for them. "Have a good trip."

I got a call from Jimmy at midnight. "Something went wrong, Hoagy. Taz can't make the cruise."

I heard myself saying: "I can drum."

"*You*, Hoagy?"

"Well, there's no one else in town who can play a lick."

It took me ten minutes to find Vic Moore over at Bradley's Casino and borrow his drums. "Sure, Hoagy, I'm not using them. I've gone social. I'm gambling with some rich broad's money."

"Keep it up."

"Can you drum, Hoagy?"

I'd never played drums before in my life. But the tourists on the *S.S. Sunflower*, spending on a rising market, didn't know the difference. And I played the seasick, rusty piano in the afternoon while the captain—a shy but over-amorous man—sipped tea and brandy with the ladies. I didn't think of law or courts or cases. We arrived in Havana, to find sunshine, stink, fun, vice, a police state, the few rich, the many poor.

5

Havana for a tourist was hot, throbbing nights, a strong legal beer, chili powder music, fat brown girls, a tropical moon, a beachcomber mood.

"Hello," the girl said it in faintly exotic accents as she came to my table.

"Hello," I said in faint Indiana accents, making an alley in the empty beer bottles before me, the better to see her.

"Sit down, señorita. Drink?" I asked politely.

She agreed. "Drinkee."

"Hey Juan, beer for us. Does it show I'm U.S.A.?"

I felt here was the real thing. The beautiful, depraved, vice-drenched item. I loved the whole idea of it. The Havana B-girl functioned much like her sorority sisters anywhere in the world. For her drink and for every drink I had, she got a ticket or chit which she turned in for her percentage of the take at the end of the night. However, I didn't care—her beauty blurred the edge of my repugnance to the hoped-for sordid undertone of our relationship. I was in a first-class blur anyway. She got up and moved as part of the music. I let her lead. The Cuban beer was strong. The rhumba (the first I had heard) gave me a kick in the groin, almost like the first time I heard Chicago jazz.

"Just grand," she said.

"I likee very much," I said.

"Me or the music? The drums?"

"Both of you, chili baby."

It was all just the way I expected: I mean the low-down place, the fans turning on the ceiling, the unshaved beachcombers— some girls pushing dollars down the tops of their stockings *and* this warm living Latin type in my arms. The two sweating, leering drummers were Jamaicans and really good. They hit a tantalizing beat and kept it with no letdown. The place smelled of hybrid flowers, rum, and busted plumbing.

"Um-m-m," said the girl, low into my left ear.

"Where you from, honey?" I asked.

"Pierre," she told me in a low taut voice.

"I don't read Pierre," I said. Obviously, though, this sloe-eyed dame was part French. (The French, I remembered, were supposed to be leading the league in *l'amour*.)

The joint was crowded, happy and under-lit. As we danced, she melted in my arms with a touch more intimate than any in

Indiana. I executed a few steps of my version of rhumba. She followed every step as if glued to my toes.

"Pierre," I murmured. "Tell me, sugar, where is it?"

"Pierre, you nut—it's still in South Dakota."

That tore it. I said lamely, "We better hit the ship." I was stone sober—and it all seemed vulgar and trite.

I wrote *One Night in Havana* in revenge, maybe. It was never published.

In Florida, I went back to the law office. It seemed to have become duller and more prosaic in my absence. My leather swivel chair needed oiling. Law books were duller than ever.

"Cookie," I said one hurricane-storm-signal day in the office, "we're doing all right, aren't we?"

"We're high on the hog. No money in the bank. But—"

"We joined the Elks, the Lions."

"And the Big Brothers, Hoagy."

"Sterling fellas—they bore the bejesus out of me. But they're good for business—eh?"

"That's right, Hoagy."

"Don't mind me."

Cookie looked at me and smiled. There was something like pity in his voice. "Sure, Hoagy, you'll settle down. Take a little branch water and bourbon to settle your bile."

6

I began to hear things through the window. "What's that?" I asked.

There was a sound of music, a haunting refrain. It clogged my mind with old memories, with solid and daffy desires a thousand times stronger than practicing law. In a radio shop across the street a sidewalk speaker was pouring out music: a phonograph record. That and nothing more.

I jumped up, shaking like a yearling maiden at the barrier. "That's *Washboard Blues!* My *Washboard!*" I hollered.

As I ran out of the office, I heard Cookie's steps behind me. "Put on your hat, you crazy loon. You'll get sunstruck!"

"I am already."

At the music store, I stood panting, sweating, watching a record go around, trying to read the name on it, going cross-eyed. Finally it stopped. It was a record of *Washboard Blues* that I hadn't known had been made. By Red Nichols. I bought it —the only copy in the shop.

I played it again and again. Finally, I went slowly back across the street. I made my way to my desk aimlessly, and started straightening up paper clips, stuffed baby 'gator, leaking fountain pens, a cracked sea shell ashtray lettered *Coral Gables.*

"I'm pulling out."

"I figured you weren't just playing with your toys."

I sat down at once and wrote Red a letter—which still exists, and gives some example of my early prose style, unpolished by college Lit. courses.

Dear Red: I just bought a sample record of *Boneyard* and gave it a good mauling. Let me rise to state that it has given me the kick of my life to see my beloved brain children *Washboard Blues* and *Boneyard Shuffle* on opposite sides of the Brunswick record by none other than the great Nichols.

Putting all the polite laundry aside, I really and truly appreciate it.

I am planning on leaving this tin-eared rendezvous of hunted bank presidents and screw drivers' union for points north on April 3. I'm about broke and will, of course, need a good steer.

I don't think there is a thing in Indiana. I would like to keep at the law but times are too bad to have a young kid like me playing hoppity-hop on the glass-topped desks for 50 a month.

But the thing that interests me most is writing tunes.

I hope to be able to make a couple of Gennett records when I get home and I could use them then. In the meantime, I wonder if you have any suggestion to make? One of them is a march one-step with a rapid lead and sort of like *Tiger Rag.* Jimmy Hartwell is nuts about it so that's two rooters. He and the boys think your records are the 'last word'.

Then I have one on the lines of *I'd Like to Shimmy Like My*

Sister Kate that's a little different. But I have no ideas for breaks, etc. . . . If you can see fit to be interested in the above and can offer a suggestion I would appreciate it immensely.

With thanks,
Hoagy

The letter done, I looked up at Cookie.

"I'm sorry," I said.

"That's all right."

"It's—" I began to clean all desk drawers by emptying them into the waste basket.

"Hoagy," he said, his voice kind but amused, "you never had a chance, you music-struck bastard."

I felt the burden of unspent time lift off me. "Maybe," I said, "I can get up home in time for the Junior Prom. I hear Jean Goldkette's coming down and he's got Bix and Frank Trumbauer and Joe Venuti and hell, all the boys will be there."

Cookie grinned and opened our liquor cabinet—an old medical case. "I need a vacation myself. I'm coming, too."

Our simple preparations for our descent on Bloomington was a suitcase of bootleg liquor with wisps of Nassau seaweed still laced into the protective burlap sacking. We were careful to get the real stuff that was then being stashed by the rum-runners at the bottom of the Atlantic and later brought ashore when the coast was clear.

We arrived newly tailored, barbered, primed and sun-tanned for the Prom. It was a night to carve on stone. Bix was at his peak then, and the violent grace of Joe Venuti sawing his fiddle fascinated us. In that complicated mosaic of his music there was no hole.

Red Ingle doodling his lyrics had us in hysterics. Off-color inanities, staccato lines, baffled the chaperones. "Do-dada-la, corkupbuttgrabuptitandslugupashot . . ."

Bix's eyes popped as he turned his head to one side, a habit he had on the bandstand when great things were coming from his horn. He said in a sultry voice his entire vocabulary of response. "I am not a swan."

The feeling of good old days was upon me once again. I had music, friends, joy, *and* poverty. The real life. No pleadings except to plead with Bix to do that *again* on his horn.

I started working on the piano. Harry Hostetter would listen silently; if I caught him grinning and rubbing his hands that meant that some pretty fair note had caught his fancy. We listened to all the new records. Frank Trumbauer was recording superb releases for Okeh. Bix, Eddie Lang, and other greats played with him on the disks. When his record of *Singing the Blues* appeared, I felt the ultimate in jazz technique was there for all to ponder. The record was a sensation among musicians even if the public didn't dig it.

Louis Armstrong was recording in Chicago and his *West End Blues* had started a real career for him. Louis had started to vocalize, a guttural style that shook us; his record of *Monday Date* with Don Redman on sax and Papa Hines at piano gave us new wonderment.

XVIII

The pleasures of the jazzmen in my time were few. Once in a while a band leader raced speedboats, or collected old pistols (that's how Russ Columbo died), but the average jazz player on his time off grabbed what he could and used it the way it came.

Usually the jazzmen had no roots; sometimes they'd get a letter, but not often—they were non-writers. They lived in a hired room with a bottle for company and maybe a pack of reefers hidden in the light fixture. Not all jazzmen were like this. Some bred to reproduce the race, had homes and wives, loyal blondes who were fairly sober too. Many settled down and tried to be like everyone else. But in the main, the average jazzman was a drifter—not rich, not too happy. And dreaming of the big break: like his own band, his name in lights over the Paramount, a solid set of best-selling records bringing in money. But as for the chicks, he was casual about it rather than ardent. To the average jazzman most of it didn't happen often, and even when it happened, it didn't last long.

The boys were human, as I knew them, and had all the human vices, and all the human virtues, as well. But many people seem less interested in virtues the jazzmen shared with everyone than in their vices, common or uncommon. It's hard to figure out drugs and their influence on the music produced. It's been over-done by sensational talk on the subject. But it's also been avoided by many as having little to do with the music produced. Some place between the two schools you could find the truth. Some of the true jazz players were a bit on reefers. I'm sure the drug is harmful, but some medical men say it has less harmful effects than hard drinking. It is the seed of a hemp-like plant that grows wild in many empty lots all over America. The best of it comes from Mexico. It's a big business; its peddlers and users push the sticks at a steady pace. The coarse leaves are ground up and made into cigarettes and the user smokes them in big puffs to get high— a state in which time seems to stand still, where the top of the head is filled with all the answers, and everything seems easy to do, better, stronger and longer. The letdown is slow. They taper off on milk and, when it's over, have some hang-over and foul breath. But I can't say it really helped the music. The few times I had it, it mowed down inhibitions, and it made an urge to be way out in a creative way. But the results were dreams, musically, that didn't work.

2

> Comin' through the Palisades
> I lost my way,
> Thought I was on the road
> Workin' for MCA

MCA, Music Corporation of America, was the bandman's boogie man. A talent agency, it had been started in Chicago by an eye doctor named Jules Stein who had connections and was booking bands into clubs and roadhouses, and then expanding. It was a time of expanding and taking over, and needing the right voice in the right place. Soon Stein was booking bands and acts into the big hotels, the theatres, and growing like a tumor till it was called "The Red White and Blue Octopus" and if you weren't with MCA, you were often out of show business. They were cold and hard, and out for the big money they saw in the new music. Most of the big bands toured for them. Some said you couldn't work if you didn't have Stein's seal of approval (for 10 per cent); anyway jazz walked through their door, hat in hand. Later, they came to New York and to Hollywood and became the biggest of the flesh peddlers. They made percentage deals, cut up action, helped or hurt people. They kept their grip on the band business and singers; even composers were signed up to feed the kitty. They had a lot to do on Broadway, then went into radio.

And people were listening to jazz.

Trumbauer's records, *I'm Coming, Virginia* and *Way Down Yonder in New Orleans*, were my favorites. Bix's choruses on them were a complete musical education. Add Bix's chorus in the Okeh record of *Riverboat Shuffle*, his work on Whiteman's *Sweet Sue* and *China Boy* and you've got it all; a digest history of a great period.

When Paul Whiteman brought his band to the Indiana Theatre in Indianapolis, Harry Hostetter and I hurried down to hear them. Bix was in the band along with Trumbauer, the Dorsey boys, Bill Rank, Eddie Lang, and Joe Venuti. Whiteman now had an orchestra that nearly made true the title "King of Jazz" (as he billed himself). That he never really understood it—and deviated from it a lot—well, that was show business.

Loafing at the stage entrance, Bix introduced us to the Rhythm Boys—Bing Crosby, Al Rinker, and Harry Barris.

Bing was lean, blond, balding—and full of personality. He held out a warm hand. "Howdy."

Bix was fatter than when I had last seen him, but looked well. He jumped with jovial success and even a neat prosperity, from his crisp bow tie to his shiny shoes.

He had grown into a handsome man. We kidded and I felt out of it. But the feeling of remoteness vanished, almost immediately. Bix took us over to Jimmy Dorsey, who introduced us to Whiteman himself.

"Pops, this is Hoagy Carmichael and this is Harry."

"*Riverboat Shuffle*—sure."

"So somebody heard it."

Whiteman was huge in those days, a mountain of suet, but cheerful, and wise to showmanship.

"What are you working on now?"

"Things," Harry said, for I went speechless when it came to talking of my creative side.

Whiteman told us a couple of his favorite stories. We laughed, enjoying ourselves. Paul grew serious. "Hoagy, that Gennett record you all made of *Washboard Blues* is a great job. It's really a good record."

"Have you heard the lyrics?" Harry asked.

"Does it have lyrics?"

"A stonecutter down in Bedford, Indiana, he heard the tune and wrote some words," I finally said.

Whiteman took me by the arm and led me to the piano. "Okay, son, you sing it."

"I've never sung," I stammered like a village idiot.

"Those are the best kind of singers."

Bix said, "Just natural voices."

Tommy and Jimmy Dorsey were at one end of the piano and Paul and Bix at the other. I sang the number the best my wheezy voice would permit.

"I told you," I said. "No voice."

There was a moment of silence and I stole a glance at Whiteman's face. It was rubicund and bland as only a fat man's face can be. He turned to his manager, "Gillette, get a ticket for this guy."

"What for?"

"He's going to Chicago with us and sing in the concert record we're going to make of *Washboard Blues*."

"Mr. Whiteman—hold it." I gulped, nearly fainting.

Whiteman laid a big paw on my shoulder. "It's going to be all right."

"Not for me."

He could feel me trembling. He laughed: "Did you ever hear, Hoagy, about the time Trumbauer was a fireman on the railroad? Fired steam for an old crock they called Cranky Joe?"

"No."

"Trumbauer was firing a boiler for this Cranky Joe, the toughest engineer out of East St. Louis, Trumbauer with a saxophone under one arm and a lunch pail of delicatessen under the other.

And he got away with it. As a matter of fact, in a couple weeks he had the engineer giving him a hand with the shovel."

"No kidding?"

"Sure, so he could get his reeds and pads in shape for blowing when they hit the roundhouse. If he can, *you* can."

"But he had practice," I said.

"Ever hear about Isham Jones?" He worked in a coal mine all day and played sax half the night. Now, you know you can't keep fit that way. One day he falls asleep and misses setting the guard set in the rails so the coal cart won't run away. There was a tired mule in front of that cart. Ish wakes up just as they're about to reach the first turn, and truck and mule fall off ass-backwards and I hear that mule's been looking all over the country for him ever since. That's when Ish beat it for Chicago and put a band in at the College Inn."

As I laughed I sensed Ish and Whiteman and myself were maybe all the same kind of people, and I wasn't betraying any mules.

3

Traveling with a big band is like being an inmate in a traveling zoo. Gags, ribs, girl trouble, money trouble, just trouble, bull sessions, card games, taking over the spare upper. Socks are traded, shirts stolen.

Chicago ran wide open. The Capone mob liked show folk. Whiteman, a powerful drinker in those days, had target practice with pistols, and beer drinking contests with some of the gang chiefs; at least, he often told the story.

In the Uptown Theatre in Chicago, where Whiteman's orchestra was playing, I stood in the wings and watched the boys go. Bing was often late. Between shows we gathered in the small basement rooms backstage and played hot jazz. Bix and Jimmy Dorsey were almost always in on these sessions. I also practiced what, for lack of a better word, I called my singing. I had a good deal of it to do in *Washboard* and the damn recording date was approaching.

Bing came around while I was rehearsing once and stood there, hands in pockets, smoking a pipe.

"Mind if I glom on to the words, Hoagy?"

"No—but why?"

"I'd just like to learn it," Bing said, expressionless.

"What for?"

"It's such a swell number, chum, I'd like to learn it."

"Well, sure."

I didn't realize until later that Whiteman wanted some voice insurance in case I bombed. He wanted somebody there who could do it if I didn't. Bing was being kind to me. He didn't hint to me I might flop. They wanted to make a good record whether I was on it or not. Bing was always kind and calm, but he was more given to living it up before he became an American institution.

So I exercised my voice and observed life backstage. Crowds of jazz followers flocked to the stage entrance to see Bix. Many were musicians. They'd crowd around him and urge him to play.

"Come on Bix—just a few bars."

Bix didn't like meeting so many people. "It's driving me nuts. I try to remember them all, to keep them straight in my mind and not offend anyone."

"That's fame, Bix," I said.

"It's bad for my nerves. I get the heebie-jeebies."

There was always a bottle in his room. I would hear Whiteman ask, "How's Bix *feeling* this afternoon?"

Bix was Whiteman's pet. He loved Bix as if he had been his own boy. But the bottle stayed.

The side of *Washboard Blues* was made at the Victor studios, with *Among My Souvenirs* on the other side. I was so nervous I ruined a half-dozen master records and the best of a double-time trio arrangement. I had a lot of vocalizing to do and the piano solo I had done for the Gennett record was included in the arrangement. It was, for me, nerve-racking, jumping from one act to another. Whiteman remained calm.

"We'll get it all on this one."

I looked at Bing to step in for me. He looked away.

The control man said, "Recording—side six."

The opening notes began. Finally we got a master that was approved. When Leroy Shield came out of the control, I thought I saw a tear on his face. We were emotional slobs about music in those days.

I was a limp, wet, wreck—so relieved I was still alive and now *silent*.

Paul Whiteman was the biggest thing in bands. His father had been a classical musician who had a high school named after him in Denver. But Paul never practiced his violin properly, became a packing house worker (our early jobs crossed here), then a taxi driver. He drifted into popular music and soon had it organized.

As the King of Jazz, he was the big name in the business, taking a fatherly interest in his men. He was a powerful liver, drinker, and worker. My being with him far exceeded anything that had happened to me musically so far. How much more it meant than the acquisition of an LL.B. college degree! College men would soon be peddling Hoover apples on street corners.

Any inner contest between Hoagy the musician and Hoagland the lawyer never bothered me from that day on. I would be forced into mundane work and might even have deep indigo periods of doubt and discouragement about my ability to succeed as a hot composer, but it was now certain that the basic pattern of my life and work was set. It was not a turning point, it was a break-through, all troops committed.

I left Chicago after the recording session in a burst of jubilation hardly comparable to anything I had known before.

Every bump home on the old Monon Line track was light with hope as we rattled through Lafayette, Crawfordsville, and points south. The upbeat was wonderful when you were riding it steady and solid.

So I finished off Hoagland Carmichael, Attorney-at-Law. R.I.P. Let *him* rest with all those sharks' heads the artist Daumier has left us of lawyers' faces.

I could use my law occasionally to sign insurance papers and affidavits. The other fellow, the composer, would follow the road of pure imagination. He'd get in there and write songs.

I found Bloomington, Indiana, in the lull between the summer session and the fall opening of the University, and quiet. The campus was deserted, so was the Book Nook. I thought of love. Of Kate. I didn't really go to see Kate. I went to her house because there was a piano there.

"It's Hoagy—the Florida lawyer."

"Just Hoagy—the song thumper."

I said she looked great and attractive.

We talked, we laughed. She was provocative and dangerous to my career plans. I loved to look at her legs; they were the sexiest I ever saw—if memory serves—and it does.

"Everybody admires your legs."

"Don't talk legs—talk music."

I always wanted to play *good* for Kate. I fooled around on the piano, something bothering me. I was thinking of Dorothy, a girl I loved—perhaps even more than Kate. Youth has these problems of emotional supply and demand. I played on.

XIX

Alone, I wandered out into the Indiana night. I sensed the town, its colors muted, its streets deep in fallen leaves; the hoot of train whistles on its horizon made a chilly shimmy in my backbone.

It was a hot night, sweet with the sad gold-red departure of summer, the brisk hint and promise of fall. A waiting night, I felt, a night marking time, saluting the end of a season.

I sat down on the spooning wall at the edge of the campus, and all the things that the town and the University and the friends meant flooded through my mind in a sentimental banal but powerful, gulping of the past gone, of time consumed, of pleasures still in memory. I thought of Kate again, the campus queen . . . and Dorothy Kelly. But why only one girl, or two girls, why not admire all girls, young and lovely? Dorothy was the loveliest. The sweetest. Maybe, but there was life to live, work to do, and I knew that with Dorothy things weren't the same as in the early days. Most people have room for *all* their loves and maybe I didn't seem to. Perhaps music was my only real love.

I had written to Dorothy when I was away. Lyrical letters about the music I was hearing. She could read the lines and between the lines if she tried.

Dorothy and myself had an understanding. Vague and wordless. More precisely I had said, "We'll let each other know when and if the blush goes from the rose."

"That's a promise, darling."

She kept that bargain. Later in New York, I got a letter, then a wire. But that was later. That night I didn't call on her. I sat on the lovers' wall alone, looked up at the sky, and whistled a tune that became *Stardust*. The demon of creation was stronger than love. Excitement held me. I ran to the Nook, fearful of spilling the tune, as if it were water carried in a hat.

"Got to use your piano, Pete."

"Sure. But—"

"Very important."

"Gotta close up. But I give you a few minutes."

The notes sounded good and I played till I was tossed out, protesting, still groping for the full content of my music.

2

Next morning, after troubled sleep, the good smell of bacon gravy woke me. I remembered. *How* did that melody go? In B-flat. And then? I sat humming it, absorbed, at the breakfast table.

"What did you say, Hoagland?" Ma asked.

I looked at her, grinned. "Nothing, Ma. Oh, mighty fine biscuits."

"You've had 'em before. Lots of 'em."

"Not like *this* morning."

Pa Robison scowled and speared a ham steak with his fork and looked up with a twinkle in his eyes.

"Something eating you—I'd say a girl and the way you wiggle, I'd say a pretty one."

A few days later I played the tune for my friend, Harry Hostetter. Harry didn't say anything much.

"It's a tune."

"I knew that, Harry."

I was looking for a job—a music job. Jean Goldkette, with a new band, was playing in Kansas City and I took a job with him playing second piano. The Dorseys, Bix, and Trumbauer had all gone over to Whiteman.

Jean said, "You'll get experience."

This new Goldkette band was mostly composed of an orchestra called the Royal Peacocks, which Myron and Lorin Schultz put together in Indianapolis. I was part of it for a few weeks but retired early when it was apparent I would have to learn a bundle of orchestrations. We hired Dick Powell, fresh in from Arkansas, as singer. He held a banjo for pictures. Dick went from there to Charlie Davis' fine orchestra and sang like a bird at the Indiana and Circle Theatres; from there to Pittsburgh fronting his own band and thence to Hollywood.

In the Goldkette band also were Andy Secrest and Sterling Bose, cornets; Larry Tise, alto; Peewee Hunt, trombone, and the great Harry Basin of Indianapolis who held the coveted "ragtime belt," as he called it, which he won in some international contest playing piano.

The band filled the new Palomar Ballroom in grand style, using Harold Stoke's arrangements. We made a couple of records for Victor and on one of these, *My Ohio Home*, I did a stylized vocal which was interesting and effective. The record sold well. I regret to this day that I didn't work more at this but I guess it was the great success of Rudy Vallee's crooning style that gave me the bum steer. At Victor in New York I sang *Georgia On My Mind, Lazy River,* and *Moon Country* through my nose instead of giving out from the guts as I finally did years later. I forgot to do what Reggie had told me to do and I was "hostile" at myself.

Jean Goldkette came to me, chewing his lower lip. "You're fired, Hoagy. The joint just can't support two piano players. Why don't you go see Don Redman on the way home?"

"I might just do that."

"I'm sorry."

"Anyway I've seen Kansas City."

I really wasn't feeling that glib. I wanted to work. So I packed my socks, my few records, somebody's shirt, Jean's ties and moved on. A musical migratory worker.

I found Don Redman standing in front of the band at the Greystone Ballroom in Detroit. He was a short bowlegged fellow directing a lackluster crew of hungover bandsmen with a drumstick. Then they came alive. The sounds bowled me over.

This was music with a solid beat and a rocking rhythm, as the five-brass team cut loose. The ensemble choruses were built around phrases that suggested knowledge of the old Negro spirituals. They used blues strains of camp-meeting chords and rode them down with the brasses. The saxophone section played with the power of a steam engine.

It wasn't all just bleating, blatant jazz. Don was writing some fine music and I was hearing some of it now.

Afterwards, Don and I gave each other the office. We agreed to exchange tunes and arrangements—but he was just being kind; he was about to create "swing" and I was still small-time.

We got along. We were both a little mad for music. He took me out to the black-and-tan speak-easies. I saw white girls loving it up with Negroes. My eyes popped.

"Look at that now."

Don shrugged.

"You come have dinner at my house tomorrow. Meet the wife."

"She like jazzmen?"

"She likes this one."

Dinner at Don's house, with his beautiful wife feeding us fried chicken, was a change of pace. I saw she waited on Don as if he were a king.

"Hoagy, what you been writing?"

I handed him the manuscript of *Stardust*. "A new tune, Don."

"I might want to play it."

"That's my idea."

He did play it but it took three years of trouping for *Stardust* to make the grade. It went from Don to Jean Goldkette and then Isham Jones was handed a lead sheet that Victor Young mooched from Jean. It was the hard way in those days. Overnight hits on radio came later.

3

I came down from Detroit and walked in on Mother and Dad. As usual, my father had found the grass in Florida no greener

A battered photo of the Book Nook, about 1918.

Above, the Book Nook Commencement Parade. Below, the first Open Job. My guest is John Hastings, now a federal judge and a former trustee of Indiana University.

My first band, 1919, at the Kappa
Sigma house, where I was eating
although still in high school.

It sounded as if I blew it through
my nose.

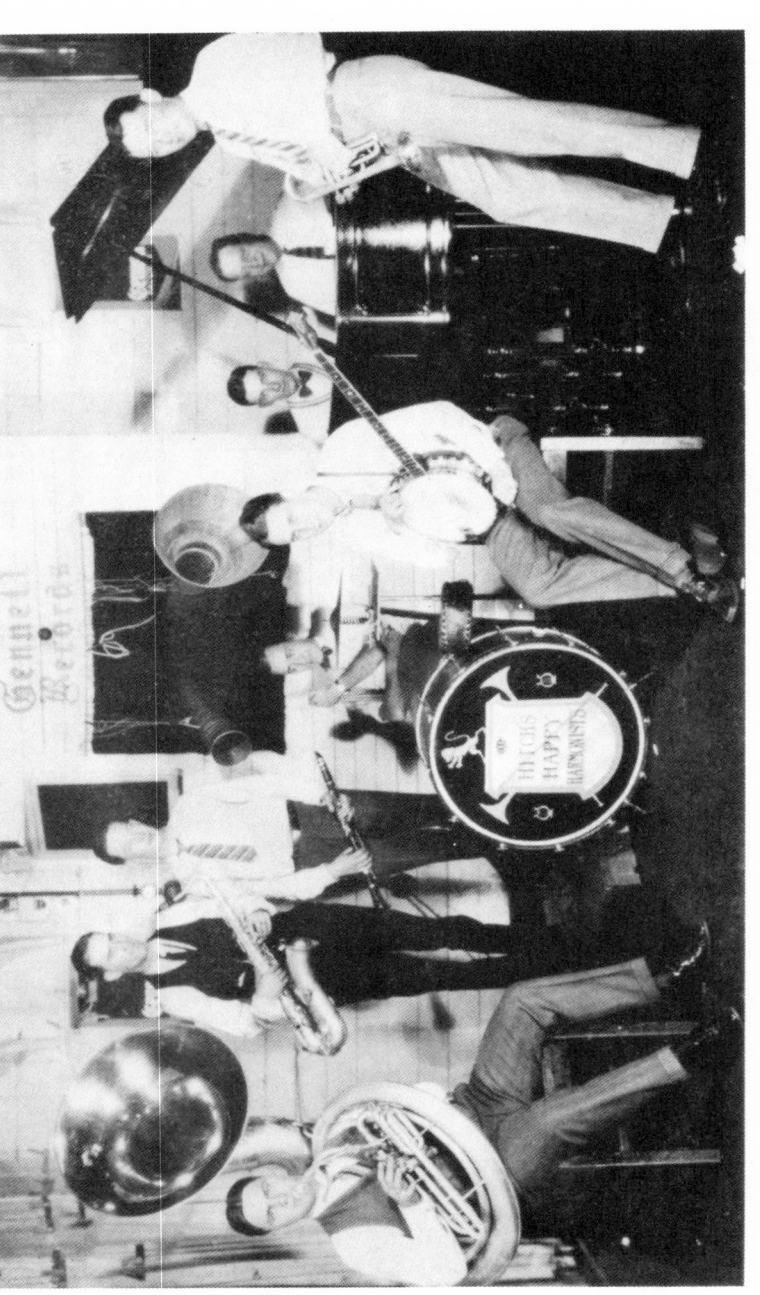

Hitch's Happy Harmonists, just before recording my *Washboard Blues* and *Boneyard Shuffle*. Left to right: Haskell Simpson, Maurice May, Harry Wright, Earl McDowell, Arnold Habbe, myself with Curt Hitch, Fred Rollison.

First visit of the Wolverines to Gennett. Left to right: Min Liebrook, Jimmy Hartwell, George Johnson, Bob Gilette, Vic Moore, Dick Voynow, Bix, and possibly Al Gande.

Bix Beiderbecke when he was with Paul Whiteman.

Left, Bix and Frankie Trumbauer somewhere in Kansas when Paul Whiteman's band was returning from Hollywood. I was a freeloader on this trip. Below, Open Job No. 2 with some of the Wolverines and a girl who was crazy for jazz.

My last college band, 1926. Wad Allen on the sax.

than it was in Indiana. They had returned to Indianapolis to take up their old life. Harry Hostetter was working in Indianapolis and boarding with my folks. I walked in and there was Mother playing cards with Harry Hostetter—and there was the piano, the old golden oak.

I said, "Love and warmth, cheer and affection—here I am."

"Why Hoagland, how nice. Harry is boarding with us now."

"He better move over to the other side of the bed."

Dad said, "I'll get the home-brew."

We talked into the night over the brew, recalling little things, the gay crazy things and the sad cold things. My mother said, "When I played on the campus when Hoagland was very little I laid him to sleep on two collapsible chairs. Maybe that's why he never grew bigger."

Harry said, "That's where he got infected with popular music. You can catch it like the mumps."

"It's a disease," I admitted.

"Ragtime on the piano were Hoagland's lullabies," Mother said.

"Did the girls like me?" I asked.

"They thought you were the cutest thing."

"Gee, to be four again."

Harry had wandered over to the piano. He had never played anything before as far as I knew. But now painfully, with one finger, he picked out a tune.

"Get up, Harry, I want Mom to beat out *Maple Leaf Rag* and *Cannonball*."

"Don't think I'll say no."

Mother sat down at the piano and she played them as well as I ever heard them any place. My father looked at me and smiled. "She's been practicing long enough to be real good, eh?"

I nodded. Harry went back to the piano and his one-finger playing. "What's that?" I asked, fogged with home-brew.

"That's *Stardust*," Harry said. "The only piece I ever learned. In case you should forget it, I learned it, too."

We all smiled and went to bed, me with Harry. He didn't snore. He said I did. But I never heard a thing.

It was good to be home, to see simple household objects again, the clock, my father's tools, and to relive a childhood not always good but very alive. I was encouraged to go on with my music. Not content with a chorus for *Stardust*, I added a verse, a piano interlude and a passage for clarinet. Emile Seidel and his band and I made the trek to Richmond to give *Stardust* its first recording.

We didn't perform wonders. It was a ragged rendition, and during the playback I felt that the melody had sustained us, in spite of our playing. I got a queer sensation as we recorded. This melody was bigger than I was. It wasn't a part of me. Maybe I hadn't even written it. It didn't sound familiar in the playback, and I lost the recollection of how, when, and where it all happened. It was a complete blackout, as if for some unconscious reason I didn't want to know, remember. Was it because I was close to Dorothy when I wrote it? I didn't know then, and it's too late to find out now. I am no longer the young man who wrote that song.

Back there in the old ratty recording studio I was vague in mood as the strains hung in the rafters of the place. I wanted to shout, "Maybe I didn't write you, but I found you." But I couldn't say anything.

All the recording engineer said was, "It's a nice lil' tune you fellas got there."

My detached feeling about *Stardust* continued. I had no idea I was already inside—I still felt no kid from Indiana, like me, was going to win the gold ring.

Walter Winchell heard a piano rendition of the tune at the Blackfeets Cafe in Greenwich Village.

"Hey, listen to that!"

Contemporary newsmen were forced to put down much needed drinks while Walter whistled the first four bars.

"I tell you it's a smasheroo—soon!"

By persistent plugging, *Stardust* became known as the Walter Winchell song. But that was later.

I was learning to write music—all the notes on the proper bars, the long-haired method of composing, not just whistling and hitting the piano keys and saying, "It goes somethin' like *this* here."

4

Late in the fall after *Stardust* was done, I wrote *March of the Hoodlums*. I made one last trip to the Gennett Studios, with my cornet, and a bunch of college musicians to record it, along with my arrangement of *Walkin' the Dog*. I was laboriously putting the notes on paper now. Stubborn as hell, not giving up. I had first picked it up in Kansas City during the time I was there with the Goldkette orchestra, aided by Pink Porter, a saxophonist. Pink explained to me what the notes on the staff meant and their relationship in the orchestral pattern.

I was weary: "Why is a B-flat on a cornet a C on the piano, Pink?"

Pink looked puzzled. "I don't know and you better not ask, just accept it."

"A hell of a way to explain music."

"Just write. Don't explain."

I figured out the only reason was a B-flat cornet's easiest fingering scale was in the key of B-flat (concert) and the easiest fingering scale on the piano was the key of C (concert). I accepted the device with some reservations. But I began to write orchestrations, putting the cornet notes one step higher on the staff than the piano notes just to make everybody happy. This was quite a concession for a non-conformist like myself.

But I wasn't going to fight Bach, Mozart, Stravinsky, and the other cats about how to write music.

My cornet solo on that last Gennett recording is not too bad unless you are a lover of good tone and the proper handling of the brass. Our cutting of *Walkin' the Dog* impressed a lot of the boys in the east. This recording ended my youthful desire to play a cornet. It left me with a sore lip and head noises.

I replaced it by a mustache about this time. I felt most great composers of the past had whiskers and lots of face hair. You hardly ever saw a bronze or marble statue of a famous composer without a beard.

I was too shy of pin feathers to grow a beard so I settled on a shaggy mustache that went off in all directions. It was a piebald off-color bit of fuzz, and I didn't keep it long, only long enough for someone to photograph it and get it printed in the newspapers. It did little to revive the Edwardian facial handlebars, and my sister Martha said, "You look stuck on yourself."

5

Fred Allen said, "California is a great place to live, if you're an orange." I laughed with the rest, but silent pictures were dying, and music would be needed, theme songs, tunes, lyrics to drown out the sissy screen stars with their feeble voices and strange accents.

I figured I'd be needed there. Wilson Mizner said, "Kid, it's just Newark, New Jersey, with palm trees."

I went to Hollywood with high hopes and a stack of compositions. Everyone said I'd return, discouraged and disillusioned. It was a land of ex-pants pressers, mental cripples, and uneducated egos. I didn't see that any disillusionment could harm me. If so, I felt it might be a man's coming of age. I bought a ticket west. I sang on the cinder-filled non-air-conditioned train going towards the setting sun. "Roll on, sweet chariot, carryin' me to Hollywood." There was a lot of Texas, an awful lot of Texas, and the colors got low-keyed; I was in the desert, a gray gritty yellowish world of tormented forms and merciless skies.

But everything was all right with me. I had an upper berth, a couple of good suits, some songs in a battered brief case.

A music publisher had whispered a secret to me. "That's where the rainbow hits the ground for composers—Hollywood."

"Are the movie stars as beautiful as they look?"

"The girls?"

"I didn't mean the boys."

"Well, good luck. And listen, write *only* hits."

I agreed they were the best kind.

We came choking out of the desert. Man had here made it green, with water; all beauty and so green. The porter said, "Pretty soon now. L.A., a fink town."

Then came Hollywood, the streets of Beverly Hills. I was glad I'd come, I told the hotel clerk.

"We bill every week, sir."

I seemed to be the only one that was glad I was there except for Chuck Chamberlain, a Kappa Sig brother, and his wife, Elsa. They are the parents of young, famous Dick Chamberlain of *Dr. Kildare*. They took me in, fed me, and reminded me that Bill Wright, another I.U. graduate, worked at Paramount. Bill was helpful but I soon learned that as far as the studios were concerned, I had: (1) The wrong address, and (2) I hadn't been sent for.

I didn't care. I walked the streets and smelled the orange blossoms. I liked the sunny warm air and hoped the studios didn't buy *all* my music at once when they got around to wanting them. Fox was going to make a picture called "Havana'" so I hotfooted it over there with my rhumba idea, but never saw anybody but the gatekeepers. Lucky, I told myself. If I had hit so early I'd end up writing sweet sob music for pictures, and marrying the boss's daughter. In those days the settled domestic scene wasn't for me.

Bill went on to become a writer-producer as did his roommate Joe Mankiewicz.

This period produced one good deed. Bill introduced me to William Powell and I was able to tell him he was Mother's favorite actor, as she had instructed.

XX

Everything that can be said about Hollywood has been said. It is dying now, to the shake, rattle, and roll of TV commercials. But in 1928 it was still alive and gold-plated and crazy. But amusing. And a hotel called the Garden of Allah was the booze set's hangout.

I didn't sell any songs, but I met the studio people and there was always tomorrow. For sound was killing silent pictures, and talking was destroying old tenor-voiced male idols. I'd wait, I thought, and enjoy the burnt umber hills, Harry's bar, and the beautiful long-legged girls. It was party party all the time. If they didn't know me I could always play the piano. Tom Mix would ride by in his big Dusenberg car with Texas longhorns on his bumpers, Douglas Fairbanks still showed all his teeth as the King, and nobody thought talkies would really make much of a change. The town was cleaner then; smog had not yet come to stay. The hills were not cut up into firetraps and mud flood-gutters. Everybody came to the Coconut Grove to be seen, the girl stars with the town stallions, the men with the vamps, baby dolls, and shebas, as they were called in those days.

It was a way of life that floated on bad booze, bad movies, good box office, and a strange idea that reality began in Pasadena and that the world needed the dream-boats made here in the hard white Hollywood sun.

Power was naked and cruel. Some producers made and broke stars for a whim. Great palaces looted from Europe, loaded with art, held continual parties. Hundreds of reporters informed the world in bad prose that Hollywood was Rome, Pompeii, Tombstone, all the sinful cities of the Bible, all rolled into one, *and* in sound. How could I avoid being part of it? It was a country boy's idea of sin, shame, sex, glamor, fat living, all available.

Only I seemed a flop. I didn't get past the right gates, I lacked the political know-how, the proper agents. I was just another hick Merton of the Movies, with a roll of music getting frayed and worn and soiled. But I didn't care. Too much. I sold a few arrangements. Paul Whiteman was in town and I knocked around with the band boys and had fun.

Paul was in Hollywood to make a movie, *The King of Jazz*, but privately he told Matty Malneck, "I want to casually and accidentally meet a movie star, Margaret Livingston." But the complications of movie-making slowed him down. The Warner Brothers were talking loudly with Vitaphone, so the screen talked —but some said the Warner boys were great kidders and practical jokers.

With Whiteman was Andy Secrest, a pal from Indiana. We got an apartment, which we shared, and I hunted up a very wonderful little upright piano for it. We stacked up on booze, beer, and food; I skinned down my life savings and bought a Ford.

Paul's bandmen leased theirs; Paul had figured out a scheme for the cars to have his famous features painted on the back. Harry Hostetter bummed his way out on the Southern Pacific to join us.

It was the old college hand shake and the old school yells. And of course before I knew it, somehow, I was the chef, and also the dishwasher. But there was also a lot of laughing and a lot of gagging and ribbing.

I spent a lot of time at the upright playing and thinking out tunes. The girls danced, the beer flowed, and the California sunshine was over everything.

I did knock out the chorus to *Hong Kong Blues* on that 'upright. It took nine years before anything happened to those blues; they went into the motion picture *To Have And Have Not*. I also acted in that picture—but I mustn't speak of my golden age in Hollywood just yet. On this trip I was like several thousand other young folk that came out to the dream-world of movies with starry eyes, some with more talent, some with less. The Warner Brothers had put a voice section into *The Jazz Singer*. Confusion was king, mismanagement was prime minister. Paul was the first man to pre-record a picture. He did the music before the movie. They had millions of dollars in new recording equipment with dozens of control knobs and with microphone wires stretched clear across the sets. But no one really knew very much of how it worked.

2

I was amazed to see how ignorant Hollywood was, how unprepared to accept a new thing, and how stupidly the old guard fought to ruin themselves. Hollywood was saved in the early talkie stage in spite of itself. Engineers kept experimenting, putting up ceilings to deflect sound, some with smooth bright surfaces, some with rough dull surfaces. With all this equipment at first they couldn't play music back to hear it after it was played. They were cutting records with a new tool, a V-shaped tool, and they played it back with a U-shaped tool. Of course they couldn't get a sound till they figured it out around some swimming pool.

In those days I would often come to the studio bandstand and find a comic was playing the drums. And at a party Charlie Chaplin would be bowing left-hand fiddle or left-hand cello (he was a lousy but fancy fiddler). The film folk all got to performing and clowning in front of their friends. Charles Chaplin in those days would take fast falls off a stand onto the back of his head, dropping five feet with a thud just for a laugh. The town had gory times and rubbed its bruises in the morning, and put ice caps on its aching minds.

What if I wasn't selling my songs?

Wild gags, practical jokes, made history. I was told that when Norman Kerry married, they put the house on skids and moved it up Hollywood Boulevard. No one left the building. A band got on the moving house; it moved slowly at the pace of a mile an hour. They played dance music all afternoon while guests danced and threw empty gin bottles out the windows into the streets with a luxurious indiscretion until the house was jacked into its new address.

A playboy silent star—no names please—gave the wildest parties. He had a lovely brawl going at his place one night, and when Harry Barris of Whiteman's singing group started to leave, an old colored butler stopped Harry at the door.

"Mistah Harry, I don't care what yo' carry out in yo' stomach, but yo' can't carry it out in yo' pocket."

Harry had a bottle of the host's gin in every one of the four coat pockets of his camel hair coat with its wrap-around six-inch belt, the proper jazzman's dress of the period.

A big star wanted to serenade a new girl. She was staying at the Hollywood Hotel (now torn down), an old broken-down farmers' hotel that was the most exciting place around. A band in the star's town-car parked under a hotel wing, and while they were playing *Lover's Moon*, somebody in the hotel yelled, "You lousy bums go home to bed!"

Someone shot holes through the roof of the town-car three times with a .45.

I said, "A music hater." The star screamed.

"No," said the hotel doorman. "Her g.d. husband is back."

But Hollywood's more picturesque adventures were beginning to lose interest for me as my songs failed to sell. Even spectacular orgies must have lost the interests of the Romans when the pattern began to repeat itself. They told me about Edna Purviance, who was Charlie Chaplin's girl once. She always drank champagne out of a huge beer stein and would sit in a corner very quietly. So quietly that people kept watching her.

I took to sitting in on the making of the Whiteman movie. I didn't think *The King of Jazz* would win any awards, but it was entertaining. Paul's boys, singing in rhythm, had no trouble to fake their mouthings to the sound track. They chirped right along and never goofed. But John Boles, billed as a "singing actor," didn't do as well. When he faked a ballad there would be holes in the song where he wouldn't sing at all, followed by long pauses. The drummer said, "He doesn't know where to open his mouth." The actor sulked till they worked out signals for him to *stop* or *go.*

3

That was when I got to know Bing Crosby well. He had come with Paul to work in the movie. Bing was born hep. He was still young and not yet Der Bingel, but he already had the high forehead, the easy, lazy way, a capacity for drink, and an interest in female company. Bing for me was always fun. He was happy to be in California. He loved it. Paul used him only as a singer, which was just as well since he didn't play any instrument. Sometimes he held a horn and faked it if they wanted the band to look extra large. He just smiled in introspective skepticism.

"I hold it right, don't I?"

The director sweated. "Just don't blow the spit out during the dialogue."

After the picture was done Bing wanted to stay in California. "It suits me."

We wondered what he'd do—he wasn't the John Gilbert or Conrad Nagel type.

"I never clicked in the East and I'm dying to stay out here," Bing said.

Paul tore up the five-year contract with Bing Crosby. "California is all yours."

The problem was to get Bing a job. They caught an agent and talked it up for Bing. "Why don't you take on Crosby and his group. They're free now."

"Why?" the agent asked.

"The studios made millions in college pictures."

"That's all over. Gangsters are in. Warners got this kid Cagney —and Eddie Robinson."

"Have they closed all the colleges?" I asked.

"We'll talk some other time. Don't call me, I'll—"

"Crosby can sing like a flock and Harry Barris is a very fresh kid with a boop boop de doop and he writes wonderful songs. Al Rinker is a good-looking kid—what you call personality. You could really make some loot with these boys."

The agent gave a Hungarian shrug. "This fellow Crosby, with those ears? That big fanny of his? He'll never make it in Hollywood."

Bing took it all casually—and went down to sing at the Coconut Grove, among all the palm leaves, the most fashionable club in town, always full of stars and important film tycoons. Opening night he sang, drank a few between the acts, and was very popular. But he didn't get into pictures. Everybody tested him. Bing said, "They spent a hundred thousand dollars in tests on me and they figured out I'm not picture material."

Mack Sennett came into the club one night to talk to Bing. "Son, you're pretty popular here. How'd you like to make some pictures for me?"

Bing asked, "How many? You're kidding, Mr. S."

"I'll sign you for four."

Mack Sennett had made millions with his Keystone Comedy Cops, his zany two-reel comedies with Mabel Norman, Fatty Arbuckle, Ford Sterling, Louise Fazenda, Marie Dressler, Ben Turpin, Charles Murray, Harry Langdon—and others. Originally a boiler factory worker who failed to get into grand opera as a singer, he came west to make pratt falls and double takes into an art.

Bing listened to Sennett and asked warily, "For how much?"

"Ten thousand dollars. Twenty-five hundred each—well?"

"Wonderful, Mr. S. Now if you just wrote that contract out on the menu here, I'd treasure it."

"All right."

Sennett did, Bing signed it, then sighed. "No, you better tear that up. I'm ashamed of myself, cheating the only honest man in Hollywood."

"I'll take care of myself."

"Everybody has tested me, Mr. S. It's no good. Too much ear, not enough hair."

"No. We'll make the pictures."

"What will I have to wear?"

"What do you want to wear?"

"Any old hat, tweed clothes, comfortable. Get it?"

"You got it."

The Bing Crosby shorts made money, and soon Bing was on his way to millions, marriage, sons, fame, glory, and an amused indifference. I still had my bundle of music unsold.

4

Mack Sennett did the same thing with W. C. Fields. They thought that Fields's pool table humor was all through, a broken-down old vaudeville juggler and whiskey baritone. Mack brought Bill back. All Fields's satire, his ire at the dentist and golf, at the world, all the wonderful old props worked. Fields was reborn and started being his mean old cantankerous self again.

"Hoagy," he said one day as he took a sip from a quart-size pocket flask, "looking around this town all I can say is, I've seen better heads on canes."

It was time I did something for myself. But how? I felt out of it, welcome only when a stray piano was around. But I wasn't getting any place. Others were.

Bing Crosby was going around with his Dixie (whom he later married). Everybody became fast friends. Margaret Livingston and Paul gave parties. Their parties became the talk of the palm tree countryside. Hollywood was socially starved—for all its free-for-all—many of the studio big shots still showed signs of their unsavory or poverty-stricken pasts. A top party had to be approved by Mary Pickford and Douglas Fairbanks to have any society clearance. Then, as now, there were few people you could count on as friends because everybody was more interested in cultivating their own existence than in building friendships. Funny thing though—as the years wore by, I found the hand shakes warmer. At the beginning we and they were a fraternity, all respecting each other and to some degree loving each other, but a very reserved lot. Oh sure, when there was a cocktail party we were as jovial and handshaking as any. Mighty damn respectable people, I might add, and interesting people, but when party time was over, everybody seemed to shy off each other. I was no exception. But now in the waning years everybody is a friend— the eyes show respect and feeling and we know that we don't have to visit with one another every week to be convincing about it. This goes for all facets of the entertainment world. We are 500,000 strong, joined in a great feeling of brotherhood.

Mark Hellinger and his new showgirl wife, Gladys, came out West. He, too, liked *Stardust*.

Hellinger was a good human being, a good journalist, a pretty good drinker, and under it all a very sad man who was a Jew, later to be buried with a Catholic holy medal in a Protestant cemetery. At the time I knew him he couldn't be satisfied until he got everybody at a party swinging high.

He was a giant compared to the successes of the town. Everybody loved him. He always wore a black shirt and white tie and drove a gangster's bulletproof Cadillac. He made a fine movie of Hemingway's "The Killers." He became very interested in making a movie of a story I suggested to him which might have been the Bix Beiderbecke story with Jimmy Stewart starring in it, but Bix's untimely death ruined that one.

Paul Whiteman kept asking Margaret about getting married. She always said, "Yes—and no." That kept him jumping all the time. "I'd have to make some kind of a demonstration. I could burn the town down, bomb the Golden Gate Bridge, or run for governor of California, but none of that would impress Margaret." He started sending her two dozen roses every hour, twenty-four hours a day. And he kept it up for a week. She hired someone to cross her name off the cards and move them on; hospitals were buried in roses. But he got his woman and they've been very happy together. But do you know *how* he got her? By dieting. Ain't that a woman for you?

As a showman, Paul was a real star-maker. The band was very popular, so it was quite natural that he would attract a lot of

young, good talent. He found room for Jimmy and Tommy
Dorsey, Henry Busse, Jack and Charlie Teagarden, Frank Trum-
bauer, good arrangers like Ferde Grofé, Roy Bargy, and Adolph
Deutsch. Morton Downey was the first singer and Mildred
Bailey the first girl singer in any popular band; then came Jane
Frohman. He also started me, but I needed more than a start. I
saw I wouldn't make it this trip to Hollywood. I began to worry
about traveling money.

You couldn't really call it living off my arrangements, but it
did help, and I'd watch out to see who was using one. I heard that
someone was going to play one of my arrangements at a party
Fatty Arbuckle was giving. Fatty was one of the great comic
stars of the silent films, and scandal had not yet ruined his career.
His parties were famous and this was business anyway; I wanted
to collect for that arrangement of mine. Bix, Harry Hostetter,
and myself got into my Ford and we started off. The car was
oiled and so were we.

Driving in California used to be a pleasure, before the invasion
of millions of cars and super-duper highways, and clover-leaf
freeways that capture you and toss you out miles from where you
wanted to go.

So we were wheeling along Washington Boulevard feeling no
pain. The sound of a siren seemed part of the proper landscape.
I turned to my loud pals.

"Now keep it mum."

"What for?"

"Cop."

The officer pulled alongside, making the famous gesture with a
leather-covered hand to get to the side of the road.

"Kid you were burning up this zone at forty miles an hour."

I said, in a very fruity voice, trying to appeal to his better
nature as a simple farm boy. "Really, was I *really?*"

It came out over-sweet and simpering. I had gone a little high.
I heard Bix choke off a laugh and the cop looked at us as if he
had stopped a nest of female impersonators.

Harry started to put his hand on his hip but I elbowed him

back. The cop read me a small lecture, shook his head, and waved us on, like a father who just didn't understand what had come into his boys.

Bix and Harry, who had been holding back until then, began to give their version of my reading of the line "Really."

I was not yet an actor.

5

Bix didn't drive a car, and neither did his roommate Boyce Cullen, first trombone with Whiteman. So they never did mix too much with the doings in the town. They hardly ever left their old Spanish villa, set high on a dry hill south of Universal Studios, where Paul was making his picture. As Bix said, "I can walk to the studio, *if* I can make that hill."

They were not the walking type, and as neither could drive one of Paul's lend-lease Fords, there is a kind of mystery as to how they got to the studio every day for the shooting of the picture.

Bix's mother came out to California to see him. She stayed a week, but I know she only saw Bix once during this visit. It wasn't something Bix wanted to talk about, and I didn't want to bring it up. There was a conflict between them, although they were very attached to each other. The visit was not a success. It may have been partly because Bix knew he wasn't very presentable and didn't want his mother to see him in that rancid castle up there in all its rusting Spanish decor, with him most likely in his cups most of the time.

I suspected she came to ask Bix to come home and give up for the time being on this band business. They were a close family given to simple, solid values, and they could not understand the kind of life Bix was living for his music, nor his drinking or other habits. It was the old corny story of the genius who didn't fit and the family whose hearts he was breaking. But he had to live out his life his own way, even if it led to disaster. If this has become corny in fiction it doesn't mean it isn't heartbreaking when it happens in life.

Bix's mother went back home, and Bix continued to burrow into his Spanish hill. It didn't do him any good to add this guilt about not seeing his mother to his other problems. The drinking continued.

Al Rinker, of the Rhythm Boys, was Mildred Bailey's brother. He introduced me to her and I went often to her house to hear her sing. Mildred overfilled an overstuffed chair by fifty pounds or more but she was a sweet sight to see when her pretty fat face and pearly teeth spoke the words in the true fashion of a singing genius. She held a can of beer in her hand during these sessions as I accompanied her at the piano and her manner of singing had such a sincere feeling I just knew she was destined for something great. We'd put on Louis Armstrong's record of *I Can't Give You Anything But Love*, listen to his gravel-voiced tones, and drink another can. I taught her *Rockin' Chair* and when she sang it at one of Paul Whiteman's parties in his Hollywood Hills palace, he signed her to sing on his Old Gold radio program. *Rockin' Chair* became her theme song.

Mildred grew to be one of the musicians' favorites—ever honest and never corny in her singing manner. She later made records with many of the greats and was one of Benny Goodman's favorites. Her record *In the Amen Corner* is a classic. She married Red Norvo, who was with Whiteman's band at the time, and we were all happy about it. A strange combo, we used to call it, but it lasted for a long time. Little fatso died some years ago and I regret that the floral remembrance I ordered (a wire rocking chair entwined in rose buds) never reached her side.

XXI

When we were bored we could always listen to Louis Armstrong recordings. They were lifters and gave life meaning again. We could always listen to Louis, and hear how great a talent could be. He's had a long history, and I see no sense in repeating all of it here—Louis had put it all down in his own book, *Swing That Music*.

In 1922, Louis joined King Oliver's band in Chicago as second cornet. It was the big time for Louis, who came and fitted right in with the music, giving Joe plenty of trouble with a good horn. But Joe enjoyed it even if he knew this twenty-six year-old boy was going to outplay him some day.

Lil Hardin, the piano player, took the gate-mouthed Louis under care. Lil had brains and education, and hadn't planned to play anything but classical piano, but here she was, making jazz history. She began by playing piano in a music store for three whole dollars a week. She played first for Sugar John's New Orleans Jazz Band, then King Oliver got her. And she fell for Louis.

In February, 1924, Lil and Louis were married. Lil worked the fat off Louis. She got a book of the standard cornet solos and drilled him. He really worked, even taking lessons from a German down at Kimball Hall, who showed Louis all the European cornet clutches. Louis just took what he wanted. He got to be a good sight reader. When he began to record, he could use the music or wipe it off. Louis played a lot of everything he had learned, but he was becoming an artist in his own right, whistling the riffs that were to become a trademark of the Armstrong style. He shifted from cornet to trumpet and back.

Louis got to New York which seemed to be the goal of every jazz player in Chicago at least. He worked at Roseland with Fletcher Henderson. It was too rich for Louis, too big; he rattled around in that band. He blew a good horn, but he couldn't just fill in or stretch out and his work was better than the band's as a whole. Louis was biding his time. Henderson was a little too sweet and soft for him.

Lil put together her own band in Chicago, Lil's Dreamland Syncopators, modestly billing: "Louis Armstrong, World's Greatest Jazz Cornetist." He blew it right; gut-bucket, gully-low horn-playing. Louis went over to the Vendome and became the singing actor, the shouting, moaning voice projecting over the hot horn and the ever-ready handkerchief. Using the big scarred lip, the smile that was to make him as famous a reciter-singer as a horn player. It's amazing the way he did it, the way he handled himself, a performance that was never ham. The guttural laugh, the husky moaning, the scatting of the words into incoherent patter. Behind it all was the horn playing, and that never let down. With horn, as the "Reverend Satchelmouth," he was always Louis. He could sing bass, had the gravel tones, and wasn't a street-corner tenor any more. He made clowning into an act.

Louis set up the Hot Five for Okeh sides, and did a lot of things, some of it sleek and smooth, often popular style, but between the stuff they cut for the public, you would find a few great records. *Savoy Blues, Wild-Man Blues,* and *Drop That Sack.* But *West End Blues* was his real beginning as an artist.

Soon, Louis was being seriously published by Melrose. *Fifty Hot Choruses of Armstrong* cut the lip of many a kid trying on the master's methods.

2

When Bix and his gang recorded *Davenport Blues* back in Richmond, Indiana, Don Murray had been the clarinet player— one of the greatest. Now we heard that he had died suddenly in Los Angeles. Leon Rapollo of the New Orleans Rhythm Kings was shut up in an insane asylum. Things seemed to be suddenly going wrong.

The worst news was about Bix. He was fumbling at rehearsals. He was often still great, sometimes as good as ever, but he was slipping and it hurt me to realize that so young a man was doomed.

I remember one of the moments of greatness back in Hollywood. Richard Barthelmess, the film star, had a birthday party, a real Hollywood hoe-down complete with everything but the throwing of Christians to the lions (they threw them to the producers instead). Paul Whiteman and his band were invited. I was an uninvited guest sitting on the back wall when Paul marched the band onto the stage built for him, and played *Weary River*, the theme song for the current Barthelmess picture. Then the sky split as they did *Rhapsody in Blue*, with Roy Bargy at the piano. It was one of those rare moments. Roy played great, Charlie Margulies on trumpet played beautifully and Hal Strickfadden handled the intricate reed parts with perfection. I've never heard *Rhapsody in Blue* like that again. Bix was there and he had his moments when they played *Clementine* and *Sweet Sue*.

Before the strange summer ended other friends showed up in Hollywood, hungry and eager. Batty De Marcus came out to learn flying. He said, "Threw my beautiful Selmer saxophone into the East River 'cause playing it finally worked loose every tooth in my head."

Andy said, "You look better this way, oh Western Branch Order of Bent Eagles, Sir."

Batty asked Horsey Hostetter what he was up to.

"I just applied for a job. How do you like my formal application?"

Horsey showed Batty his letter:

I need a job. I once shook hands with an Indian and I'm a close friend of the Spanish-American War. I haven't any experience but my mother has. . . . She used to comb my hair and pass me the potatoes. I represent a line of hog farms, frog arms, iron dogs, fog horns and frog ponds. Since then I haven't been six years old.

Yours,
Harry Hostetter

P.S. I have a dog named Fred.

Batty rubbed his big freckled hands, stood erect and solemnly said, "Brother, let's pray!"

When Paul Whiteman's special gold-painted train (his sponsor, Old Gold cigarettes, did it) left for New York, I bummed a ride from Paul sharing a berth with Bing Crosby, who was still with us.

"Good thing you're scrawny," Bing told me, when I climbed into his berth that first night. "Maybe you should have stayed and hit the studios again."

"If I'd stayed, Bing, till I got a studio job, I'd be able to sleep in a piccolo case."

"It's a racket. Let's cork off." And he did. Bing had gone to sleep in a wink of an eyelash, snoring slightly in perfect pitch to the train whistle, as we rumbled through the desert. "Awhoooooohooo," said the train. "Awhoagyeee! Toooo Badddd, Hoooagy!" Meanwhile, I worked on an arrangement of my *Manhattan Rag* on the train platforms with Frank Trumbaùer to record for Okeh in New York.

I still didn't care too much for New York. I eyed with distrust all its fish-belly green people who were so hurried and ill-mannered. I found Stu Gorrell, a friend from college days, living in the Village with some other I.U. boys and they gave me a cubbyhole. "Fellas, it looks like the place generations of janitors have crawled off to die in."

3

There was a musicians' speak-easy on Fifty-second Street that was a hangout for us, an upstairs smelly place where, if you sat long enough, you could meet all the jazzmen that were around New York, or hunting a job, or passing through. It was in one of these hush-hush saloons that Bix got a beautiful black eye—over nothing, really. I couldn't understand it, because Bix was not one of those brawling drunks who look for a fight. He avoided anything violent and turned his back when someone said they could lick any bandman in the house. Maybe he just stepped in between and caught one intended for someone else.

The place we hung out in was one of the first speaks on Fifty-second Street, and it started the vogue for joints that made the street famous and notorious. The bartender asked me to put up a thousand clams to help him start a new place across the street when prohibition ended. I finally reneged and lost the opportunity of being the co-proprietor of the Famous Door. Red McKenzie's and the Spirits of Rhythm opened there or at the Onyx—I don't remember which—and the street was on fire. Red got his start playing a kazoo on a big-selling record of *San*. Other places appeared and soon every new jazz artist or singer had a place to hang the hat. Lee Wiley and Martha Raye more or less made their names on the street, as did Billie Holiday. Mildred Bailey showed up, too, and the roster of guys who brought that street to life is unending: Pee Wee Russell, Joe Bushkin, Artie Shapiro, Sidney De Paris, Sidney Bechet, Muggsy Spanier, Zutty Singleton, Red Allen, Sid Catlett, Jess Stacy, Fats Waller, Dave Tough, Wingy Minone, Bud Freeman, and Stuff Smith with Jonah Jones, to name only a few.

Stuff wore a battered top hat and Jonah wore a derby. When Stuff got the feeling, he would change his fiddle bow to an inverted position so that he could saw on all four strings at once. Then he'd start pumping four beats to the measure while Jonah and the others did their work. One chorus would lead to another. It was a welling thing that led to pandemonium and a breaking point at about the fifteenth chorus. A brain-washing delight.

Leo Watson played ukelele and other instruments with the Five Spirits of Rhythm, but his big act was scat singing. Louis Armstrong and singers before him had been scatting for years (and Red Ingle and I had done imitations), but Leo was fantastic, with inflections and nuances of imaginative color.

When the college boys, down for the weekend, got too thick, most of us left.

But something else happened on that street. The Club 18 opened with Al White as M.C. comedian and Pat Harrington from Canada as his stooge drummer. This was the first and finest ad-lib comedy in the country.

XXII

I found some comfort in Harlem. It was spreading out, and was a good place to hear the real raw jazz. I explored it and got to know it. Negro shows and revues were in work and Harlem was jumping, becoming famous and fashionable. There were two Harlems, one the phony one for the thrill seekers, the other a sometimes sad, sometimes gay slum that loomed big and wide, with its fancy places and its low places. It sprawled but it had music.

I saw Harlem wasn't a unit or a city within a city. It was a country, a colored country surrounded by New York City, and like any country you can't label it by any one of its parts. The heart of Harlem was big, noisy, dusty, and centered around 131st Street and Seventh Avenue. The corner where the colored house-wives passed with their shopping bags, where the numbers boys and the poolroom characters stood, where the lovers of women and horses loafed in the sun, resting between pleasures. I could walk along The Stroll—that block between 131st and 132nd and sense how much progress the music was making. Kelly's place with the fey lipsticked characters playing it for smutty laughs. The Rhythm Club with the droop of a trombone being played all alone, before the boys got together as a group. The Barbeque with the good smells, and the upstairs halls where they shuffled for jobs, stole music, and rehearsed. An out-of-luck jazzman could put the bite on Erskine Hawkins, Jimmy Lunceford, or Cab Calloway on the stairs. The Lafayette's backstage door opened on the alley near the bar of the Bandbox, where you could treat the girls to a drink, where there were always a few of the boys with a horn in a paper bag, or where a small player was lugging around a bass because he still hadn't found anywhere to lay the two of them down that night.

"Bury you now—dig you later."

"Lay the skin on me."

That was Harlem as it was, that and the society white folk, in tails and white ties, hunting jazz, or the newest verse to *Minnie The Moocher*. They were snobs, but they had money and everyone was usually mighty hungry.

I listened to the music coming from coldwater flats where they slept six to a bed. Freebee food, men on street corners full of smoke. A woman with big sad eyes, holding onto a kid with rickets and a spot on his lung, trying to sweet-talk someone out of a bottle of milk. And all the time they were making music, blue music, hot music. Harlem jazz, New York style—an American music, smoky around the edges.

I was learning something from Harlem. And, as I already said, from Duke Ellington. He was servicing jazz in a fine way, transforming the ugly image some people had of it into beautiful fantasies. His *Mood Indigo*, I kept telling people, was the product of true genius.

I'm getting a bit ahead of the story, but perhaps I should tell you here a thing that happened in 1934. Six of us, dressed to the teeth, went to a new place in Harlem, a cellar joint. My friend, Willy the Lion, was playing piano—great piano, a commingling of ragtime and jazz with counterpoint. Willy accomplished this with a cigar in his mouth at all times. The place was crowded and Lazelle Rafferty was fascinated with the antics of a young Negro at a table nearby. She kept staring. Suddenly the Negro flicked the contents of a glass of whiskey at her. All hell was about to break loose and everybody was on their feet. Fortunately, I appealed to Willy immediately and he was able to get us out of there without mayhem.

2

I broke the Harlem spell to visit Bix at his hotel. I met a maid in the hall.

"What's the matter with that fellow, anyway?" she asked.

"He's sick."

"He ain't been out of his room for three days."

The last time I had seen him his pivot tooth fell out when he leaned out of the hotel window to yell "Good night" down at me. We searched for it frantically with matches burning our fingers—so he could play that night.

"No tooth, no music."

Bix was sitting at the piano with a phonograph beside him. The speed regulator was pushed clear back and he was memorizing each slow note as it whined off the disk.

" 'Lo Hoagy."

"Why don't you go out for air, Bix?"

"I can live without it now."

"Nobody can."

"I'll go take a music lesson."

He was in no condition to take a music lesson—Ravel's piano method.

I remembered what his teacher back in Davenport had said to him. "Tell your mother that your theories of harmony are such that you can learn nothing from me. And I mean that as a compliment, my boy."

Bix just shook his head. "A teacher should know everything."

Later, Bix and I sat on the floor, listening to the *Fire Bird* while I kept thinking how it had been in the past with him, doodling with Bix under the pavilion in Indianapolis when he was with the Wolverines. Bix blasting the night air with an incomparable horn. The night we drove to Richmond to make the first records. Bix up on the bandstand, night after night, week after week; creating great music, hot and lovely, every time they turned him loose. Bix, maybe a genius, but a sad sack of a human being, subject to the ills of the flesh and marrow, the self tortures of the spirit. And he had no way to say it but with the horn and I knew now the horn wouldn't ever say it all.

A few days later, I visited him again in his ill-kept room.

"Hi, Hoagy." Bix in the semi-darkness was lying on the bed,

partly dressed. He looked bad; there was something wrong, as if part of him were detached, indifferent to life in the dark.

"Hi, Bix." I sat down on a rickety chair, pushing soiled shirts off it. "How's it going, fella?"

Bix smiled with a waxy grimace. "What are *you* doing?"

"Been listening to the publishers tell me, 'It's not commercial.' And working in a bank to make up the difference."

Bix looked away, stared at the stained wall. Then I heard his muffled voice. "Don't worry, boy. You're . . . ah, hell . . ."

Then he said, "Hey, that new tune of yours is pretty good."

He meant *Stardust*. It had just been released (Isham Jones on Brunswick) and I smiled at Bix. It was the second time he had ever given me a compliment. The first time was back in Indiana, when we were on our way to record *Davenport Blues*.

I'd have liked him even if he hadn't liked my music. There was a deepness to Bix that would have attracted anyone who was trying out the new music and wanting to know more.

I asked him to come out and have dinner with some folks from Indiana. "They love you, Bix."

He just stared at me and said, "Yeh."

It was the wrong thing to say. Everybody "loved" Bix, but he was bothered by that, so I changed the subject. "No horn, no piano, just a fine chicken dinner. And we can sing if you want to."

But he didn't accept. Perhaps he didn't have the energy for it. He wasn't eating, and if I had had any gumption I would have loaded him off to a hospital. (Later Paul Whiteman sent him back to Davenport and the family tried to put him on his feet.) Here, in his room, he worked on his wonderful piano compositions— *In a Mist, Candlelights, Flashes, In the Dark*, and others.

The country, too, was in the dumps. The crash, the muttering from President Hoover that prosperity was "just around the corner"; the great depression was on us. Many all-American bands got lost in the shuffle of unemployed feet. The public stayed home and made do with what they had. They listened to the sweet and simple radio music: the Vallee-Lombardo schmaltz. No one would have any of us. Songs weren't selling, the Tin Pan Alley goons shouted. "The people won't listen. Jazzmen, real jazz dies! Jazzbos walk the street. Hot Horn men sell apples. Steel down ten points. Rails off. So never you mind, a lot of characters out of a job."

There was a kind of desperate urgency that took over all of us in the early 1930's; everyone who could tried to shut out personal loss, the depression, and carry on as if the era were to last a thousand years. It was a hell of a time to be part of; not a place for a jazz composer to be trapped in. But there I was.

Men out of senior societies at Yale used to come to hear us play, their girls dewy from Bryn Mawr. The Hotsy-Totsy Club still did big business, and there was Guinan's and Mario's. I'd be walking home late at night, and the fashionable crowd would pass in a fleet of taxis on their way to the Club Richmond, or Helen Morgan's, and later they would form parties to go to the newsreel theatres to hiss Roosevelt.

Sometimes I would go down to the French Line pier to see the great luxury ships on sailing night—all wild fun, lights, and gay streamers. Those sailings at midnight were the last romantic gestures of a wounded economy. I guess our music was its *Grave-yard Blues*. It seemed such a long time before we heard *Happy Days Are Here Again*.

3

I moved into an apartment with Stu Gorrell and Cookie in Jackson Heights, where there were trees. Not far from us lived Harry Shackelford and his wife Lucy, who had both been several years ahead of me at Indiana University. Also living with them was Bill Shattuck, a few years my junior at the same school. Bill found me and invited me up for dinner. Naturally they all loved music and asked me to play their nice piano, too. This was the beginning of a very warm and helpful friendship. Eventually, they helped me get a job in Wall Street to add to the meager earnings of the music business. Finally, I was spending most of my time answering the frantic telephone calls of elderly ladies, who seemed to blame me personally for the depreciation of their bonds. Johnny Green, later musical director of MGM, was also working there—as a clerk.

Good old Burns Rafferty (another product of I.U.) worked there, too. He and his lovely wife Lazelle spent a good deal of time together with me window shopping on Madison and Fifth Avenues. We were all clothes conscious but we had very little moola to buy anything in those days. Burns and I sold the entire bond-purchaser list of S.W. Strauss and Company to some sharpie in Wall Street for $500, a rather shady deal—but we needed that dough bad, and what the hell, maybe the guy could help some of the ladies dispose of their bonds. Burns is now head of a two or three million dollar lumber company.

S.W. Strauss was one of the biggest bond and bank houses in the world, but by 1931 they'd had it. They had bonds out on forty or fifty big buildings; the amount of money involved was perhaps $500 million. Soon the whole $500 million could have been bought for probably $20 or $30 million. Any man with the needed cash and courage then could have bid for all the bonds to be the richest man in the world. I figured he'd need $10 or $15 million to start—then *zing*, a billionaire. But I lacked the capital.

I dreamed of big deals. I loved the Waldorf Astoria Hotel because it was made out of Bedford limestone from Bloomington. I watched the hotel go up. And one day I realized the $1,000 hotel bonds were down to $110. I said to myself, I wish I had some money. I was thinking in big figures, wishing I could buy a hundred of them. There was another issue against that hotel; they were debenture notes. Two thousand of these $1,000 notes were selling on Wall Street for from 25¢ to 50¢ apiece. They weren't on my list—I didn't know about them, otherwise I'm sure I would have bought a bundle to paper my bathroom and to protect Bedford limestone. Later they were paid off in full. I could have bought a hundred of them for $25.00 and cashed them in for $100,000 in twenty years time.

"That's even better than buying western Indian land in the early 1800's," my father said when I told him later.

When I did get some cash I used it to dress up. I went to one of the best tailors in New York on Fifth Avenue. I had them make me a double-breasted suit with a narrow lapel, not the wide peaked lapel that everybody else was wearing all over town; an innovation of having the overlap only four inches wide instead of the customary six or seven. This made me look taller; most of the boys were looking shorter with those fat short coats. Twenty-five years later this became the fashion. In 1938 I designed an ascot type shirt with the ascot attached like a collar. This I wore on the stage but now I wear them for every occasion. Recently (1962) many haberdashers have stocked a poor imitation of the same, but they seem to be selling. Naturally, I didn't patent my idea. So don't feel lonely, kind sir, if one of your ideas has been misappropriated, too.

I had a date with a Miss Peggy Johnson one night. She was a wonderful brisk girl from Muncie, Indiana, and I was very fond of her. I had a clean starched shirt and my tails were pressed and the wrinkles were snapped out of my top hat. I was feeling as dapper as Jimmy Walker that night as I called for Miss Johnson. (As a matter of fact, I was often mistaken for Jimmy Walker. We both had a long lean head, the skinny shape, and we held our heads cocked to one side when we were interested, so that with a few drinks, we *could* be taken for each other.)

Miss Johnson's apartment was cozy and warm and she greeted me with an Indiana smile as she looked over my finery.

"You do look the dude, Hoagy. Where shall we go? Smalls? Cotton Club, Savoy?"

She was ready to go, wearing a wonderful gown, daring, gold lamé, all the rage then, and she filled it well.

Her piano intrigued me. I lifted my tails out of the way—the way Noel Coward would—and I played the piano. Played for hours. Later I left and we'd had a wonderful time going no place.

Two years later Miss Johnson married a man from Phoenix,

Arizona, named Barry Goldwater. I record all this to show what a lady's man I was.

Goldman Sachs, RCA, and U.S. Steel fell, but I managed to compose two or three things. *Georgia On My Mind* was one of them. Frank Trumbauer prompted me to write it. One day he said, "Why don't you write a song called *Georgia?* Nobody lost much writing about the South."

"It has a good sound, Frankie."

"It ought to go 'Georgia, Georgia . . .' "

"That's a big help."

Later I sat down at the Shackelfords' piano, gave it some thought, and wrote it out, note by slow note. A week later I was playing it and trying to think up lyrics for it. Stu Gorrell, one of my roommates, pitched in and gave me some help. As a result I gave Stu an interest in the song.

"How much in cash, Hoagy?"

"You'll have to wait like the rest of us."

As it turned out, a few quickly dashed-off lines made Stu many thousands of dollars and it presently is paying his daughter's way through college. His only song.

4

Bill Shattuck and I moved into better surroundings, an old, creaky walk-up in East Thirty-first Street. The lure was that it had a grand piano in it, the first I ever had in my own place and an excuse for a big party. Anything was an excuse for that.

One of the first things we did was to go out and buy our winter's stock of liquor, eight bottles. Then we phoned the actors for our housewarming party. There is not much that's clear beyond that point in my memory. Reports were it was *some* party. When I woke up the next morning and started feeling my way around the apartment trying to find a recovery drink, I discovered there wasn't a drop left.

We laughed. "The whole winter's supply of whiskey gone in one night!"

It was worth it I decided, holding my hang-over. And so was the apartment. I held rehearsals in it for the all-star studded records I was to make for Victor. Bix, Jack Teagarden, the Dorseys, Pee Wee Russell, Bud Freeman, Benny Goodman, Gene Krupa, Joe Venuti—they were all on deck. The apartment became the hangout for every free-time jazzman in town. I must admit I loved it. It was the atmosphere that stimulated and inspired me. I was no solitary for an ivory tower.

The place was also a Hoosier hangout for visiting natives. A group of old classmates decided to look me up. All they had after a few days hard pleasuring was the name of my street and some approximate idea of the number of my apartment. In good Hoosier hog-calling voices—well oiled—they walked up and down the length of two blocks yelling, "Hoagland, HOAGLAND!"

I heard and leaned out of one of our windows.

"Hello. Come on up."

They rallied to the stairs with cries of "Liberty Hall!" It was a warm feeling to see college faces, remember old times, talk of how this and that had gone wrong after all the big talk on the campus, of what we'd all do once we got out and grabbed the world by the short hair. I'd sit and watch the boys drink and sing and I would think: anyway, I'm not alone.

Wad Allen and his new bride, Bette, arrived from Indiana. After Wad had had a few too many we laid him out on the black bedspread in his neat grey suit with hands over his chest and wrote his obituary on the beautiful marble mantle that had graced the room for a hundred years:

"Here lies a mother's boy."

The next morning we talked about the 1928 Prom at I.U. when Don Redman and the McKinney's Cotton Pickers played for it. Don and the boys were great and they got a kick out of watching the college kids do the "finale hop." After the ball was over, the entire band piled into my apartment. It seemed that in those days the local hotels had no rooms for the race.

All I could recall of those wee hours of the morning was the passing of the bottle and the eight dark forms draped over chairs and sitting in corners waiting for train-time back to Detroit early the next morning. A rugged life then for musicians.

Bill reminded us of the Bent Eagles Book Nook Commencement which followed the prom that year. When school was closing, the Bent Eagles gathered from far and near for their burlesque of the graduation exercises of the university. Wad Allen —the out-of-town speaker—arrived complete with a live white hen and copy of his speech.

The exercises began with a parade, organized in East Third Street, which proceeded to the Book Nook gathering crowds en route. Wad, in a frock coat, top hat, and with the hen under his arm, led the parade. He stood on a huge empty bus. Directly behind the bus was a cornet jazzband led by the sardonic Semite who dealt in secondhand clothes on the campus. He beat out the rhythm with a yardstick and we of the band, clad in bathrobes, came behind him.

Next came Eddie Wolfe, one of the newer and most ardent contributors to the order, and Bill Moenkhaus. They were symbolically arrayed in long black robes, to which were attached huge white eagle wings. Their mode of locomotion—a strange contraption swung between large wobbly wheels—was drawn by a swayback white horse, a horrible-looking creature. Pete Costas, the proprietor of the Book Nook, and a large following of Bent Eagles brought up the rear, dressed in pajamas and bathrobes.

We filed into the Book Nook and found it jammed with students eager to hear the out-of-town speaker. Wad delivered his address from the balcony and the charter members of the Bent Eagles assisted Pete Costas in delivering diplomas to those of the student body who had spent most of their time in the Book Nook during the school year and showed other promise of holding aloft the mystic torch of the Bent Eagles.

Wad's speech was an inspiration to all. It was as insanely futile as a Bent Eagle's idea of posterity, as senseless as a Bent Eagle's idea of time. Wad ad-libbed part of it and the speech is lost. I recall that it went something like this:

"Ya Lord and ya Lady Bent Eagles, friends, Foleys,[1] birds, and ya graduates; as the sheaves of years go passing by, comes this large class broken in mind and body seeking, through that limitless waste of years, those beautiful and intimate secrets known only to us Eagles.

"Seated as I am, on a silver dollar, it seems that I should flap my wings. Some of you I do not know. There are others I do not know. In fact I am a total stranger.

"Some of you will go away. There are others who will go away. Some of you will Sembower.[2] Perhaps this means Cogshall[2] is not here. Leap, Cogshall, leap!

"Ya Lord and ya Lady Bent Eagles, friends, Foleys, birds, and ya graduates, let me charge thee; I who from yon mountain comes to life; I from whom Mac Whore Ben Wilson. Let me charge thee three dollars."

As a concluding gesture Wad threw the flopping hen, mystic symbol of the true Bent Eagle, into the throng before him and the diplomas were then handed out.

Monk closed this solemn conclave, this session of spiritual rejuvenation, with an appropriate poem.

5

For better or worse I was falling into a pattern of life that was to remain, often for long periods of time, my way of life. After a day doodling or listening to music, I would gather friends around me and often go out on the town. There was a lot to see, and times were such that it didn't take a lot of money, which was just as well since we didn't have much. A lot of the time we were on the cuff.

If we weren't jamming in some smoke-reeking room with the chicks listening on the bed, their shoes off, and the brew moving around, there would be a rent party and somebody singing it out, husky and low-down.

[1] Ringer of the Chimes
[2] Professors

One felt in key with Bessie Smith:

> Check all your razors
> An' your guns
> We're gonna be wrasslin'
> When the wagon comes.

Always there was talk: to write jazz down, or improvise. The big talk against writing it down was that jazz was not composed music, but improvised in performance. Therefore, anyone who wrote it down was out of the true jazz tradition. Which was like saying only blue-eyed men were members of the human race, while brown-eyed men were only trying to be like blue-eyed men. There is room in jazz for the written, we would say, and the improvised.

"You don't improvise from nothing. You take a phrase that exists in mind, or on paper, and you improvise *that*."

In the end the blues are not the paper they're written on, we agreed, it's the horn and the slapped bass, it's the singer and the voice, it's the smoke in the room, it's the people listening, bent forward, eyes closed or shiny, it's the time and place and the ache inside that matches the ache in the words and music. It isn't something to take apart too much, to analyze. It's:

> When I got up this mornin'
> Blues walkin' round my bed,
> I went to breakfast—
> The blues was all in my bread.

That's how we lived in those no-good times—and the thirties ran along with millions unemployed. The hungry jazzmen would drop off the freight cars in Jersey City and report on all the towns in the sticks they'd been vaged, given one night in jail, a bowl of bug-infected soup, and moved with a kick in the ass and a last look at the sign: *No Outside Unemployed Allowed, Chief of Police.*

In the grim thirties. I rattled around, got to be known. And the new music, too.

6

Star Dust had sold over 100,000 copies so far, and a couple of new records were being made. Irving Mills of Mills Music wanted to put me under contract with a twenty-five dollar a week drawing account against royalties. At least I didn't accept that deal, but went to Ralph Peer, who had just formed Southern Music Publishing Co. Ralph had found out that he could go to some of the record companies and pick up new songs that were being recorded—just by being there and handing out contracts. In this way he picked up a good many western songs and eventually thousands of Latin-American compositions. It is now one of the biggest firms in the world.

Ralph had picked up my *Rockin' Chair* through the influence of LeRoy Shield, the then A-and-R man for Victor. Ralph agreed to pay me thirty-five dollars a week and I very joyfully handed him *Georgia On My Mind* which Stu Gorrell and I had written.

Along about that time Okeh Records were giving the country the best in jazz, including Frank Trumbauer's great records with Bix and the Louis Armstrong sessions. Tom invited me to make *Rockin' Chair* with Louis. I sang the straight part and Louis ad-libbed. Those blubbering strange sounds he made at the mike in front of my face tickled me to the marrow. Then Louie played a special cornet chorus. Jack Teagarden was there to lend encouragement although he didn't play on the date.

"Hey, Mr. Hoagy," Louis said, "that's a purty good tune."

Rockin' Chair, at this writing, is practically Louie's theme song, too. He took it up where Mildred Bailey left off. *Rockin' Chair* sold a bit and a few bands started playing *Georgia On My Mind.*

And now a nice thing happened. I was invited by the Victor Recording Company to make some records for them. What a break! And fortunately it coincided with Bix's return from Davenport. Victor wanted to record a corny thing called *Barnacle Bill the Sailor* and agreed to let me include *Rockin' Chair* for the first session. A later session was to include *Bessie Couldn't Help*

It and *Georgia On My Mind*. Did I get a band together? You betcha, and what a band!

I had Jimmy Dorsey, Tommy Dorsey, Jack Teagarden, Gene Krupa, Benny Goodman, Bud Freeman, Joe Venuti, and Bix, to name a few. This was probably the greatest aggregation of names ever assembled at one time and all they got was twenty dollars each per session.

I wrote the arrangements and fortunately stumbled onto the idea of switching the march tempo of *Barnacle Bill* to one-step on occasions so Bix and Benny Goodman could do their stuff. The composer sang his *Barnacle Bill* and I sang a weak version of *Rockin' Chair*. These were not great jazz records except for a few spots here and there. We had the men to do it and I could have made the orchestrations accordingly, but Victor was rather intent upon commercialism. For instance, Jack Teagarden and I had worked out a fine opening chorus of *Bessie Couldn't Help It* but when the A-and-R man heard it he said,

"I want to hear the melody."

Jack said, "Man you've got it."

But I noticed in the rendition that he slipped in a riff or two here and there.

And Bix—he looked fine even though Paul Whiteman had not taken him back into his orchestra. I noticed that Bix was a wee bit nervous for the first time. I caught him rehearsing a small passage behind the studio drapes on one occasion. For this reason, I didn't give him quite as much to do as I should have and now I am sorry because when he did play it was the old Bix and he gave the music the lift it needed.

At the Victor plant I found a pressing of my *One Night in Havana* that Fred Waring had made a year before. It was the first American attempt at rhumba with gourds and sticks. Of course, none of us were too familiar with this new expression, but the record sounded good to me. The Victor Company in their strange wisdom refused to release the record. Marked across the face in red chalk were the inspiring words: "Not Commercial."

XXIII

I don't want to give the impression that the thirties were all gloom, nail-biting, and worry. I was starting to catch on as a song writer, and while the big golden flood hadn't begun yet, I was beginning to perk up and take an interest in the town's social order—a polite way of saying girls, booze, parties, and lots of laughter.

My Thirty-first Street roommate, Bill Shattuck, and I, almost as soon as we got on our feet in New York City, ordered for ourselves full-dress midnight-blue evening clothes. We went all the way: tails, white gloves, top hats, canes, the white tie, and even if we could not afford it, a flower, a white one, of course, in our buttonholes. Bill and I would often dress, even sometimes if only to stop in at the Automat. But we were getting invited around to real good parties, and out would come the tails and the top hats and off we'd go to studio, ballroom, parlor, or soiree, young men on the town, fresh and full of juices; even the thirties didn't scare us. Bill loved the opera and talked me into going to the Met to hear Wagner, Puccini, and so forth. I liked it, and even stood for minutes at a time applauding in the proper manner. Dressed, of course.

Harlem was a great place to dress up for. All the smart, jaded, bright people were discovering the Negro and his music. Bill Shattuck and I would tilt our top hats on the sides of our heads and go to listen to Ellington, Satchmo, Dicky Wells, and others, sit in grime and blue smoke and amber spotlights and hear the new music—not so new now—catch on. Marge Everson, Bill's cousin, and I would dance to the Duke's music till our legs were

limp. Marge was the best and we loved to do variations of the
Lindy Hop, Suzy Cue, Rhumba, the Toddle, with some old
Friars Inn steps, in a conglomeration of fancy foot work. Duke
and the boys got a kick out of it and sometimes they would play
just for us. Louis Armstrong was at the Savoy Ballroom and
sometimes he too would play just for us, or so we thought.

I ran into Bix in a speak-easy and he had a beer. I proposed
again that he come out to the Shackelfords with me for dinner.
Of all surprising things, he accepted. He refused a drink at their
house and I could tell it wasn't easy because visiting with strangers
was a tough go for him. He did play a bit of piano but it was
rather listless. We didn't push him.

After dinner Bix and Bill Shattuck and I went up to a small
park to sing barber-shop harmony. A cop came along and said,
"Time you guys got home. The neighbors say you're a nuisance."

We thought we were damn good and Bix was slow in taking
orders, whereupon the cop billy-sticked him one you know
where and we were on our way.

"Fine thing, you can't sing in a park," and Bix said a dirty
word. It occurred to me then that he seldom if ever used dirty
words. On occasion I'd seen Bix talking to himself as though he
were very dismayed about something, but no dirty words came
out.

I don't claim to know what it was deep down that ate off Bix,
but when you know a human being and you see him suffering,
there is the idea in you to try and get him out of his mood. It
doesn't work, of course, and none of us can really change anyone's destiny too much, but we try; oh how we try, and how we
get in trouble.

Here's a bit that our host, Harry Shackelford, didn't tell me
for many years. He had forgotten to.

He and Bix sat back in a bedroom while I was doing a few
songs for the girls in the livingroom. Bix told him that he felt
uneasy among women folk. I am sure he didn't mean the younger
set but after all some women are a bit anxious to please and con-
descending. Perhaps, this is what he meant. But mainly, he inti-

mated to "Shack" that his style was a passing phase and that he was "through." He also used the expression "has-been," and Shack told me that Bix's manner was that of a melancholy boy. Of course he was not a has-been and maybe it was because Whiteman did not take him back that got him thinking this way.

Bix came back into the livingroom and said, "Ran into a girl the other day. She's going to fix me up in a flat out in Sunnyside."

"Great, how's for bringing her over to my kip some night?"

"Any time," and we made a firm date.

2

Bix and the girl came to my apartment two weeks later. She was Bix's kind of girl. A bit mothery, maybe lost herself, but neat, willing to put up with Bix's habits. I liked her. We didn't have a drink. We didn't talk much music, and it became apparent that this girl had no idea who Bix was and why he was the way he was. It was just two strangers meeting. Perhaps she knew he was a musician, but that was all. The thought struck me —later—I didn't know Bix either. He was my friend, yet intimately, deeply, warmly, I didn't know him. He was unfathomable, the bit on the surface hiding the deep-lying man.

He stepped out of the room to get some cigarettes. "Listen, honey," I said, "if Bix ever gets sick, if anything happens, *let me know*. Let me know right away!"

"Sure," she said. "I'll let you know."

"He doesn't like help—you have to force it on him."

She nodded, bit her lower lip, and lowered her head till I couldn't read her eyes.

"Yeah, I know."

When Bix came back, he seemed to want to be sociable.

"You still with Irving Mills, Hoagy?"

"I do some recording, but it's not a living," I said.

"What do you do for cakes and java?"

"Working for an investment banking house."

"You won't quit music, Hoagy?"

"Uh-uh. I don't think so."

"I won't either. But I'm still right back where I started—at liberty. . . ."

The girl showed interest. "Sweetie, where'd you first start?"

"Buckley's Novelty Orchestra, a million years ago. We got a job at the Terrace Gardens in Davenport. There was a union band there and we had to join the union. To join the union you had to read music. I didn't."

"What happened?"

"I memorized everything cold. But cold. And we got up there and I looked at the sheet and blew right good. And then they double-crossed me. They stuck up a sheet I hadn't learned. You got a drink around, Hoagy?"

"No," lying. "How'd you get around the new sheet?"

"I played exactly what the piano played. I was right behind it on its tail. Of course, I was supposed to be playing the orchestration. I got canned. Jesus, I felt so low-down about it."

"What you were doing was a hell of a lot harder than reading," I said.

"Must have been," the girl said, patting his arm. "And you don't need a drink."

"Don't need it, baby, just happened to think about it."

"It must have been great music."

Bix's shy grin lit up his face. "You know I never did learn to finger that bugle right."

I was pleased Bix had a girl. And I had an old girl again, too —Dorothy Kelly. But I knew at that time that music, the ambition to live it and write it, could not merge with a life of simple domesticity. I couldn't live on two sides of the coin at one time.

Dorothy and I corresponded and as her labored affection for me seeped away in her letters, my replies became harder to write. And finally it was hard to react—it was impossible. I have a draft of the last letter I tried to write. The one I couldn't mail after the wire came from her, saying that she was to be married.

Dearest Dorothy: The snow falls through the stripped branches of the maples in Bloomington, and it's beautiful. The snow takes away every harsh tone and the snow rounds out all things soft, immaculate. The snow falls here in New York, people grind it into a dirty pulp. It doesn't matter to a mug who is in a roaring subway car riding up to Harlem to hear the Duke do things no other man can do. The guy in leaky shoes on the subway is me.

This letter is about you and me, about all the things we dreamed of, about a house on the hill and the vines. But there is the music, I like it, too. I have to have it. I have to have New York right now. It's exciting and it makes me want to be somebody. I am still nobody. I couldn't bring you here to a fourth floor cold water walk-up, papered in unsold sheet music.

Last night I went to hear a five-piece band work in a speakeasy on 52nd Street. You'd like this way of life for a while, but not for too long. It's going to take me a long time, Dorothy, and I'll have to spend half my time rattling doors, chasing indifferent people; because to me it is urgent. I can think of you now, write what I want, because I know I won't send this letter on to you.

I keep telling myself that I can't love music more than a girl like you and I know that I'm a fool. But I could also be a liar the way things are, and I'll write you about that some day (but I know I won't write you again). I'm going out tonight. Louis Armstrong is in town. He's going to show me purty notes. And so I'll learn some more about composing.

I hope that you are happy,
                    Hoagy.

3

And here comes Harry! I had moved again in the traditional Carmichael fashion and I might say in the manner of most young people who live in New York, and Harry Hostetter had wired me from Houston, Texas, "Have Tux will travel. Look for baby."

"Baby" arrived in the form of a satchel that looked suspicious. Harry arrived by freight and I immediately burned his clothes while he took a bath. What was in that satchel brought him a few bucks and I am glad the F.B.I. didn't come sniffing around our house. I was making home brew beer which smelled to high heaven so that is all we could have been arrested for, anyway.

Harry met a lot of musicians in the Broadway area and he came running to me one night.

"This guy, Sidney Arodin, plays a pretty clarinet, and he's gotta tune you gotta hear, Hoag."

"Where?"

"Over on 56th Street in a clip joint."

We went that night. It was a shabby brick-front walk-up on the second floor and the only customer was a balding man of about fifty-five with a hired girl on each arm, drinking champagne. They must have clipped this gent for five hundred dollars at least before they let him out. Harry and I were guests of Sidney's, so none of the girls glanced our way.

Sidney played his tune and I was highly pleased. I knew Harry couldn't be wrong. In the ensuing weeks I wrote a verse and a lyric and titled it *Lazy River*. The ambition of every song writer was now accomplished although I didn't know it then— that of having in his folio something on the order of a folksong that could be played and sung in most any manner, something that could be sung all the way through by drunken quartets or by blondes over a piano bar.

Soon, I was recording this one, too, for Victor with Tommy and Jimmy Dorsey, Joe Venuti, and Red Norvo on vibes. On the reverse side (*Moon Country*, written with Johnny Mercer) Jimmy Dorsey picked up a cornet he brought along and started to ad lib during the last and final take. This was not part of my orchestration but it worked out all right. Didn't know that boy could blow a cornet!

Southern Music published it and to date, it's one of the biggest money makers of all time.

The soup and bread lines grew longer. Washington issued the news it was only "a temporary setback" as a lot of jazzmen put cardboard in their shoes.

I sat by my phone in the musty post-depression office of an investment house, hoping the publishers would call and tell me that *Stardust* was selling. I was afraid to call myself, afraid to ask.

The phone rang. I picked it up. It was Wad Allen. "Bix died, Hogwash."

"When?"

"The other day. I just saw a squib in Winchell's column."

It was a blow right between the eyes. "Little girl," I said to myself, thinking of the promise I had extracted from Bix's girl, "why didn't you call me?" I couldn't shake it off. I just sat and stared at the grim, grey city out there beyond the unwashed windows. He had looked so good just two weeks before—and I had been full of hope for him. Now even his body was miles away and I had not even had a chance to be of help.

He hadn't survived, picking up radio one-spots like the Camel Hour. Casa Loma had wanted him, but Bix could take only four nights of their involved, exacting arrangements and tricky ensembles. He did some recording.

His only recreation for some time had been motion pictures. He loved *Wings* and *Hell's Angels*. Occasionally he would visit the city morgue. "It's restful and no tourists." He had recorded *In a Mist* for Okeh Records and Paul Whiteman's great arranger, Bill Challis, would pester him to get all of his compositions on paper. Thanks to Bill, they are in published form.

He got a bad cold that hung on but he and his girl friend went to Manhattan for a rehearsal in spite of the fact that he was running a fever. In a few hours he could hardly stand and she took him back to the apartment in Queens, where a doctor in the same building examined him and said he had pneumonia.

His resistance was low and in a short time he drifted off. On August 7, 1931, he was dead at twenty-eight.

I felt dreadful over his untimely death but I knew the little any of us did to help him couldn't stop the drive to destruction so many great artists seem to have. I respected him and loved him at his best—and I leave the enigma of the inner Bix Beiderbecke for others to figure out if they can. But I don't think the searchers will find much more. Later Bix's girl sent me the iron mouthpiece of his horn, and I have it under glass before me now.

4

Even in hard times ("If F.D.R. is elected, you'll see grass growing in the streets") the cult of the hot jazz, the tempo of those
who refused to regard commercial corn as significant, was alive
in subtle ways. Those who had heard the early Bix Beiderbecke
recordings realized that there was something more to jazz than
pretentious arrangements and red lights and tailored jackets. If
you were a lover of Bix, Louis Armstrong and Frank Trumbauer
in those years, you felt at times as if you were a member of a
secret society in a world of sweet popularization.

It was us fanatics, pure and unadulterated, that kept the genes
of jazz alive through every miscegenation with popular fancy
and demand. More important, it was this blood line that survived
the economic and moral ups and downs of a badly bruised nation.
Because of its low-down, gut-bucket gully-ho origins, jazz received a bad press for thirty years before the intellectuals rushed
up with fancy theories to defend it. And the old Dixielanders,
Kansas City, Chicago, Harlem schools were later dismayed to
find that the "critics" and "experts" and "historians" had cut in
on a thing that once was something beyond "critics" and exclusively their miserable own.

The early thirties still found me musically up the creek with
my music manuscripts as a feeble paddle. The people who
thought my tunes were good were many, and I was thankful to
them. I got encouragement but little cash, free drinks but no
great popularity. New York City and the nation were sliding
deeper into the Great Depression. I remember the sad mood of
the period and I am convinced that I would not have survived if
I had not had some musical talent and a limestone-hard Indiana
character.

About my music I was stubborn, contrary, tenacious, and reso-
lute in the fight, punching away. There wasn't anything else I
could be. If I didn't love my music I was just another kind of
Okie beating my way, another soup kitchen hobo with nothing

ahead but the dust bowl. I just wrote what I God-damned wanted in my own way.

Folks with a reputation for stubbornness, contrariness, are most often likely to be hunch players. We gamble for no reason, with no intelligent analysis of the odds against us. When the hunch pays off the gambler gets credit for perspicacity. When it doesn't, and for the vast majority of us it doesn't (even for Hoosiers), we shrug it off.

There were dreadful soul-grinding, morale-destroying moments of doubt. No one could add up such a long succession of disappointments as mine and not have moments of disillusion on the fairness of all odds. I never had the easy Norman Vincent Peale smile that made it easy to peddle my wares.

The world seemed to be tumbling down when F.D.R. came in. For me it could have turned into a private gold mine, by accident. I had a girl friend who went to a fancy party and a U.S. Senator there liked her so much he asked her to sit on his lap.

"Baby, you know what's going to happen the day after tomorrow? No? F.D.R.'s going to close the banks and that will raise the price of gold."

"Senator, you say the funniest things."

But she came running to me with the news. A tip like that should have started me off trying to get my hands on some gold stocks that would leap in value as collectors' items. But all I said was, "You're crazy. No senator would give out with that kind of news."

But it was true and I stood aside to watch the gravy train roll by. "The great Train Robbery" some people called it.

I missed this one but not the next one. Senator(?) Carmichael told a bunch of his friends during the fourth of July weekend of 1934 that at eleven A.M. on the Monday following the stock market averages would hit rock bottom and prices would end much higher at the close. The market did just that. I bought a few shares and by September the tickertape was late on the upside at times. Few people made much because they had so little to invest in those days. To risk a dollar was to risk the baby's milk!

5

In the grim gray world of the aftermath of the twenties, some hope seeped down to us disinherited. We even had a kind of social life on the edge of the volcano. An informal but potent New York society known as the Sons of Indiana was organized, as if the depression was not enough. It became immediately popular with hungry Hoosiers during the worst years ahead.

It was an informal society that could laugh at the mess the world had made of itself. It was ashes to ashes all the way; no wonder the Sons of Indiana tried to make its membership by-laws cheerful: "Any sassafras drinker of the male sex, who has nursed a hang-over through Elkhart and can name the city where the Soldiers' and Sailors' Monument is located, is eligible for membership. Men born and raised in Indiana are also eligible."

One article of the constitution declared: "The object of the organization is to promote friendly relations among Indiana men, resident or temporarily adjourning in or about New York City, and to cherish and perpetuate the memories of the State of Indiana."

It was an all-male organization. Their annual Outstanding Hoosier awards over the years have included such names as Wendell Willkie and Ernie Pyle (and much later, Hoagy Carmichael).

Ernie dropped into my Fifty-second Street apartment once (up from Washington, D.C., I think) and, after we had had a beer or two, chatted about nothing in particular. I wondered how he was going to write a column about me. But he did in his easy, know-how manner.

As my music caught on I did expand a bit, but I was a strange combination of free spending at times, but at other times, holding onto a buck when I got frightened the worst of the depression was not yet over. But when I went wild, as over race horses, money seemed printed on snowflakes.

In 1929 I had bought my first insurance policy, bought it from a banjo player who worked in an orchestra at the Columbia Club.

"Hoagy man, you'll have a rich ole age."

"I haven't read the fine print yet."

I made my first trip to Louisville, Kentucky, to attend the Kentucky Derby. I drove to Cincinnati, Ohio, and joined a private party on a river boat. Girls and jazz all night—floatin' down to Louisville. I picked the horse I liked because of name and colors: I have found this to be as scientific as any other way—and just as damaging. I picked Little Colonel. It was raining that day and mud was on the track. I bought a $2.00 ticket and had to be shown how to do it. For this little innocent, Little Colonel walked in and paid $62.00. An easy way to make money that cost me many, many thousands of dollars in the future. I'm a good form reader but I'm a bad bettor. I do not plunge at the right time. In horse racing you have to be patient and bet only one horse to win. When you're a winner, leave. My advice is: If you like horses, the merry-go-round ones are harmless. I like roulette. It's intriguing and less nerve-wracking. Numbers 34, 4, and 17 are my favorites but they have never performed like the number 26 did one night. That number came up four times in a row right in front of my eyes. Practically a million to one chance and I'm proud to say I had a few chips on it the third and fourth time it came up. But a real gambler would have bet it heavy the third and fourth time at the wheel. Remember, one dollar on that number, left to ride for four straight, would make you $1,336,336 in five minutes.

I was born with a broad fat conservative streak. In the stock market I would invest a few thousand dollars and make a few dollars, then pull out. I never had the courage to stay with it. Too many of my ancestors buried their loose change under the fireplace or kept it in an old sock under the mattress. And we never had a lot, so I was careful.

6

First success was now real, but it took me a long time to admit it was there, and mine. So I didn't really savor it properly at first.

The world was changing and I with it, fight it as I might. The 1920's were gone, gone for good, but for their echoes, and later their glamour would come back to us badly distorted in films, in books, in stage shows. It was somehow not the real twenties, but something people wanted to believe was the twenties, or a time when everything was permitted and everything had a shine and an edge. In a way it did, but not the way we remembered it. We left out the cold hard moments, the sad lonely times.

Meanwhile, there were the 1930's mounting up before me, hurrying along in dance time. The girls looked different to me, and they were. Backless evening dresses appeared with godets and drapes near the floor, the V-necked sweater was every place, but the car of the period was still square with its flat radiator, although the running board was to go soon. It seems odd to think of a motor car as an object to remember, to love in memory, but those square old crates still command a strange affection in my heart. My ideal was the National—a sports roadster, 1920 vintage, long, big hood, brass radiator; dreams were made of such stuff as that beauty. Wilson Mizner had one in Florida and I rode in it. That's when he said, "Son, hitch your wagon to a star—a rich Ziegfeld beauty." He looked me over and I knew he was just teasing, but I thought about it. And somehow the images of most of the girls, too, have faded into one composite shot of a type.

In the early thirties, I walked to where the old Waldorf Astoria Hotel had been. The new giant, the Empire State Building, was going up. Later I could become a bore talking of *my* New York City, no longer being the New York I knew. Radio City was still a series of wet holes in the ground, and the musty, malty old speaks in brownstone cellars were already memories or turning into 21 or Toots Shor, or onion soup dives. We no longer sang *Singing in the Rain* at Tony's or heard Rudy Vallee do a jew's-harp version of *Vagabond Dreams* through his nose.

The best escape I found was still the movies, where one could be warm, romantically nudged, while the hero (was he Rod La Rocque or Ronald Coleman?) took on the features of Hoagy Carmichael as I watched. Radio, I saw, hadn't killed off the theatre, the films or the night spots, even if the average radio still cost $135.

As a Republican, I read where Mr. Coolidge had retired from the White House and, frugal fellow that he was, had taken a house in the country that cost him thirty-six dollars a month in rent, although he got a dollar a word writing for the newspapers. People read with interest his remarks on a problem of our day: "Unemployment results when men are out of work." I counted the words at a dollar each. I could have said it myself if I had thought of it—and much cheaper.

Stardust was growing in popularity. I heard Edgar Hayes play it in Harlem, and that set it off again. Other songs started pushing for escape from my mind.

I had made a great discovery. I could write tunes. Write as *good* as anyone doing it, and at times my ego said why not better? I also found out I didn't write them, really. Each tune just wrote itself. The time had to be right and I had to be right, but the tune came out all on its own. I didn't care much for writing lyrics, but I could turn from knocking out a tune on a piano and shout, "Isn't that great!" Not great maybe, but I knew it was good.

7

I was getting fame. People were hearing my songs and remembering me. Radio was then the poor man's night club, and my music was on it more and more, and even I appeared on it.

My friends and I would go up to a little golf club about sixty miles from New York City. They had tennis, a little lake where they had boating, but none of us could really play golf. We couldn't hit our hats, didn't know how to hold a club. Anyone could beat me at tennis, but I took some lessons and eventually got so I could beat a few people.

I tried to play hockey at our little club and the only pair of skates I could find were a pair of ladies' size 8. I was able to get into those although my toes protested. I'd never played hockey in my life. Everyone was wildly laughing. I wondered why.

They were laughing at me. I was so excited about the game I hadn't noticed my ankles had given way and I was running around that rink on the insides of my ankles.

"Hoagy, you don't need skates, just ankle guards."

I also went to more parties. Jules Glaenzer of Cartier's threw the best ones. At one, George Gershwin was there; he had finished the score of *Porgy and Bess,* but it hadn't been produced yet. After I gave up the piano stool, George began to play his new music. People were interested, especially Jules, but only a few were listening to *Summertime* and the wonderful transitions he was playing. But most kept grabbing cocktails and yelling: "Play some of your show tunes!"

Finally, deadpan George played *Rhapsody in Blue* just with one hand, doing it very well.

I could see it was what they wanted. I grinned at George.

"I know just how you feel. No matter *what* I write they want me to play *Stardust* all the time."

George said a dirty word, lit a cigar, and made 'em listen. He liked to control a party when he sat down to play.

George Gershwin was a dapper lean shark of a man, happy in his success but wondering just how good he really was for all his huge lump of ego. A long time after that I saw George just before his untimely death—a young giant of popular melody cut down in his green prime.

He said, "Funny, Hoagy, I've written better things than the *Rhapsody,* but the *Rhapsody* is still the trade-mark for me to the public. *Porgy and Bess* is a big step beyond the *Rhapsody.* The *Concerto in F,* musically, is, I think, a bigger thing. Why aren't they as popular as the *Rhapsody?*"

I made a shrugging answer. I felt the *Rhapsody* showed most his borrowing of original jazz themes.

"Hoagy, I wrote the *Rhapsody* for a highly specialized orchestra for rhythmic dexterity. All symphony orchestras are not good for it. I mean, you can't get terrific rhythm out of 115 classical men. You need a great sweep and a certain personal rhythm."

I said, "You need jazzmen."

He looked tan and alert; he had it made in Tin Pan Alley, on the stage, even in concerts.

"You like concert forms, George?"

"Dr. Damrosch commissioned me to write for concerts. First the *Concerto in F*, and then *An American in Paris*. I'm not sure they ever played the music right. I don't think the symphonies can. It needs a jazz band."

"Could be."

"Just as soon as I finish a moving picture score, the next thing I'm going to write will be for a jazz group."

Later we had one of our sweaty, not-too-good-to-watch tennis matches at Rip's court on Park Avenue and we solemnly swore we'd never write a Hawaiian song. Recently, I broke that promise, but since it hasn't been published or recorded I still feel in his good graces.

There never was a "next thing" for George. With nineteen chances out of twenty for a successful brain-cyst operation, the twentieth chance caught him.

Looking back to the thirties when George was so good and so popular and giving all those parties in his penthouse, rushing around courting the girls, learning to paint in oils, collecting modern art and free-loaders (Oscar Levant stayed around to rush down for corned beef sandwiches, George told me), I don't think he was ever really happy.

George wasn't a real jazzman and he knew it. He was out of Tin Pan Alley, with a great gift, and a desire to make concert music out of new forms.

8

People were beginning to ask me to entertain. I was always quick to show off a new tune. I made believe I was seeking opinions, but I knew whether I liked it or not. Like all young men, I accepted praise; on the other hand, I listened to criticism very little.

Georgia On My Mind was a song that rose in popularity slowly but definitely. It became a hit that musicians liked to play. Mildred Bailey and Louis Armstrong were keeping *Rockin' Chair* alive. Mildred used it as her theme song and everybody was listening to Louie's version, too, which he played often because of the record we had made together. *Lazy River* was a hit at first and hung on, but was not quite as big as the other two. *Stardust* was doing more for me than anything else.

Times were still hard for the average citizen—like my father—but the cost of things was low with so much unemployment. My family in Indiana managed to survive. Dad had a job, but the real problem was how long he'd be able to drive a car fifty miles a day to keep that job. They almost said prayers when he showed up unbanged and unhurt. I helped my sister, Martha, go to college where she wanted to become a drummer. My sister, Georgia, played piano for dances and did the adagio.

I was feeling older but maturing slowly. My college days were long behind me, I felt, as I looked at the new breed of college creatures. They were hatless now, fur coats were out, and racoon skins gathered moths in closets. Girls no longer went in only for sleek silk; they wore those clumsy ankle socks. The dinner jacket was standard, sending most tails into storage—although I remained a rebel till my tails turned green.

Mae West was making the curve desirable again. *She Done Him Wrong* was the rage. No crystal ball told me that I would soon be writing songs for one of her movies.

It wasn't my college world any more. As I stood drinking with friends the night Utah became the thirty-sixth state to ratify the end of bootlegging, I knew I was getting on. My world had changed.

9

It's not easy to write of my songs, but since this is for the record, I have let memory dredge up some of the excitement of the period when I wrote them.

Judy was written about this time and became a musicians' favorite immediately. They all played and liked it, but not enough. Or sung it enough to be a favorite of the public. I wrote the melody in 1928 and it was so weird, so modern in style that Wad Allen named it *Birdseed*. It had no lyrics but six years later we published it because we thought musicians would understand it. They did. Sammy Lerner wrote words to it. Good words, too.

A song plugger introduced me to Johnny Mercer. He was a young, bouncy butterball of a man from Georgia. He hadn't had a song hit, but I could tell that he could write. Johnny had married Ginger, a showgirl sweetheart, and they lived in Brooklyn. We did write a couple of things that weren't too important but then one day he strolled into my apartment and said,

"I'd like to write a song called *Lazy Bones*."

"Sounds fine—let's start."

Actually, in twenty minutes we wrote the entire song.

Two weeks after Southern Music published *Lazy Bones,* and Ralph Smitman, their song plugger, handed copies to Kate Smith and the Casa Loma Orchestra, I made my first trip to Europe in search of new musical sounds.

Cocktail time in Geneva found me in a little bistro listening to a three-piece orchestra playing *Rockin' Chair*, and at the New York Club in Budapest I heard the orchestra playing *March Of The Hoodlums*, another tune of mine. Paris was playing nothing but American songs so I came home empty handed, but I had a hell of a good time. When I got off the boat a friend told me that Southern Music had to put on extra help in order to ship copies of *Lazy Bones*. It had become an instant hit while I was gone and was selling 15,000 copies a day. A sweet, surprising bit of news, indeed.

At this time you could look down on Times Square and count all the people present in a jiffy, but the success of *Lazy Bones* seemed to generate new confidence in the music business and within a year Times Square started to look itself again. In 1933, *Lazy Bones* won an ASCAP special award of $1,250 each for Johnny and me.

"All that spendin' money, Hoagy. Let's do more!"

We were elated and started writing more, several things that didn't set the world on fire, and soon Johnny was with Paul Whiteman and writing with others, mainly Matty Malneck. It was a disappointment to me because with the proper guidance and diligent work, Johnny and I could have flooded the market with hit songs. We were atune and I knew he "knew" and he knew I "knew." But the chips didn't fall right. Probably my fault because I didn't handle them gently.

My demon spurs me to direct action. I've had an impulsive nature all my life. I reason well about most things but in those years I was overanxious regarding music and the need to make money, especially in the years when the early poverty still stung me. In the eyes of many I was an easy mark, a strange sort, or a fool. The conventional rules of conduct, even in business dealings, I'd throw aside when the going got tough or when I got overanxious. I was too eager, and yet did not have gumption enough to seek good advice, or ask if I were making an ass of myself.

Many times I did make an ass of myself. But I was never obstreperous, just reckless and impatient. I needed to make money in those early years. It was the tangible reward we were judged by. Young men mistake rewards for progress. I did.

If I was busy composing, learning business, growing up, the times were busy, too. But people sang songs, and *The Music Goes Round and Round* was the biggest nut hit since *Yes, We Have No Bananas*. Major Bowes, a toad-nosed old city slicker, had a radio show called *The Amateur Hour*.

As times got better for the nation, Roosevelt-hating became good upper-class form. I was a Republican, but I didn't enjoy talk of "that crippled s.o.b." Out in Locust Valley and Greenwich, where I'd go for parties, they had regular Hate-F.D.R. sessions. He was rarely called by name, but referred to usually as *That Man*.

In music we were talking about something called *swing;* the old Dixieland Jazz was changing and people who stuck to it were called moldy figs. The jitterbugs, convulsed in the Big Apple, had heroes like Teddy Wilson, Gene Krupa, and Count Basie. And Benny Goodman was preparing to take on the mantle of King of Swing. I was ready for it, ready for anything.

FOUR

"The Music of the Years Gone By"

XXIV

The middle thirties were great times for song writers, although the early twenties were probably the best: fewer writers and piano music used to sell in bundles over the five-and-ten-cent counters. In 1915, when I worked in a five-and-ten in Bloomington, there was a girl there who could play a bit of piano to help sell sheet music. At closing time, she would play the new songs for me and I would listen and learn and marvel that the names on the sheet music could write these wonderful things. Later, in Indianapolis, I haunted the five-and-tens and a music store on the Circle. These girls played well and loud and occasionally a song plugger would come to town to sing the songs behind the counter. I never bought anything because I couldn't read the music but I picked up a lot of new songs by ear.

Those of us writing songs in the thirties were not making the money that writers had for years before. Radios, phonographs, and movies had replaced the old upright piano. The baby grands came along but, unhappily, most of these were used as furniture.

But there was ASCAP (American Society of Composers, Authors & Publishers) which some song writers, including Victor Herbert and Gene Buck, had organized a number of years before for the purpose of collecting money from various sources, mainly the radio stations, for the use of our music. Payment for public performance of music under the Copyright Act is the main function of this organization. It was a lifesaver to writers and publishers and I doubt that we would have had half of the great songs that came along through the years if it hadn't been for this support. The big broadcasting companies couldn't stand to see all this money leave their till. They organized a competing organization called Broadcast Music, Incorporated. When I say "all this money," I am kidding. In respect to the networks' gross or even net income, I doubt that the amount paid to song writers was any more than 0.5 per cent.

What with *Rockin' Chair, Stardust, Georgia On My Mind, Lazy River,* and *Lazy Bones,* to name a few, there was a year or two when my music amounted to about 1.5 per cent of all music played on the air. If I had been paid on a performance basis, I would have been making $50,000 a year from this source alone during the depression.

ASCAP's system was to place writers in classifications according to the importance of their works and distribute the funds quarterly in varying amounts, according to the writers' classification. Once you attained a higher classification, you were certain to retain this classification for a considerable number of years whether you wrote more hits or not. It was like an annuity and we thought it was a good program. A few young disgruntled writers were unhappy about it and they took their message to a former violinist who was then in the U. S. Justice Department in Washington. This was the beginning of the end of ASCAP's first payment system. Now, if a young fellow writes a big hit, he is paid mainly on a point system for all the performances of the song on radio and television. He might receive $25,000 or $30,000 from this source in one year and, of course, pay the government a big hunk in income taxes. In my opinion, the other system was better. In recent years, anyone could fashion some rock-and-roll song, with little or less originality and make more off of it in one year than *Smoke Gets In Your Eyes* earned for the late Jerome Kern during his lifetime.

In the depression years I had enough income to live comfortably and most of my friends from Indiana were employed. I got some jobs on radio. I was one of the few writers who could both write and sing songs. Harold Arlen, Willard Robison, Johnny Mercer, and Benny Davis are a few other writers who could sing a bit.

I liked New York. "You've never lived at all," I used to think, "if you've never lived in New York." Fiftieth and Park Avenue is one of the most beautiful pictures in the world—where the church stands across from the Waldorf Astoria. An area six blocks long and six blocks wide, from Third Avenue to Eighth Avenue and from Grand Central Station to Fifty-second Street also held enchantment for me. In this neighborhood a song hit could be made in a few weeks; it was the center of a trade that fanned out over the entire nation. All the publishing houses, good orchestras, and broadcasting stations were huddled together here. Musicians and writers lived in the area. Being a bit different, I chose the brownstones and various walk-ups in the Fifties, east and west of Park Avenue.

I've already told how I happened to switch music publishers—from Mills Music, who had offered me a twenty-five dollar a week drawing account against royalties, to Southern Music's Ralph Peer, who agreed to give me thirty-five dollars a week. So Peer got *Rockin' Chair, Georgia On My Mind*, and soon *Lazy River*. These songs went far in establishing him as a major publishing house. He gave me on paper 1 per cent of the gross business after *Lazy Bones*, but I asked for my release in 1935 so I could go over to Warner Brothers' publishers, Feist, Witmark, and that 1 per cent went out the window. I was a bad businessman. Too anxious to go ahead quickly, I went to work for Buddy Morris, who was running the business, and Stanley Adams (now president of ASCAP). We wrote *Little Old Lady*. It sold 650,000 copies at sixty cents each. When an opening to write songs in Hollywood came up (my primary reason for joining the firm), they sent Johnny Mercer and left me home to tend the store.

My apartments had gotten better, in spite of the depression. I had acquired on Fifty-second Street a second-floor walk-up with a fine balcony, high ceiling, good kitchen, a large dressing closet (which I had never had before), king-size bed, and a beautiful marble fireplace, all across from the Ambassador Hotel. I worked to fix it up and bought a Fisher grand piano. Steinway once had his piano factory on the corner of Fifty-second Street and Park Avenue. Someone remarked, "Steinway would turn over in his grave if he knew Hoagy had a Fisher grand here." There was a good restaurant downstairs and Tony's was right across the street. It was here that Johnny Mercer and I wrote *Lazy Bones*.

The agony of success was stained by an inner worry: "Will it last? Or am I just one of the passing freaks, like flagpole sitters and Channel swimmers?" But I was on my way and practically any song I wrote would be published.

When Dick Huber moved in with me in 1934, we got acquainted with the Sherman Fairchilds and through him and the Powers Agency, we met and dated some of the most beautiful models in New York. They were a fine, healthy, well-stacked lot but, unfortunately, for bachelors, almost all of them just wanted to model. For me, the most beautiful model we entertained was a girl from San Antonio, Texas. Her face was seen on all the best magazines. She did our place proud as fine decor and we had lots of dates. She left New York and later I heard she was to marry the man who shot Dillinger. He was a mighty brave man dealing with Public Enemy Number One, but not so brave with the ladies; he didn't show up for the wedding.

2

To keep the place in order, we advertised for a maid who would cook and late one afternoon, around six o'clock, in came Eva Ford.

"Where you from?" I asked her.

"Originally Boston, but it sure got dull."

"It's not dull here."

"No—it don't much look it."

Eva had a wonderful smile. She was quite young, no more than nineteen. I liked her and hired her. When she met my roommate, she said, "Mr. Huber, I like him, too."

Eva saw me through what was called a heart attack by some, but may have been only indigestion. I had gone to a Swedish place on Third Avenue with Hank Wells—smorgasbord in a basement, a deadly mixture. Afterwards, as I was walking up the two flights of stairs to my place, all of a sudden I felt this thing hit me—as though someone had put a two-hundred-pound weight on my chest. I stayed in bed two weeks and went on a diet.

Eva took care of me as if I were rare crystal. When I had visitors, she'd do a dance to amuse us, the Suzie Q.

I recovered and through a friend, Ann Graham, I met the girl I was to marry. Ann was a very beautiful girl from Wabash, Indiana. She came to New York and the only person she knew to call on was me. She called.

Ann introduced me to her roommate Ruth. George Gershwin became very fond of Ann, who was quite an inspiration to him. They were together a lot of the time when George was writing *Porgy and Bess*. Ann went to Europe with a show and while over there, she was discovered by a young Greek shipping tycoon. Ruth would come over to read me Ann's letters, but she had already told Ann about me, "That's the man I'm going to marry."

Ann seemed to be having a wonderful time with the Greeks. "It sounds that way. Is he a rich Greek?"

"Very."

It was natural, with Ann in Europe, that Ruth and I would spend a lot of time together, and in that way we became very fond of each other, the usual result, I am told, of being young and meeting often. If I seem unable to explain it with more detail, the truth is that I wasn't at all sure of myself, or serious—as yet— to the point of falling in love. Ruth made me think of domestic life and I resented it a bit; I was having so much fun as a bachelor.

I was aware that Ruth meant more to me just then than any other girl I had ever known. I admired her looks, walk, talk, wit, charm, vitality: I liked being with her, wanted to be with her when I wasn't, and I thought about her when I should have been working.

We grew closer, grew to understand each other, or that part of ourselves the courting drama lets us see of each other. For— it seems to me—we are never truly ourselves during the mating dance. We prance and strut our best stances, give off our clearest laughter, our most poetic tones. Only to lovers does the prattle of small talk take on a glow of value just to them.

"Did you read Winchell this morning, Hoagy?"

"Yes. What are you reading?"

"*Life Begins at Forty.*"

"Silly girl."

I suppose we could have used a dialogue writer, but not really; we liked it corny.

3

Meanwhile the Greek shipping king had finally corralled Ann and married her. Ruth went to London to visit them, and Bill Shattuck and I decided to travel, too—to Barbados. We had never been. Ruth wrote she'd like to come along. She took a boat from London to Barbados and met us there. We fixed up a tennis court, cut grass and limed it, and took pictures of us playing.

"It's heaven, Hoagy."

"It's the British West Indies."

"You've been to the bar."

"Let's go back."

A fourteen-year-old Barbadian boy named Buttons was bartender. He could make any kind of a drink we wanted. That and enjoying beach and the sun, watching a black fisherman with a sixty-pound net, throwing it from the beach to catch one little fish none of us could have seen with a telescope.

I said, "Ruth, marry me," as we sat on a park bench.

Before we left Barbados, we wired the news home and bought several cases of the finest Scotch and a little monkey we named Harvey III. My mother was once given a canary by some musicians and she named it Harvey. One day it was found with its toes turned up in the cage. Not long after, Harry Hostetter sent me a horned toad from Texas in a box. I reached down and found I had hold of a spiny horror. It was in a state of winter hibernation. I put some water on it, but then I realized it didn't want water but warm dry sand. I built a little cage and fed it flies.

With Tommy Dorsey at the NBC radio show in Indianapolis when Mother played *Maple Leaf Rag*.

With the Firehouse Five at the Mocambo on Sunset Strip.

CBS Radio, with Buddy Cole, one of the country's greatest pianists and organists, and my friend and helpmate on in-numerable programs and recording sessions. Buddy died of a heart attack as this book was going to press.

"Cricket" with Lauren Bacall and Walter Sande in "To Have and Have Not."

Above, Ruth, Dad and friends when Dad came to New York to the 1939 World's Fair. Below, Mother at my home with Randy Bob (left) and Hoagy Bix.

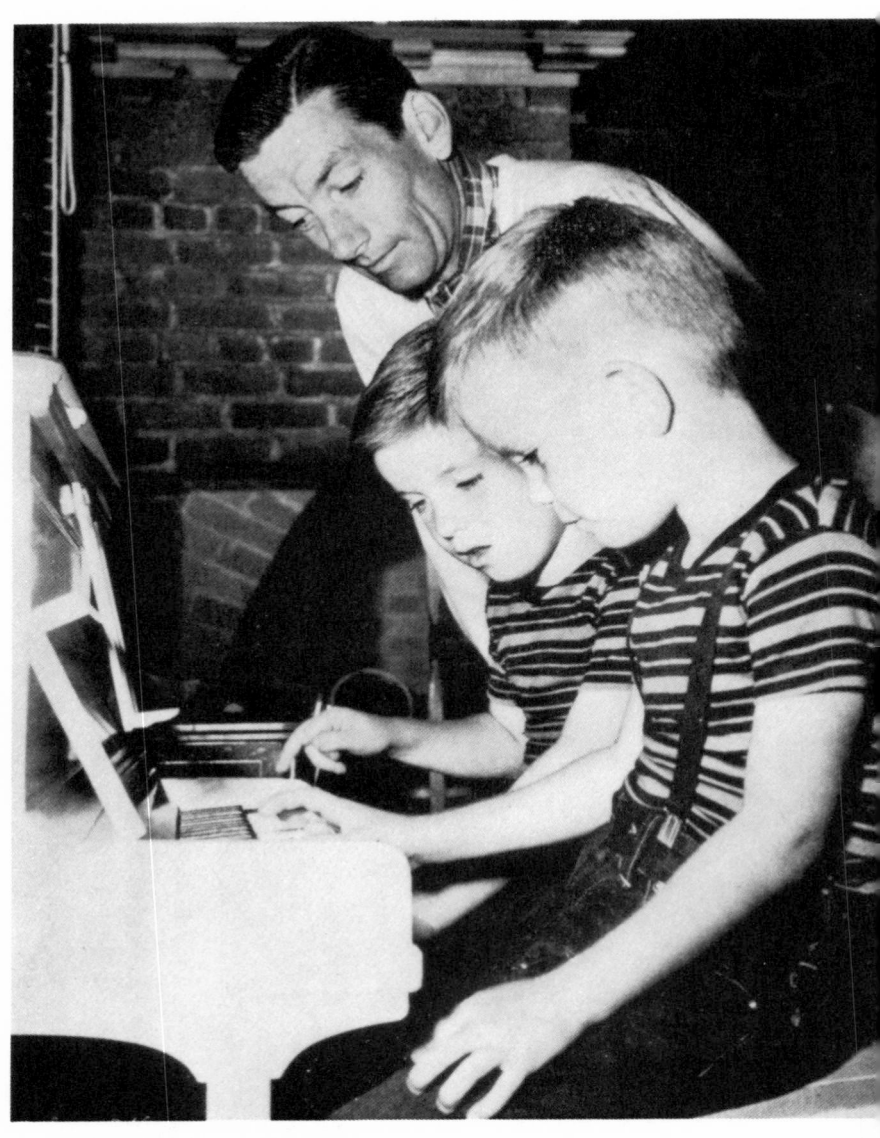

A mess of nuthin', but Randy Bob became a good piano player and Hoagy Bix took to the drums. Photo taken in 1948.

Above, the house at Palm Springs. That nice looking lawn belongs to the Thunderbird Golf Course. Below, with Arnold Palmer (left) in 1957, just before he became a top name in golf.

Partridge

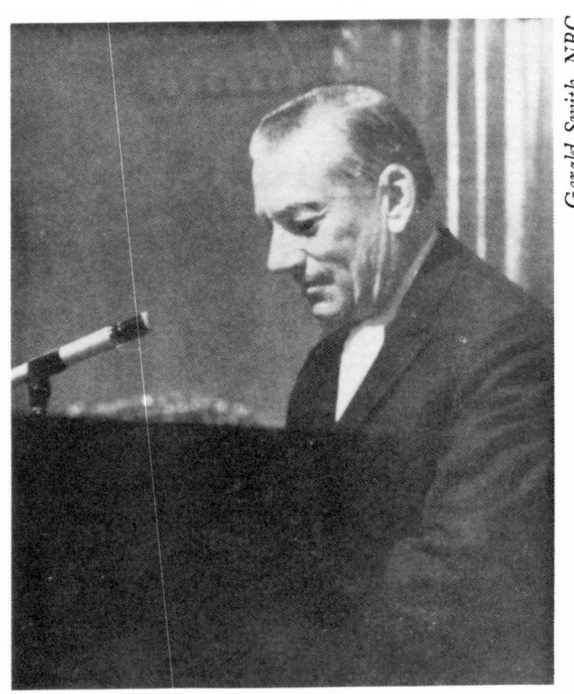

Gerald Smith, NBC

A couple of recen
shots, one of then
taken in my presen
apartment.

Duncan Schied

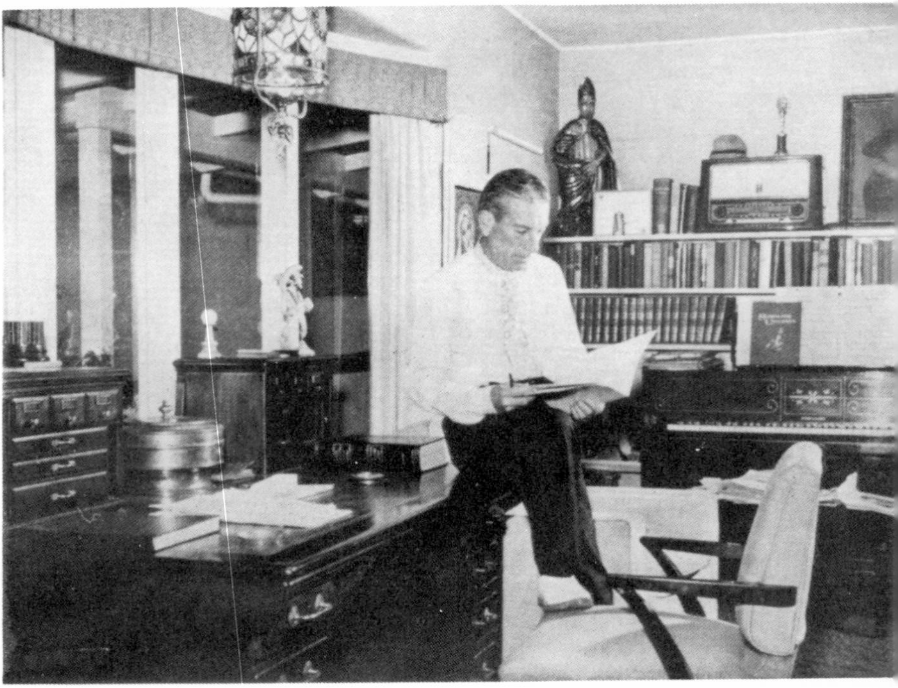

We had it for a couple of months and Mother liked it, too. Occasionally she'd put it in the oven to warm it up a little. Once she overdid it. *That* was Harvey II. The monkey was Harvey III.

Harvey was a lot of company and we'd play together for long hours. Harvey could get drunk, too. If anyone left a cocktail around, he'd lap it up. We'd know when he had gotten into something alcoholic because he'd make a jump from the divan to the back of a chair and miss it, then get up and rub his eyes as though he couldn't understand what had happened. When he was sick, we treated him like an ailing child.

I was a bit jumpy—not as much as Harvey III—about being a bridegroom. And back in New York the press got hold of it. Walter Winchell broke the news on radio and we heard him on shipboard, sailing home:

> New York *World-Telegram*
> Friday, March 6, 1936.

HOAGY CARMICHAEL, NEW YORK
GIRL WILL WED NEXT SATURDAY

Hoagland Carmichael, Indiana University graduate and composer of *Stardust, Lazy Bones* and other songs, will be married next Saturday to Miss Ruth Minardi of New York, in his apartment at 121 East Fifty-Second Street, New York City, it was announced yesterday. Carmichael's parents, Mr. and Mrs. Howard C. Carmichael, who live in Indianapolis at 3120 Graceland Avenue, will attend the wedding. Intimate friends of the couple will be invited. The announcement was made after Carmichael's return from a West Indies cruise.

The next few days for Ruth and me were passed in a scented fog of parties. I had fittings, rehearsals, hand holding, and more parties. As my hazy, overwound impression of the wedding is most likely not the true one, I shall let the press report it:

CARMICHAEL WEDDING MARCH
(Associated Press)

NEW YORK—Hoagland Carmichael, the man who composed *Stardust,* married the girl on the magazine cover today.

It was a wedding of art and music. The bride, Miss Ruth Minardi, has posed often for McClelland Barclay, the painter, and he gave her in marriage to the song writer. Howard (Wad) Allen was best man.

George Gershwin played piano—a recital of his own latest tunes—at the reception afterward, and Conrad Thibault, the baritone, sang. A "jazz" band furnished stomp music in between.

Carmichael and Miss Minardi marched to the altar of the Fifth Avenue Presbyterian Church to strains of one of his own unpublished numbers, *The Wedding Song.*

> "Hand in hand, giving our love to
>   this endeavor,
> Heart and soul, vowing this tryst
>   will be forever;
> I take thee as mine, dear,
> Take me so as thine, dear,
> God has said we may this day be
>   wed. . . ."

At the reception, Carmichael's mother, who taught him piano as a boy, played *Maple Leaf Rag* in the family tradition. Gershwin followed her to the piano, asking first what she wanted to hear and finally playing the entire suite of his *Porgy and Bess* folk opera.

"Gershwin was playing just for mother," Carmichael said with delight later.

Explaining his choice of "Bunny" Berigan and his Famous Door Five for the occasion, he added: "That's just the best band in the country."

Berigan borrowed "Bud" Freeman from Ray Noble's Orchestra to play saxophone and Carmichael directed several numbers.

The reception room resembled a meeting of Indiana University alumni. . . .

There were New Yorkers, too. Among them Condé Nast, publisher, and Sherman Fairchild, aviation executive. . . .

The bride, a native of Chicago, attended the University of Georgia. She is a brunette, 23. Carmichael is a staff composer for a motion picture firm. . . .

No more surprised bridal couple emerged from a church door than Mr. and Mrs. Hoagland Carmichael. Surrounded by a group of rice throwing friends, they expected to be whirled away to their recent wedding reception in the gleaming limousine which had conveyed them to the First Presbyterian Church.

Instead, an old-fashioned hansom cab—a relic of the Mauve Decade—smote their vision. The vehicle was decorated with white ribbons and in true Main Street style a large placard on which was written in huge letters "We have just been married" dangled from the rear.

Attracted by the unusual sight, a giggling crowd held up traffic at Fifth Avenue and 55th Street. When the bride and bridegroom appeared, the spectators greeted them with a cheer. Even two "striking" scullery maids who were patrolling the Gotham Hotel forgot their woes and joined in the vocal demonstration.

But Mr. and Mrs. Carmichael were "sports." They climbed into the hansom, while photographers snapped them. Friends substituted the obsolete equipage for the automobile while the knot was being tied.

As for my wedding, one thing (among others) the newspaper account didn't print was that Mother's piano playing caused Dad to take me aside and whisper—much too loudly: "Your mother plays better than that Gershwin fellow."

"She's very good."

"She's *better!*"

"George is supposed to be one of the greatest in Tin Pan Alley."

"Pshaw," my father said in disgust and turned away to smile at the bride.

Bill Shattuck filmed the entire wedding in detail—but as was excusable in the excitement, forgot to put film in the camera.

Such was the start of a marriage that was to have a fine beginning and many happy early years. I was past my middle thirties when I married a young, beautiful, impressionable girl.

XXV

While most American males marry in their early twenties, I had been a bachelor a long time and lived the life of the modern musician. Housebreaking me was a task and I was never fully domesticated. I retained my inner core of loneliness which diminished in time but didn't entirely disappear. And I lived away from the world a great deal of the time in the cloaked enigma of the music man, bent over a piano probing for some secret voice.

But outwardly I was the shiny success, the well-tailored popular song writer, the crisp creases of New York styling hiding what was still in many ways the Indiana country boy on a lucky spree.

I had a lovely bride and a contract (Buddy Morris finally came through) to go to Hollywood and write for films when *we* were ready to go. And I was wanted now, not just going out on hope. They were sending for me, on my terms, and the wasteland would be milk and honey, caviar, palm trees—and even some day a place of our own. We wanted children.

"Honey, kids grow big out there!"

"It's the orange juice or the sunlight, or the loose clothes they wear."

"Everybody is growing taller."

"Not as tall as out there."

When at last we got to the coast, Hollywood in 1936 was booming like a thousand wildcatters hitting oil all at once. The frightening studio millionaires had fully recovered from the depression in their rosewood suites and Cadillacs.

Society for us had a wide spread, a big range. We knew the

best people in the big clubs in Pasadena. We went to the society parties and knew people who were blood kin to the Huntingtons and the Stanfords. And one of our hostesses was mistress to a rich oil man who couldn't let her live in his guest house. "How, honey, can I ever explain you to Hoover when he comes to dinner?"

Soon we knew the town along Vine and Hollywood, sat in Musso's on the high bar stool in the favored back room, at the Gotham in the little bar, or in The Brown Derby where the people were something special. Everybody watched everybody else, and about eleven, people on the prowl would come in there to pick up the sound of local jazz. We sat in the sun at The Players, legs crossed, our drinks cold. Everybody knew us and came over and said, "How is it going?" And Don the Beachcomber drank with us. (I am #44 on their credit list.)

It wasn't really such a sinister town when I got to know it better. A lot like other towns and other places, it had the good little eating places where you ran up bar bills, the beaches where you sat and got done up brown, and the shops where you ran up more bills. The liquor man liked you, the grocery man liked you, and the dry cleaners liked you. Everybody liked you and gave you the greeting. "How is it going?"

There were harbors where some people had big boats and invited you aboard. And there was Emerald Bay down below, where they hunted back three generations before they let you in. We were there weekends and met popular Buick dealers and men who owned gambling boats.

The town was also Eagle Rock and Inglewood and the homes of the Lockheed workers in the valley. And the big tracts where everybody lived like everybody else. There were even times when somebody would dig up an old Bessie Smith record:

"Oh, tell me how long, how long must I wait
Oh, can I get it now or must I hesitate—"

Then all the glamor, and sunshine, and suntanned bodies would fade out and I'd think how much Bix liked to hear Bessie sing.

2

Hollywood had changed, of course. I remembered the old days of my failures there, when I felt I'd never make it and the orchestra was playing dance music for other people.

The town had been a pretty wild place. It had been fun for me in those earlier days with all the bootleg liquor and all the babes in short skirts and rolled stockings. Dog stars. Tom Mix's horse, Mack Sennett's bathing beauties, the big parties on the big white boats, and if somebody got shot or tossed overboard—well, that was part of the fun too. Valentino's "Falcon's Lair" was amazing —and I didn't believe it when I was told some people put radio music into their tombs at Forest Lawn.

Being in Hollywood with a wife was not like rousting about with the Paul Whiteman boys back in the late gin-soaked twenties. It was the social scene now, exclusive parties, and name people; lots of name people, and I shall not try to list most of them. The columnists kept printing items about us, but I don't really regret that I didn't keep a full social scrap book. All I remember is that we were accepted, mainly because of Ruthie's charm, and in a few years time we were attending at least half of the big social events of the times. By 1950 there wasn't a movie star, producer, director, or columnist in town that we didn't know personally. Some were intimate friends and it was good fun.

Success in California, or that part of it we lived in, was measured by one's credits (screen or ASCAP), one's income (studio contract or dividends). There was the rigid English set, too, and the literary messiahs who bunched around Aldous Huxley. Jean Hersholt (a collector of first editions of Hans Christian Anderson) was there, and other brain types, such as H. G. Wells ("a delightful sex maniac" several pleased starlets reported). Elinor Glynn, rather shopworn, traveled with a portable tiger skin and IT.

We ourselves fitted in best with the people who liked to be amused, enjoyed parties, played golf and tennis, and had to get up in the morning to go to work.

I follow with some press clippings that may give you some idea of what our life was like:

> Hoagy Carmichael recently signed a 52 weeks' contract to write musical scores for Paramount at a salary of $1000 a week. Hoagy's newest song, *April In My Heart*, which he wrote for Paramount, is a sequel in melody form to *Stardust* and will be his greatest hit since the latter song, the composer predicts. The lyrics were written by Helen Meinardi, sister of the composer's wife.

This was a paid advertisement because I had hired a press agent. Come to think of it I never predicted the song would be bigger than *Stardust*. And I'm glad; *April In My Heart* was a bust.

HOLLYWOOD PARADE

Just prior to the sad and sudden passing of Lottie Pickford, Pickfair was the scene of a farewell party for Buddy Rogers, who is opening in New York next Friday as guest conductor at the Loew's State Theater.

Revealing was the fact that, whereas social events at Pickfair in other days were characterized by titles of nobility, this party featured a lilting aggregation of Buddy's musical colleagues and song writers, such as Cole Porter, Ray Turner, Hoagy Carmichael and Sam Coslow.

Following cocktails and hors d'oeuvres in the Western Room, amid Mary's prized relics of '49, the dinner buffet was served up in the dining room. Then Mary started something when she asked Composer Carmichael to play her favorite tune, *Stardust*, which she recorded the while on the recording machine.

HOAGY MEETS HOPE

Paramount Studios decided Mr. Hoagy Carmichael was just the one to write the music for a certain scene in a Bob Hope picture. For two days and nights Mr. Carmichael hammered and scratched away and came up with a hit: *Two Sleepy People*. [My press agent didn't seem to think it necessary to mention that I wrote the music and someone else wrote the words. It was Frank Loesser.]

Don't Speak for Days

"We didn't speak to each other for two days," interposed Mrs. Carmichael, formerly Miss Ruth Meinardi, New York artist's model.

That often happens, they said, indicating that life in Hollywood is no "rockin' chair."

"My contract with Paramount hasn't even started yet," he said, "but when they want things done out there they want them done. It certainly is far different from writing songs to please yourself."

Goes Into "Trance"

Mr. Carmichael, asked how he could turn out music to order, said he didn't quite know.

"You have to go into a sort of trance and get into the spirit of the sequence, and then write whatever you goddamn please," he said.

The Carmichaels, after a year on the West coast, are Hollywood boosters, although Mrs. Carmichael admitted "you have to get away from the place once in a while."

Approximately 99 percent of the conversation centers around moving pictures, she indicated, adding "that gets tiresome."

Appears in "Topper"

Mr. Carmichael seemed unimpressed by the fact that he not only is a song writer for the movies, but now is on the screen himself. He made a brief appearance in "Topper," will have several "spots" in "Road Show."

3

The Paramount Pictures' Music Department was a boiling, roaring madhouse during the late thirties; musicals were in vogue but I don't think they needed quite all the song writers they had under contract. I felt I could have written many more songs than they used.

Leo Robin and Ralph Rainger were their top team when I was put on salary. Their biggest hit had been *June in January*. They were good writers and very fine boys.

Harry Warren and Al Dubin (fine writers) were holding down similar posts at Warner Brothers, while Yip Harburg, Nacio Herb Brown, and Arthur Freed were taking care of MGM's song problems. Harry Revel and Mack Gordon teamed up to do the chores at Fox. Musicals were in and everybody was eatin' high on the hog.

Out of nowhere came a young hopeful named Frank Loesser. He had written a few songs with the tunesmiths that weren't too well-known. Eventually the studio more or less teamed me with him. Our first song was *Heart and Soul*, which wasn't even used in a picture. Frank said he wanted to write a song called *Small Fry*. I said, "Sure," and we did. The day we completed it, we walked around the corner of a building to visit Wesley Ruggles, a producer. We had heard he was making a picture with a youngster in it. He invited us into his office and there sat a pixy named Donald O'Connor, twelve years of age. We put the demonstration record of *Small Fry* on a machine and Wes listened to the song. He looked at Donald. "The song is it."

Frank, I often felt, had some sixth sense about what might be needed. This was true of *Two Sleepy People* which we actually wrote on our own. It just happened to fill the needs of the Bob Hope picture. By 1939 Paramount had so many song writers moving in and out they had to build soundproof stalls so they couldn't steal from one another.

Ned Washington dropped into the studio one day and Sid Kornheiser, the head of what we always called the "song-plugging department," asked him to write a lyric to a melody I had written expressly as the musical theme for Mickey Rooney's picture, *Midsummer Night's Dream*. Ned came up with a fine lyric called *The Nearness of You*. There was no place in the picture for it, said the producer, so Sid sent it back to New York for publication and asked his contact men to give it a go. Lately, *The Nearness of You* has been giving *Stardust* a run for its money.

Sid was a right smart man about what made song hits and the best of contact men in the thirties and forties. He was the only man in Tin Pan Alley who would touch a very difficult song of mine called *Blue Orchids*. He also published my *I Get Along Without You Very Well*.

Frank Loesser interested me. Frank was gifted and most energetic but he was very flighty at first in his choice of lyrics. It was a good thing that he worked with me for a while; I had a sobering Indiana affect on him. He had a tendency to want to write things "way out." This may be because he was so packed full of ideas then that he was overloaded. We did one score for a motion picture in Miami in the terrible heat of a tropical summer. It wasn't too successful. Later, Frank was in the Army, writing words and music, such as *Praise the Lord and Pass the Ammunition* and *Slow Boat to China*. Eventually he wrote Broadway productions and started his own publishing company. It is quite likely he will surpass Irving Berlin, if his energies hold up, in the number of songs he has written and published.

4

Tin Pan Alley is almost too much for a writer to try and talk about in detail. It was a strange and magnificent part of the American scene. A factory in one sense, big as all the U.S. Steel plants. It was certainly run differently. There was never any real organization. It fed on many uncertainties, risks, some thievery, heartbreaking disappointments, and at times, great jubilation. The hundreds of youths and men who ran wildly about to plug a song worked hard. It took a lot of fortitude on their part to stick relentlessly by a song and insist that it *must* be played, sung, or recorded. Continually in competition with each other, they all remained friendly.

A real sour note about Tin Pan Alley was the fact that song writers were overanxious to get their songs published and so publishers were prone to buy cheaply and issue contracts favorable only to themselves. They would often buy a song outright for twenty-five dollars because the writers were desperate for money. Most of their contracts did not contain a clause whereby they were bound to publish, and they clung to the old royalty rates of the early 1900's, even though gross selling prices had gone way up. Even today their rates are practically the same, as are the royalty rates that record companies pay publishers—hardly ever more than two cents per record. I have always wondered why the publishers have never banded together to increase this.

The record and broadcasting companies in this country have made millions. In percentages, the men who write the song and the men behind the song have profited very little in comparison. ASCAP has never been able to collect money anywhere near reasonable for performances. I once figured out if every man, woman, and child in America were taxed the amount that publishers and song writers receive from ASCAP, the amount would be about 12½¢ per head per year for the privilege of hearing music on radio, television, Musak, or in theatres and nightclubs.

This may explode the old folk belief and dream that the way to get rich is to write a song. No more than one out of a hundred songs makes any money. This average may be a little higher today because records are in demand and the quality of the song is often not quite as important as the rendition, the electronic tricks, and the arty album covers.

The best touch I had with reality was my family. On March 1, 1939, the newspapers carried a headline:

HOAGY CARMICHAEL RETURNS
FOR MOTHER'S RADIO DEBUT

It seemed only fair and logical that my mother, who had done so much to inspire me musically, should have some fame of her own. She was a very fine piano player, and in some other time and setting, with a different destiny, she could have become a star performer. While I was certainly aware that it was my own fame that had now brought her forward, I didn't give a hoot how it was done, as long as it was done. I was one boy who didn't give his mother's apple pie preference over her handling of the ivories.

The press was very kind, and what is more, pretty accurate, a fact not always true about American journalism scenting a story:

HOAGY CARMICHAEL LISTENS. HIS MOTHER PLAYS

Hoagy Carmichael, the Indiana boy who writes songs the nation sings, came home yesterday afternoon for the most exciting event of his mother's life.

Mrs. Howard Carmichael, housewife, 3120 Graceland Avenue, will make her radio debut with her famous son and Tommy Dorsey's band in a broadcast on the NBC-Red network from the stage of the Lyric Theater at 7:30 and 10:30 o'clock tonight.

His mother will play a special arrangement of the *Maple Leaf Rag*, Hoagy declared. He'll play a "little piano" himself, he said, featuring a number of his own compositions, as he did in a similar broadcast with Dorsey in New York several weeks ago.

Hoagy was excited himself at the chance of presenting his mother to a nation-wide audience. "She played for the same Indiana University sorority and fraternity dances in 1903 and 1904 for which I played 20 years later," he declared. In the meantime, Mrs. Carmichael raised a family but "she can still play the piano today to my Dad's satisfaction."

The author of *Stardust*, *Lazy Bones*, *Little Old Lady*, *Small Fry* and numerous other universal favorites will join Dorsey in tonight's program in paying tribute to the memory of an old friend and associate of his Indiana University days, the late Bix Beiderbecke, whose genius on the cornet still is a marvel to bandmen. They will recall their early recording dates with Bix in Richmond, Ind.

Hoagy didn't bring his family with him this trip. The infant Hoagy Bix Carmichael was not considered big enough to travel and remained at home on the coast with his mother. Hoagy is anxious to get back to them, but has business in New York which will keep him in the East for a couple of weeks. He may get to Bloomington this trip only for a couple of hours to visit with his grandmothers Thursday. Later that day he will leave for New York.

There he has several irons in the fire which bear watching. He has to see about a contract to write the music for a new show and has a picture deal under consideration. He recently completed a "short" for Paramount, in which he introduces a new song, *That's Right, I'm Wrong*. It will be released in about two months.

His latest hit, *I Get Along Without You Very Well*, will be featured Saturday night on the Hit Parade radio broadcast. This song was based on a poem given Hoagy by a friend 10 years ago. When the song was written, he conducted a quest for the author of the poem, with the aid of Walter Winchell, They finally found her—Mrs. Jane Brown Thompson of Philadelphia, Pa.—but she died Jan. 19, the night before Dick Powell introduced the song on radio.

Hoagy and his mother were having a little rehearsal at home last night. They were to rehearse with Dorsey and the band at the Lyric at midnight, after the last show. Mrs. Carmichael, who taught Hoagy the first things he knew about the piano, was rising to the occasion beautifully.

"This is the price of fame," she sighed as she held her pose "just another minute, please" for the photographer.

5

When it came time to go on the air, it was Dad who appeared jumpy. He kept repeating, "Oh. I don't know, I don't know."

I told him: "Go out and cool off till you do."

Mother was very calm in appearance. I had sent her a lot of flowers, and so had other people.

"They burying me or praising me?"

She looked like an old pro and if she had the butterflies in her stomach she didn't show it. A huge crowd had turned out to see the actual broadcast, and it was like an opening on Broadway. Mother was taking it all as if it were coming to her, and in a way I am sure it was. For every ten-day wonder or celebrity in the limelight, there are the dozen people or so who paid his way, worked things out to send him along. And then they stepped back into the shadows to live out their lives, often drab hard lives, while the strange bud they had nurtured went out and had all the best of it, the material best anyway.

My mother charmed the press, and they responded properly:

HOAGY'S MOTHER
"SWINGS THAT BASS"
IN RADIO DEBUT

A capacity audience that had gathered hours in advance whooped and hollered, whistled and clapped for Hoagy Carmichael and his mother, Tommy Dorsey and his band, as they broadcast an NBC radio program from the stage of the Lyric Theater at 7:30 o'clock last night.

An estimated 1,500 persons who packed the sidewalk in front of the house while the show was on then moved in to witness a repetition of the program for Pacific coast stations at 10:30. The second audience was slightly more sedate, but nonetheless enthusiastic.

The popular Indiana composer, trapped by autograph hunters in the alley behind the theater, escaped through the stage door just a few moments before the broadcast began. A great cheer greeted his entrance.

Hoagy, Dorsey said, is a composer who has a definite idea behind each of his tunes. He had his two Indiana grandmothers in mind when he wrote *Little Old Lady*. After joining with piano and voice in a medley of *Judy* and *Small Fry*, Hoagy began to reminisce. He and Dorsey talked over their first 'jam session' together, a recording date at Richmond, Ind., with a pick-up band when Hoagy was a student at I.U. and Tommy was "trying to learn to play the trombone." They will never forget that day because then and there *Davenport Blues* just "popped out" of Bix Beiderbecke's head and they all joined in. The program came to a sort of climax when Edythe Wright, another vocalist with the orchestra, sang the ever popular *Stardust*.

Then it was Mrs. Carmichael's turn, called to the stage mike by Tommy. Hoagy said "Mother, swing that bass," and Mother did. She played *Maple Leaf Rag* with the full band. The audience loved her, applauded for over a minute, stopping the show. The producer, Herb Sanford, was happy for mother but very unhappy about trying to get the rest of the show off air on time.

Many of the jitterbugs present came early in the afternoon and brought their lunches to be sure of good seats. Many also came early but forgot that they had to eat. Dorsey, the sentimental gentleman, sent out for sandwiches and milk to still the yearning stomachs of 12 youngsters in the front row.

And guess who was taking bows and was the most proud— Dad.

Returning to New York, Johnny Mercer and I were invited by the Shuberts to do a Broadway musical called *I Walk With*

Music, starring Simone Simone, the best talent in the show being Mitzy Greene. We all liked the score but the show was too weak to give the songs much exposure. Jake Shubert got under my skin on a few occasions and most of us were disturbed anyway because we did not think enough thought and money was being put into the production. Soon after the opening it appeared that one of our songs was not going to work out and in an impertinent manner Jake yelled at me, "Write another song." I'd had it. I followed him up the aisle, took him by the coat lapels and shook him.

"Don't ever talk to me that way again," I said.

This bit perhaps explains why I was never invited to write another Broadway show. He was a wheel—or did I misspell it?

6

People have called motion pictures—among other things— leaping snap shots. And that is what they are on the basic practical level. Little collections of footage, running for a few seconds to a minute or two, with cutters pasting them together and song writers creating music for them. A composer whips up a score to set the mood of a picture, so that the weeping or laughing a movie causes in a theatre is often the music catching the customer's heart and tear-glands off guard, rather than what he is seeing badly done on the screen. Good pictures need music, too —but not as badly. I was just as pleased to remain behind the cameras rather than in front of them. It wasn't the hard work of film acting I disliked—it was the long boring waiting while someone changed a light, or make-up was repaired, or the star got over a hang-over, or the actress took a little time off to get a new divorce. Most of a Hollywood actor's life was passed sitting on a dollar canvas chair with his name lettered on it—if he was important enough—waiting for the director to decide which side of a table he wanted photographed. Besides I wasn't built to give Cary Grant or Tyrone Power any worries. Yet all of us have sat in a movie theatre and seen ourselves in place of the people on the screen. That's why we like it.

Hollywood directors, some of them very fine craftsmen (and geniuses), had the skilled knack of taking almost any hunk of human material in not too gruesome a shape and bringing out an impression that this creature was acting. There are, of course, fine actors and actresses who could command respect on any stage. But in the main, the ex-shoe salesmen, gas station valets, and waitresses who were boosted to stardom had to be led by the hand, told just what to touch, when to turn, and how to breathe. There was the story I heard of a girl from the cow country (she later became a great star and married a famous producer) who was so unused to chic city ways that they had to teach her to use bathroom tissue. But I suspect that item was a press agent's stunt.

It was during these first years of our marriage that changes were taking place with the family. Georgia had gone to California to establish herself as a Practitioner and then as Teacher of Religious Science; she eventually married Jack Maxwell, another Practitioner. Martha had left the girls at the Tri Delt House at Indiana University and gone home to work as a newspaper reporter and then as top-flight secretary with the newly formed National Labor Relations Board. And then Dad died at age sixty-nine of cancer, his lust for living finally spent. He'd seen his grandchildren, his daughters educated, and seen me achieve a measure of success that was satisfying. His trips around Indianapolis as an inspector for the city were very boring and tiring. A sad note, though—when he asked me to bring a bottle of beer (which he dearly loved) to his bedside and he couldn't even take a tablespoon full of it without nausea, I thought what a little thing to be denied and what a pity.

Much to our surprise, people came in droves to his funeral— even the mayor and the governor, and it was not due to my bit of fame. A man whom we had loved but never quite understood had, with his oversized generous heart and robust laughter, made the people of Indianapolis his friends. And we were humble.

The worn set of playing cards and lap boards on which Dad used to play solitaire were put away.

XXVI

My big acting break came and in an oddball way. I am by nature, when at home and working around the place, rather a natty dresser. But during the war, short of help, I let down and settled for a frayed pair of pants, a tired-out shirt, and a good two-day growth of beard.

I became an actor by scaring a friend of my wife's. The friend was sitting in the Carmichael lanai chatting with Ruth, when in walked an apparition. I came in wearing a pair of shorts, with my hair hanging down over my forehead, muddy knees, looking as if I had been doing some hard work in the garden—which I had. It was a good two minutes before the startled friend recognized the apparition as the usually well-groomed Mr. Carmichael. By the time she did, it had occurred to her that I "ought to be in pictures."

The friend was Slim—that is, Mrs. Howard Hawks, whose husband was at the time looking for a different type to play the role of a honky-tonk piano player and singer in the Warner picture *To Have and Have Not*.

Slim asked Ruth, "Who's the character?"

"That's no character—that's my husband, I think."

"Howard will—*must* test you. Bogart is starring—and that new girl, Bacall. The part of Cricket fits you."

I turned up at the studio very nervous and excited, wondering if I could go through with it. But they never even got to me. I just sat there all day, watching. At the end of the day, they told me they wouldn't need me for a week.

I decided then and there that acting was the life for me. I had earned a week's salary just by dressing up and smearing a little grease paint on my nose and cheeks. It was certainly an easy living.

I ended up by writing all the background music for the picture, as well as supplying the songs, *How Little We Know* and *Hong Kong Blues.*

Eventually, of course, I also had to make with the acting I'd been hired to do. My first scene required me to sing *Am I Blue.* *Am I Nervous* would have been a more appropriate title.

I chewed on a match to help my jitters, and when the time came to shoot, I asked Howard if I could keep the match in my mouth. It was a very noisy night club set, and Mr. Hawks couldn't hear me in all the confusion. I thought he said "yes" and started the scene. By the time it was finished, Mr. Hawks decided to let it go through. So from then on, in addition to all his other problems, he had my match to worry about. But he was kind—he kept me from overacting.

The match was a good decision, it turned out, because it became a definite part of the character and helped make it an outstanding one. But it was a grave responsibility to me.

One morning I had a scene with Humphrey Bogart. Bogey walked into the scene chewing on a match. My heart sank. What can you say to the star of the picture when he's apparently intent on stealing your stuff?

I didn't find out until the next day that it was a rib. Bogey let me go on thinking they had actually shot the scene that way.

RKO paged me for the role of a philosophical, singing cab driver in *Johnny Angel.* I sang my own composition, *Memphis in June,* in the picture. The lyrics were by Paul Francis Webster, with whom I was doing a considerable amount of writing.

I'm very amused about my singing voice. A strange style, a sort of chant. A little to my surprise, the bobby-soxers discovered me and kept me busy signing autographs.

"Maybe they'll call you The Voiceless," one of my friends suggested.

After that I was mentioned for every picture in which a world-

weary character in bad repair sat around and sang or leaned over
a piano. I took several of the parts but felt I was being type cast.
It was usually the part of the hound-dog-faced old musical
philosopher noodling on the honky-tonk piano, saying to a tart
with a heart of gold: "He'll be back, honey. He's all man."

2

When I was offered the script of *Canyon Passage* to read the
part of Hi Linnet, I saw that while I still made music, I did it
outdoors—on the back of a mule. And most of the action took
place out among real trees and rocks. It seemed a change and I
took the part. It pleased me. No piano either, just a phony mandolin.

Until the part of Hi Linnet came my way, I was practically
piano-bound on the screen. It was getting so that if I moved more
than ten feet from a piano in a movie, I felt like Esther Williams
might without a swimming pool. So naturally the picture *Canyon
Passage* came as a welcome change. Walter Wanger was the producer.

Just me and my mule and my fake mandolin. I just pretended
to play it. In a sense, the mule was a fake too. Anyway, he refused
to cooperate and we had to rig him up with a set of invisible wires
to make him stop and go on schedule.

The character of Hi was just as unreal as the mandolin and the
mule's apparent obedience. But Hi was nice unreal. He was a sort
of fairy-tale boy, the kind of person you never meet, but wish
you could. Hi wore odd clothes I designed myself from historical
pictures—and ran a sort of second-hand store. People liked him.
I certainly liked playing him, especially after the writer took a
few tucks in the part to make it fit me better. Work on the original script really saved me from being the face on the cutting-
room floor.

In *Canyon Passage* I had a chance to sing several songs and
sitting up all night with Jack Brooks, a lyricist, we got a bolt
from the blue that turned out to be *Ole Buttermilk Sky*, just
handed to me as a gift.

I'm reminded that Howard Hawk's wife, Slim, and my wife, Ruth, used to call Howard "The Great White Father." He was a little older than all of us, had grey hair at middle age, but was tall, handsome, and quietly severe. His manners were always so correct that, I believe he rather awed the picture business fraternity. It seems that he had a way of making them respect him once he had made one or two rather successful pictures. This also goes for Victor Fleming, his bosom friend during the formative years in the picture business, who had many of the same characteristics that Howard had. They became ruthlessly undeniable as success came their way and I believe it was good for the picture business. You will find that there are many of the type I have just described, such as William Wellman and Henry Hathaway.

Hawks had found a girl named Betty Bacall in Brooklyn and had stashed her away in a Hollywood apartment, hoping to make a star out of her. He saw something in her that I did not see when I first met her at his home. He was giving her help a couple of times a week on how to be an actress. He made her scream for long periods several times a week to make her vocal chords become husky. Howard always liked husky-voiced women. In Beverly Hills, I would see a bewildered Lauren (Howard changed her name), leading a sad little poodle around the streets, both wondering what this was all about.

When we were filming *To Have and Have Not*, I would often pop, unannounced, into Lauren's dressing room—to tell her some new story, or to pat her on the fanny in a much too familiar way. Humphrey Bogart would usually be sitting there making grimaces at me. Later I learned that Humphrey was very much in love with Lauren and there was a marriage coming up. The picture was a tremendous success. *Hong Kong Blues* was a big hit. Howard Hawks sold Lauren Bacall's contract to Warner Brothers for something in the neighborhood of a million dollars. As they used to say in vaudeville, "A very good neighborhood."

I worked with Harold Adamson of *Around the World in Eighty Days* fame and wrote two songs for him that appeared in the picture *Gentlemen Prefer Blondes*. Jane Russell sang *Ain't There Anyone Here For Love* and Jane and Marilyn Monroe sang *When Love Goes Wrong Nothing Goes Right*.

For another picture we wrote another song for Marilyn called *Down Boy* which might have turned out to be a sensational thing. Mr. Zanuck, head of the studio, vetoed the song, much to Marilyn's disappointment. We had rehearsed the song together and she loved it. I felt it was her first chance to become a song stylist and soloist like Mary Martin after her singing of *My Heart Belongs To Daddy*. Marilyn had tears in her eyes when she came to tell me the bad news.

I think she really liked the simple life and was not as ambitious for success as most of the big stars. At the time she was making *Gentlemen Prefer Blondes* she was interested in a young man who worked in the music department of Fox Studios just because she liked him, not for what he could do for her.

3

Writing about Hollywood in those years of the forties and fifties, politics have to be talked about. The left-wing boys were pretty much in power, and somehow I was always tangling with them. What I put down is personal knowledge, not hearsay.

Humphrey Bogart was a bit confused politically in my opinion. He shouted a tirade of abuse at my Republican stand one night at a big party. I invited him outside, coats off, fists up. I weighed 135 pounds, he 150 (he was not a tough man off screen at all, in my opinion). My wife, Ruth, broke it up.

There was a very strong leftist contingent in Hollywood then. Once my wife Ruth and I were at a dinner party where this became very evident. Lee Bowman and his wife Helene were there also and the four of us looked at each other in astonishment at the conversation going around the table.

I was invited to play a part in *The Best Years of Our Lives*. William Wyler was the director and Fredric March was one of the stars. Myrna Loy was in it and so was a young sailor from

Massachusetts named Russell, who had had both hands blown off during the war.

Russell wore certain metal attachments on his arms made to serve as hands, and he was pretty good with them. I devised an attachment, which was made in the machine shop, that would enable him to grasp a golf club and hit the ball. I had hoped that this episode could be brought into the picture but it never made it. The whole picture was an odd experience to me. When Sam Goldwyn introduced me as a member of the cast at the Academy Award show he called me "Hugo" Carmichael. This Goldwynism was profitable to both of us. It was the best joke in the Academy show and Jack Benny invited both of us to his radio show to repeat the episode.

Night Song was a very sweet picture that Louella Parson's daughter Harriet produced. Dana Andrews, Merle Oberon, Ethel Barrymore, and I played in it—and it's one of my favorite pictures. I enjoyed working with everyone. The little scene in which I taught Ethel Barrymore to play gin rummy was a delight. Of course, she ginned on me three times in a row.

Making the film *Johnny Angel* was a pleasure. Bill Pierara was the producer. Bill is now a famous architect in Los Angeles. He was a good producer and I admired him for having the foresight to call the director and me into conference to see how I could be worked into the picture intelligently and interestingly. My major contribution to this picture was a stick with a propeller on the end, which would whirl around like mad when I rubbed the stick with another stick. One of the ways to be a success in a movie, if you are not a great actor, is to have a gimmick that people will notice. George Raft used the idea to make himself a star by tossing a quarter in the air and catching it. When I played in *Las Vegas Story* with Jane Russell and Victor Mature, I worked a stunt that all the croupiers in Las Vegas can do to perfection: the business of holding two silver dollars in one hand and quickly flicking one over on top of the other. This isn't easy to do but I learned how. When Vincent Price was in the middle of one of his stirring dramatic scenes in the picture, I was not so innocently in the background flicking dollars. Vince is an old pro in the movies. Without looking back, he stopped the cameras.

"I will not proceed until you get rid of that clickety-clackety scene stealer behind me. Something tells me his name is Hoagy Carmichael."

4

I enjoyed working with stars and directors. They are usually intelligent people and often witty. Sometimes actors are a little too quick-witted and the director or producer is disturbed; the people on the set are wasting time trying to ad-lib wisecracks. I was never a funny man with a quick quip. I'm usually intense about the matter at hand and the wits would often bore me; I thought they were trying too hard to be funny. The job of the comedian is a tough one and the moment he sounds as though he's trying too hard, he's a flop. I was puzzled, too, by the exaggerated attempts of people on the movie set to show how fond they were of each other. Sometimes these are premeditated phony dramas. There has been more public off-camera kissing in studios than there ever was in all the movies.

Of the movies I made, *Young Man With A Horn* was a favorite of mine because my character was well-written. The part of Smoke, a piano player who rolled his own, seemed to lend some authority to the character. I honestly felt properly dedicated to the part as a musician. Possibly some of this rubbed off on Kirk Douglas. He, too, looked like a music man to me as we played the parts together. The picture was panned by critics because they didn't bone up enough to realize that Mike Curtiz, the director, and Jerry Wald, the producer, were not trying to make the life story of Bix Beiderbecke—they were merely making a story of a musician, written as a novel by Dorothy Baker of San Francisco. Her story was fine except for one thing—no ending. The story conferences became so intense that they even called me in to see if I could think up an ending. Mike Curtiz's idea of just letting Kirk die of alcoholism finally won out.

Betty Hutton was a star at Paramount. Buddy De Silva, the song writer, was then head of the studio. He called me to ask if I had something for her to sing. Paul Francis Webster and I had completed a song called *Doctor, Lawyer, Indian Chief*. Betty's record for Capitol of the same song was a smash. Later Paramount had a film idea, *The Mack Sennett Story*, for Betty Hutton. They hired Johnny Mercer and me to write the musical score for Betty. Paramount had spent $300,000 on the idea. Betty and her agent had already made up their minds that she was not going to go into the picture but instead was going to do the Cecil DeMille picture, *Greatest Show On Earth*, so Betty could swing on trapezes. I saw this from the way in which Betty received the song demonstration that Johnny and I attempted. Betty turned down the picture.

Eddie Sutherland was once directing Mae West and Louis Armstrong in a picture. He called me for a song that Louis was to sing and play in a big street parade. I went to the studio and played everything I could think of for him and Mae West. Not a nod of approval.

Finally Eddie said, "You go over to my house now and have my butler dust off the grand piano and you sit there all night and compose until you come up with the right tune."

The butler did not get a wink all night either. I figured out a tune and sleepily played it at the studio the next morning.

"No, darling," Mae West said.

"Well, how about this one?"

In my sleepy state a tune I had forgotten all about started to roll off the keys. Jubilation ensued among the listeners ("Yes, yes, darling"), so we named it *Jubilee*. Louis played and sang it and it was a complete bust. This song writing isn't easy.

Adolphe Menjou and I were together in a picture called *Timber Jack*, another picture in which the owner of Republic Studios *and* husband of an ice skater, named Vera Hruba Ralston, tried to make her into a movie star. Vera was a very nice person, and I am pretty sure she knew that the necessary talent was not quite there. But she tried hard. Adolphe and I were roommates at a lodge on Flat Head Lake in Montana, the locale of the picture. We would play gin rummy for hours at a time. When a question as to how I was to play a certain scene came up, Adolphe would say, "Pay attention to your card hand, this picture will never be seen anyway." He was right, except for its showing on television. People kidded Adolphe about his money, of which he had plenty. The old bromide about "He's got the first nickel he ever made" could have been true. He pulled a nickel out of his pocket one day to flip a coin and there it was—a liberty head nickel in perfect condition. At his funeral, many of the motion picture moguls for whom he had made millions were conspicuous by their absence.

5

In 1936 I had taken up tennis with a vengeance and Stanley Adams and I put in many an hour on the court behind the Chateau Elyses Hotel where we were staying while writing a score for Columbia Pictures. By 1937 I was taking lessons consistently from Johnny Faunce, a professional, who for many years was considered one of the great doubles players. Through his associates I met and played with some of the big names in tennis; of course I was not their equal at any time, but occasionally I could hold my own on a doubles court to some extent and occasionally beat some pretty good amateurs at singles. I played with Jackie Kramer, Louise Brough, and Don Budge. My last day of serious tennis occurred in August of 1942 when I played one set of singles against Dick Skeene. Dick had beaten Don Budge on the circuits. Naturally, Dick beat me to the tune of 6-2, but I keep telling everybody that there were three games of the eight in which I had Dick 40-love at one point but lost all three of them.

That was the day Lee Bowman and his wife Helene suggested I take up golf. Dick and I had been playing at the Bel Air Golf Club tennis courts, and since Lee and Helene were members of that club, I put on a tattered old sweater and walked into the reception desk to make application for membership. A Mrs. Smith was the most important cog in the machinery of running Bel Air Country Club. Joe Novack was the pro but it didn't seem to make too much difference who was president because Mrs. Smith was the business office.

"Hello, I'm Hoagy Carmichael."

"Hello, I'm Mrs. Smith," she said, looking me over carefully.

"I would like to make out an application for membership in the Bel Air Country Club, Mrs. Smith."

"You would?"

"Yes, Mrs. Smith."

"Are you sure?"

"I'm sure."

"Well, Mr. Carmichael, that is your name, isn't it?—I had better inform you that all the members of this club are millionaires."

I said, "Oh, I'm sorry," and backed away in my shabby tennis attire. I had to go to the president of the club to get an application.

Some don't approve of the Joe Novack system of teaching golf, but Joe made me a ten-handicap player in six weeks of lessons. Randy Scott talked me out of Joe's system for hitting a golf ball. I eventually became an eight handicapper, but I might have even obtained a better rating had I stuck with Joe's rigmarole, as I called it. His system is sound and you'll never shank if you swing and sway in the Joe Novack way.

My last trip to Glasgow, to do a week's performance at the theatre, found me on the local golf course a couple of times. I was getting my rented set of clubs together to play a few holes and I overheard an elderly Scotsman say, "I wish Joe Novack were here to straighten me out." Naturally, I got into the act.

Way in the back of my mind was this thing some were still talking about. Television. A friend of mine from New York dropped in for a visit. He was Leonard Hall of CBS and he knew his way around.

"Hoagy, watch television, and get into it."

"I hear this talk and I wonder, just *what* is television?"

"You'll be surprised when it gets rolling. Don't muff it."

"Who has sets?"

"More people than you think. Get in it."

I did get into it in a small way. A few artists got talked into doing something on the first TV station in Hollywood. The whole station was a jumble of controls on top of a hill above Hollywood. Nobody was sure just what one did on television. The man who seemed in charge told us, "It's doing something the eye will follow."

This wasn't much help, but we tried. The comic artists in the group did some funny cartoons. When it was my turn I suggested I draw a map of the United States in four minutes and indicate the capitol of each state. I missed by ten seconds. The entire audience of eight people, mostly coat holders, gave me a great hand. But I wasn't smart enough to run to Washington and reserve a channel for myself.

6

We made more friends, we went to more parties, and in time, we had two sons. First Hoagy Bix, and then Randy Bob. I don't have to explain that my first son I named, in part, after my memory of Bix. We were a happy family group, and flourished. And in time we even got that dream house that everyone wanted in California, with all the trimmings. It was two and a half acres in Holmby Hills, a fancy part of town. Bogart and Bacall, Lana Turner, and other stars eventually were our neighbors. I'm not too good at describing things like houses so I'll just quote someone who took the Carmichael tour:

"Informality keynotes the three-bedroom, one-story rambling ranch house. One can almost sense how the dwelling has grown into an ideal place for a famous composer to work and play. It also is arranged for full-time family fun and easy entertaining.

"Everywhere there are trophies, keepsakes, and mementos of the Carmichaels' life together or of their association with dear friends. In wandering from room to room, one sees many treasures from the past and present of Hoagy's America.

"Priceless items—like Bix's mouthpiece—the antique plates which once belonged to Hoagy's great, great, great-grandmother; or Hoagy's 'Fascinatin' Paintin' that he made recently in his 'spare' time; the game table which once belonged to Lucky Baldwin; the fine linens and art objects Ruth had found.

"The bedspread on Hoagy's bed—embroidered by his mother —carries part of the score of his world-famous and ever popular *Stardust*. On a side table was one of his son's versions of how to depict in wood Hoagy's famous song, *Lazy Bones*.

"The bedroom suites overlook the swimming pool terrace. From there you can see the lanai, centered north, the south kitchen wing and the separate cottage to the southwest in which are quarters for his two sons, Hoagy Bix and Randy Bob.

"Due east of the foyer is a spacious living room with fireplace, and the music-den which is to the north of the foyer.

"The west wall of the music-den is graced by a fireplace, on whose mantel one finds more keepsakes. Included are Hoagy's prized 'hole-in-one' golf trophy, a silver cup he won in the California State amateur golf tournament, a tennis trophy, and a collection of brass miniatures."

One thing this reporter failed to mention was the "utility" room. I was in there every other day to fix something.

Compared to some over-ornate Hollywood homes, our place was Dogpatch, but to us it was wonderful.

7

I found out there are ghosts in the California sunshine. The past is pushed aside, but you step up to a bar and there is a ghost —an old unemployed director who makes the past come alive.

"Sure, a great town, Hoagy, when the going is good."

"So I hear."

D. W. Griffith stood around for years in bars, a lonely guy picking up talk with strangers. He lived in a lousy hotel room and couldn't get enough money together to fix a parking ticket. He, the giant of the early screen. Chaplin fooled them; he saved his money. But people not fit to shine Griffith's shoes avoided him, crossed the street when they saw him coming. But he made whatever history this place had.

"Remember when F. Scott Fitzgerald died? The golden boy of your Jazz Age, Hoagy? There was nobody in the undertaker's parlor where he lay. The man there asked me if Scotty had any friends in this town. They stole his smart young people and his sad young men and his schools of flappers a million times, and they wouldn't come."

"It doesn't matter," I said.

"They named a street after Lasky, DeMille has a street, and Ince has one, but you can't raise a dime on those honors. Thanks, I'll have another double."

One wonders sometimes if California is not an ironic trick, something someone is laughing at and not much concerned about. The curse of this place is that one must run, pant, and sweat, play a good game of tennis, feed the tanned, smooth, dry flesh, and never be granted resignation. Everything eludes them—and they do not care, for the jobs will be bigger tomorrow, the pay more, the girls more beautiful, their skins tanned like leather even though the smog is dulling the sunlight. And then I remember—I shouldn't say *they*—I should say *we*.

I must admit that it took me a long time to say that *we*, for I was still really a jazzman. I felt temporary about it much of the time. It may be for this reason that I wrote *Stardust Road*, which was published in 1946 by Rinehart and Company of New York. This little book incorporated all of the lonely feelings, memories, and incidents of the "Bent Eagles," all the early frustrations of my own personal contribution to the age of jazz. It was never a best seller but a copy today is almost a collector's item.

In those days before the jet age, California was still four days from the New York water hole via the Santa Fe Super Chief and its bone-jolting dash across deserts. But we exiles knew what was happening in civilization: swing and boogie woogie's popularity came out to us through the radio and the news items. In 1938, there was a riot in Times Square when Benny Goodman opened at the Paramount Theatre to give a swing show. Thousands stood in line all night to get in and the police had to close the doors on the place after 4,000 kids jammed the theatre howling "killer diller" and "in the groove."

The nation, I saw, was becoming jitterbugged, and their terms —square, hep cats, and alligators—were the new inside slang. Men like Tommy Dorsey, Teddy Wilson, Gene Krupa, and Count Basie were accepted in the best places now.

8

The world was real out there. I'd sit by the fireplace with Ruth, and the voice of Edwin C. Hill and H. V. Kaltenborn would talk of our world beginning to smolder at the edges, ready to burst into flames, and if we didn't take Hitler and his Germans too seriously it was because there was talk of a recession and of the new sit-down strikes. I didn't expect the world to break down.

The World of Tomorrow at the New York World's Fair and something called the Oomph Girl were getting a lot of free space in the news. It was still for me the kind of world where a man could raise his children, write his music, and find time to do a little painting on the side. Lots of people, we knew, were in trouble someplace far away, but some of us felt safe here. It was the last time Americans were to have that feeling of security, for soon technology was to do away with distances, time, and clean skies.

It was better for me, I felt, to turn to the musical scene and study it closer. In a world I never made, I did make music. Jazz never retreats in the nihilism of just noise, or the sterile world of the mere sound-benders. The true jazzman is introspective, tough, and oblique. He will continue to be so, to remember that both seed-time and harvest in music are not a matter of the usual sowing and reaping. It's real, and it says something.

When the news was bad—when World War II was just around the corner—I could say to myself that jazz was still alive and kicking with the gestures of New Orleans or Dixieland, trying to get the feel and the taste of living into its notes—and not politely either. After being a dog for a long time, it grew—only to have everyone say that its best days were behind it or that no one was writing real jazz any more and who needed it, anyway? But it wasn't true. Jazz isn't dead, just some of the great players and inventors. There's a hassle about what was right and what was wrong with jazz, but the reasons don't matter if you can turn up a Louis Armstrong; turn up a lot of him and turn him loose.

Jazz just got too fashionable for a time. It moved over to France, and the same mob that had almost buried modern art with their explaining of it moved in to explain how great jazz was and why America just didn't know it. The best one of the mob, Hugues Panassie, wrote two books about it, *Le Jazz Hot* and *The Real Jazz*. He got himself into a knot with the first one when he overlooked all of the early Negro jazz in New Orleans. He got better in the second book, but somehow Basin Street doesn't translate very well into French. It was a serious try and did no harm, but it was feeble stuff—long-distance guessing in my opinion.

Nobody knows how many recordings were made, how many masters are still around for original pressings. But a lot of cataloguing has been done. Charles Delaunay did the best job with names, dates, and players in *The Hot Discography*.

The avant-garde boys didn't do much damage and they saved a lot of old records from the ash can. The Hot Record Society published a magazine around 1938, *The Rag*. The United Hot Clubs of America did a lot to separate the hot from the sweet schools.

It is not true, as some critics said, that the center of jazz remained constant. It became a small expanding universe. Critics would want it to be constant, but actually like any living art, it changed—and should have changed—as it grew. As to what jazz is, that will always be a question. It could be the feel of a speeded-up tempo while still keeping the old tempo, or a collective improvisation, rhythmically integrated; it certainly could be answered the easy way by calling it syncopated syncopation.

I like it best when it is very personal, made of chords and extemporaneous rhythms all set in the art of real improvisation. I can judge it only by my personal reactions to its freshness, its profundity, and its skill. Mere skill is fine—so is surface freshness. Every man is his own boss as to what is profound in jazz, and what isn't.

To me, jazz in its purest form is simply the mind in its contact with itself—to steal Aristotle's definition of intuition. And in Hollywood, I wondered just how much of my mind could be in contact with the outer, walking, talking, drinking, breathing me.

9

There were periods, as troubled times filled the world, when California was too much to take, when life there seemed dry and sterile. I knew then that I had my father's yen for far places, a senseless desire to change and move on. At such times I would visit New York, but I always came back. When away, I had a feeling that none of it had ever happened on the coast, that the coast itself did not exist, that there was no California. I could remember, but could not swear any of it was true. It had dropped away like a dream; nothing could ever have been like the things I thought I remembered.

There was no season and no changing to seasons, and even the leaves did not fall. Life left no marks. It was all parties, all record-playing, all drinks in what the film people called a "montage," one of those arrangements of objects: bottles, faces, train wheels, clouds, all pumped full of music to take the place of real action, to advance the plot without telling anything in detail— symbols of life, like Chinese characters that once were pictures, but no longer.

A trip east was always a kind of parting with that whole unreal world, the train gathering speed, moving again for the long climb to the blue ridges above San Bernardino. In the failing light the orange orchards dropped quickly away.

I sat watching the tracks pass in the blue gloaming. The sun setting in the west, setting over all the fine hills, and the dry hills that would some day be fine hills if real estate values held. Setting on the tar-stained beach where the birds stood at nightfall all facing the same way, their feet in water, while the last seagull swooped down on the flickering moths. The sun was soon a thin edge of orange, and the pitch and lurch of the speeding train was a shaking rhythm rocking as it climbed up out of California in a hurry, with the click of the rails.

Johnny Mercer also made the trip many times. He wrote *Blues in the Night* and *The Atchison, Topeka, and the Santa Fe*, on railroad rhythms. I always wanted to write a train song, but I never did. But it is easier for me to dream out my melodies and lyrics on a train, or on a plane. The click of track, the monotony of air flight, drives out reality and I turn away from everyday things and search for inner sounds someplace in my mind and spirit.

XXVII

When the dismal shock of Pearl Harbor came, I was wondering if I was to be a soldier in my second world war. But the wiser powers in control told me to go on writing songs. I did, all through those fearfully scalding years, all through the long agony of seeing my friends go off and some not come back, of wondering—as my sons grew up—what was I doing to make this the last war. But I knew how futile any one man's efforts can be against a great and stupid madness.

There was little I could do but give the world something to *hum*. I sent a lot of my songs to the wars, and they were the least harmful of all the things that went into battle. Echoes of their comforting skill—their memories in simple pleasures, of home places came back to me in tattered letters in flimsy envelopes from many crazy places where kids—GI's and nurses—waited out the war or fought desperate battles. All these people wanted me to know that my music had made life bearable during some hard time, some fearful moment, some unquiet desperation. There were those other places where men were stationed for months, even years, in some desolate, lonely outpost. There was often only some short wave music or a hand-wound record player rasping out songs on worn shellac to keep the boys from madness. For me to know of this was a great reward. I made over a hundred personal appearances in camps, barracks, and hospitals.

When we'd first written *Ole Buttermilk Sky*, I didn't feel it fitted into *Canyon Passage*. I pleaded with producer Walter Wanger to leave it out of the picture. But he insisted, claimed it had merit, and said it was in. At the time I thought he was stubborn, but I thank him now every time I see him.

It won me in 1947 a fancy bit of paper reading: ACADEMY OF MOTION PICTURE ARTS AND SCIENCES. *Certificate of Nomination for Award. Ole Buttermilk Sky.*

I didn't win the gold-plated hammer-headed little doll *that* year, but in 1951 I won the Oscar, with Johnny Mercer, for a song called *In The Cool Cool Cool of the Evening.* Bing Crosby sang it in the picture *Here Comes The Groom.* The betting and studio pressure play had been for *A Kiss To Build A Dream On* by Harry Ruby and Oscar Hammerstein, II. Advertising and press agent gall doesn't make an Oscar race pure as the driven snow. But we had planted our song not once but several times in the picture, and I carried home, fairly won, the golden nude statue with the sword. Many are cynical about Hollywood awards, and rightly so. There is too much jockeying and lunch buying, gift giving and ad taking. But I didn't do anything but sit back and wait after writing the music—a creative item often overlooked in that busy place.

My good friend Jane Wyman was in the picture with Bing and sang *Cool Cool* better than I thought she knew how to sing. She and Danny Kaye did the song at the Awards dinner and in very good style.

An ironic note re *Buttermilk Sky*—my old song writing pal, Johnny Mercer, beat it out in the Awards of 1947 with his and Harry Warren's *The Atchison, Topeka, and the Santa Fe.* A few years earlier I had shown Johnny a couple of tunes I was quite proud of. He took them home and I didn't hear from him for six months; he is the original "Don't call me, I'll call you" guy, in reverse. But this time *he* called and sang to me over the phone two wonderful lyrics—*Skylark* and *The Old Music Master.* Quite some kick to sit back comfy like at the telephone and listen to two new hits aborning!

2

Of course there were musical defeats, too. I think I earned one in 1951 when I let some gabby Hoosiers talk me into writing a serious long hair symphony for Carnegie Hall. The press was fair and the experience taught me to know the limits of my talent:

HOAGY CARMICHAEL IS GRADUATED— TAKES CARNEGIE HALL'S PLAUDITS FOR NEW NUMBER

INDIANAPOLIS ORCHESTRA PRESENTS HIS 'BROWN COUNTY IN AUTUMN'

New York—Hoagy Carmichael, of *Stardust* fame, was graduated to symphonic rank on last night's program of the visiting Indianapolis orchestra in Carnegie Hall.

Along with the graduation, the "Hoagy" part of the popular composer's name was billed as "Hoagland," and there were one or two other points of difference between the song writer and the symphonist.

After hearing Fabien Sevitzky conduct his new *Brown County in Autumn*, I am more convinced than ever that *Stardust* was a great song. Mr. Carmichael ought to write more like it.

What Mr. Carmichael didn't get over in his *Brown County in Autumn* was the very thing he got over in *Stardust*—that he had something of his own to say and his own way of saying it. . . .

Mr. Sevitzky gave an agreeable reading of the novelty and then led the lean and beaming composer out for a bow. Mr. Carmichael clasped his hands together and took the plaudits in true boxing style. . . .

Differing from the critics was André Kostelanetz, who said of Hoagy's first symphonic work:

"Carmichael must be very encouraged. The audience likes it and it was played so beautifully."

A wise child, I have since then stayed within my more familiar spheres of activity. I have done a thing for a large orchestra called *The Johnny Appleseed Suite* (twenty minutes) which was performed on the Bell Telephone Hour. But it is more melodic and more within my scope. A trial run by the Indianapolis Symphony last year led to the Bell performance.

6

In 1948 I received a telephone call from Mr. John Bates, who wanted to see me.

"Hello. What's on your mind?" I asked when he arrived.

"I want you to do a radio show for one of my clients, Luden's Coughdrops."

"How much?" (He told me.)

"When and where?"

"CBS, right away."

"What do you want me to do?"

"Anything you want to do. Agreed?"

"Agreed."

Just as slick as that. We had a drink and started talking about something else.

I wrote the script—little simple things pretending that I was in my library working with my secretary and rehearsing new songs, some mine but mostly others. I used Sherlee Turner, who was the secretary at Decca Records, as my girl Friday. I had heard her voice on the phone and it was the most pleasing I had ever heard. Instead of one piano we used two, and to back me up, I engaged the great Buddy Cole, who had made many records with me at Decca. There was a bass player and that was all. I am sure Mr. Bates would have reneged on the whole deal if he had seen my first scripts but they were so simple and intimate and so quietly done that the listening audience felt as though they were eavesdropping. I had always wanted to try this out and it worked. This show soon gained ratings far above many shows costing $25,000 a week.

A word about Buddy Cole. He has probably done more recording, both for records and movie studios, than anybody in the country—and deservedly so, because he is a great talent on both piano and organ and is a happy person to have around. He could even imitate *me* playing the piano, which has come in handy on occasion.

By 1953 I had a successful TV show, *Saturday Night Review*, and there was talk of my taking over the *Show of Shows*. Television is a strange and dangerous monster. From Madison Avenue to the newest vice-president's Ivy League tailoring—it's booby trapped every inch of the way. So I gave out a lot of Indiana-country-boy-type interviews to the press:

Hoagy Carmichael was talking about his new job of taking over the *Show of Shows* time on Saturday evenings over NBC-TV for the summer. His hour-and-a-half-long program is *Saturday Night Revue* and he's the emcee. But the more he talked about it the more it seemed he was trying to get out of the whole deal.

"Don't tell anybody," Hoagy commented, "but I'll never know how I got into this. Me taking over an hour-and-a-half show! Why, something's gone wrong somewhere. Somebody gave me this job just to see if I had any talent. I can't sing, I can't dance, I can't play the piano, and I can't remember lines —so what am I going to do?"

NBC-TV is quite contented with the set up. Perhaps because they don't know that Hoagy just doesn't know a thing about show business. After all, the guy has only written dozens of hit songs, he's been in a good many pictures, he has done several TV shows with notable success. It looks as though the network has been fooled into hiring a rank amateur with no experience at all.

So how did all this come about?

"I've got a good agent," Hoagy grinned. "He and I had been talking to NBC for about a year-and-a-half trying to get together some kind of show. . . ."

3

It was to be my show. And at first it looked that way. There was a meeting of the minds in my patio, the TV brass representing the stations, the agencies, and the sponsors. I explained my idea of the show so they could accept or reject it. They said they liked my ideas, such as the playlets showing how songs were actually written. There was some doubt on their part when I explained I wanted to end the show each time with some young boy we'd pick, so that between our talk and music, the show would end on something like a heart note.

It was the kind of thing that can't be put too well in words, and I could see the brass lifting an eyebrow here and there at the idea, which they would strangle someplace along the line long before it went on the air.

When they left, I went into my den and looked at the cold TV set. I hadn't watched much TV, but it seemed a good idea to see what the kind of people I had just been talking to put on the air. I flipped the switch and walked away from the set to brood a bit. I heard a Spanish-sounding voice singing *Who Shot A Hole In My Sombrero*. I really got a shock. If this damn thing was psychic they could have me in for witchcraft. *This* was the boy I wanted. He was Ricky Vera, and when I put him into my show he was one of the characters that made NBC's season in 1955.

It wasn't easy. The writers came up with fearful humor, much of it obscene, and I'd rant, pull weight, and get the writers back to their machines. Often it was just air time before we had a proper story line. There was also Ricky's mother, who would often suddenly demand fifty dollars more—or NBC would try and pay fifty dollars less. And *who* ran after mother and son— and often pulled them from the bus to come back into the studio? Me.

I sadly learned it wasn't really my show. It belonged to mysterious people, to directors, cameramen, and stooges. But if I yelled I got things done.

This became George Gobel's chance, but they were photographing his zipper instead of his face. I yelled and finally they gave him close-ups. He'd a died otherwise.

There were other news items:

REPUBLICANS GET NEW PIANO PLAYER
IT'S OUR HOAGY

Washington—More than 1,000 Hoosiers, by the most conservative estimate, arrived in Washington yesterday to witness the inauguration of President Dwight D. Eisenhower. . . .

Governor and Mrs. George N. Craig, Senator and Mrs. William E. Jenner and Senator and Mrs. Homer E. Capehart, and the Indiana Republican congressional delegations were feted last night at a reception given by a group of Indiana visitors.

They laughed when the little man sat down at the piano to play.

The little man, Hoagy Carmichael, had just said: "You can tell this is an Indiana party—only Hoosiers could be having so much fun—just being Hoosiers." . . .

Hosts and hostesses for this one were nearly a dozen Hoosier couples who found a free moment on the busy inaugural schedule for a social affair. The guests included just about everyone from Indiana or anyone who ever passed across the state or ever heard it mentioned.

Such folks as John Foster Dulles, the new Secretary of State, and Martin Durkin, the new Secretary of Labor, dropped in to visit the Hoosier party. Morton Downey sang.

Carmichael described his unusual garb as an "Eisenhower formal cocktail" outfit. It was a battle jacket tailored out of evening coat material.

4

There were a lot of snake-dancing people from the old college down there to cheer and dance, and I noticed suddenly we had mostly passed the half-century mark and were getting etched by time. Some of the old gang were paunchy, some bald; the ladies had fought time the hardest and most successfully with diet and dyes, with girdles and clinical attention, but it was no use. Close up, we showed that for us it was Indian Summer.

I remembered Ma Robison saying, "Some folk say: time goes. Well, always remember Hoagland, it isn't true—it's time that stays, *we* go."

Writing of Ma, of time staying, and of old loved faces going, I'd like to put down here some of the last notice the world took of my two grandmothers. They were strong and sterling women, and life had been both hard and kind to them. It pleased me that I could do a little to make their last years ones in which they had a kind of fame of their own as inspiring one of my songs:

> Mrs. Taylor Carmichael, 4302 North Capitol Avenue, who is one of "Hoagy's" two grandmothers who inspired *Little Old Lady*, received a special tribute at the Mother's Day Service at the University Park Christian Church. While the song was played, Mrs. Carmichael was presented with a potted hydrangea and was introduced by Rev. S. Grundy Fisher. This "little old lady" is 85 years old. The other grandmother is Mrs. Alex Robison and she lives at Bloomington. Recently Hoagy dedicated the song to them.
>
> The dedication was a surprise to both. They had been informed by wire to "listen in" on the program without knowing the song was to be played for the first time.
>
> "How did you like it, Mrs. Robison?"
>
> "Must be a pretty good song the way people clapped."

When 1955 came around, it was the twenty-fifth anniversary of *Stardust* (or *Star Dust*—it's right to me either way), and the old tune was stronger than ever. *Time* magazine did some research on the background and the far-flung popularity of the song, so I might as well let them explain it:

> In Italy it is called *Polvere di Stelle*, and ranks with *O Sole Mio* as an alltime favorite. In Japan it is called *Sutaadasuto*, and is one number record stores are not afraid to overorder. In England, where professionals call it a "gone evergreen," no song has sold more copies. In the U.S. it is called *Stardust*, and is the nation's most durable hit—comfortable as an old shoe, and yet rare as a glass slipper.
>
> Its publishers are currently celebrating its 25th anniversary. Actually the song was born in the summer of 1927, but its fame was delayed. It bothered almost nobody until Bandleader Isham Jones recorded it in a haunting *lento*. Jones's violin soloist "played it pretty," says Hoagy, "with feeling—to bring out the melody—and pretty soon it began to make a noise on Broadway." A rising lyricist named Mitchell Parish was commissioned to write lyrics, and *Stardust* became history.
>
> By 1933 most people seemed to be singing *Who's Afraid of the Big Bad Wolf?*, but a 20-year-old Indiana girl, mortally

wounded in a shooting, asked to have *Stardust* played at her funeral. Three years later the record business was stirred almost as deeply, when RCA Victor dared to release the song on two sides of a pop record.

Stardust has already brought Composer Carmichael, 55, a fat $350,000 in royalties, earns him $25,000 a year. But Carmichael, who has long since branched out into the movies as an actor (*The Best Years of Our Lives*), would hate to be remembered as a one-hit composer. "Actually," he says with legalistic caution, "I have what is considered, in the minds of the musical fraternity, 35 hits."

5

Legalistic caution or not, for this text I must make some kind of statement about the recordings of my music and my voice. My songs have sold by the millions, and though I was not always in the mainstream of modern jazz music, jazzmen have continued to find inspiration in my songs. Almost before a tune of mine was off the juke boxes it had become a jazz standard.

As for my voice—not so long ago I did the *Hoagy Sings Carmichael* album. It was backed by an orchestra of modern jazzmen: Art Pepper, Harry Edison, Don Fagerquist, Harry Klee, and Jimmy Rowles. I sang ten of my own songs. My native woodnote and often off-key voice is what I call "flatsy through the nose," and if that is new to music history let purists take warning. When I hear my voice on recordings, I get a bit depressed, but my phrasing and enunciation is a redeeming factor. Strangely enough, I sing better now at age sixty-three than I did at thirty-three.

When I'm pinned down as to what recording really has the best quality, I am not ashamed of my singing in the Kapp album called *Ole Buttermilk Sky*. I made it at the age of fifty-nine, and I think it the best vocalizing of my life. A friend hearing it said, "Hoagy, you have courage. Most choir singers have given up by the time they reach your age." I liked the *Hong Kong Blues* records, most of the early Decca album, and the album of children's songs I did for Golden Records.

An English magazine, *Vocal Jazz*, had this to say of my singing —and I'm willing to accept their viewpoint as about the best I'll get:

As a vocalist, Hoagy is unique. He can give his pallid and well-pitched baritone voice an endless number of shades which are real escape valves for his refined artistic sensibility. His voice is captivating, his inflexions are of a notable musicalness, his refrains have a freshness, a spontaneity and a purity which are really charming. He sometimes sings as if in secret, close to the microphone, with an endearing sort of nonchalance which cannot be found in any other artist. From *Washboard Blues* to *Judy*, Hoagy's vocalising has always been one of the most delightful artistic expressions it has been possible to hear in the jazz idiom.

By way of a pleasing novelty, someone at Broadcasting House recently made an accurate statement concerning jazz. Over the ether came the remark that Hoagy Carmichael was the only present-day popular composer with a genuine jazz background. And it is that fact, above all else, which puts his singing in a class by itself. No better, of course, than many of the acknowledged greats such as Armstrong, Teagarden and the rest, but more peculiarly subtle—one might even say more subtly peculiar—than any other jazz singer.

6

Once the ball gets to rolling, what with many radio appearances, movies and records, the inevitable happens. Your business manager tells you that you must go on the road. This means either one night stands at fairs, big auditoriums, and cow palaces throughout the country with five or six supporting acts, or a two-week personal appearance in Las Vegas or in various hotel cafes, night spots, and large theatres. Well, I did them all. It pays good money (of which the government gets at least half) and most of the time you are very pleased that you have been able to please others.

I am not unhappy that I did it, but it certainly becomes a drag. I have always felt that for the effort you put into it you have entertained too few, unlike television.

In 1948, *Billboard Magazine* elected me the "male singer of the year in the United States." Of course, this was a big laugh, but since this election was based upon the number of records sold that year (*Ole Buttermilk Sky, Huggin' and a Chalkin',* and *Hongkong Blues,* to mention a few), it evidently was a fact, thanks to the late Jack Kapp and his confidence in me. At any rate, this led to my first personal appearance in London.

Here again I used my own imagination as to how to present myself. I wore a hat on the back of my head and no tie, with a cigarette drooping from my lips, and I lazied through the entire performance. This is entirely contrary to the accepted routine of show business, but I was remembering how I used to applaud many a poor act at Keith's Vaudeville House in Indianapolis just because I was nervous for them. It worked. I could sense that the audience sat back and relaxed because I looked relaxed. Actually, I wasn't so at all times, but I did keep up the front. They tell me that I broke the record at the Copley Plaza Room in Boston, at the Nicolette Hotel in Minneapolis, and at the Chicago Theatre. Because of this I was invited to the Palladium in London for a two-week engagement. Judy Garland was to follow me. While dining and dancing with her and her husband a couple of nights before her opening, I could sense that she was very nervous about the whole thing because this appearance was to be her try at a come back.

"Judy, all you have to do is to start singing one of your big picture songs and you are in, Flynn. Come sit in the box at my matinee performance and see how easy it is to please this wonderful London audience."

She did, and I over-lazied my act to the point that the management almost used the hook to get me off. Judy opened with a big song hit, promptly tripped on her gown and took a prat fall. The rest is history.

XXVIII

There is a great deal more I could write about the fifties—new songs, new honors, new faces—but it would merely repeat in some way what I have already put down so far. A man's life after his youth moves often in cycles—and it's hard to change to a new track. I came out of the fifties with all the pleasant burden of popular approval that a man can take. I cannot honestly say I didn't like it, even if I blush when I give an autograph. I had made a place for myself not only as a song writer, but as a folk artist; I had created certain song forms that will live on, they tell me, long after I am gone.

I had money, and that has given me comfort, made me able to live in a way that most would have cherished. I recall again the death of my baby sister. Being poor, we couldn't afford to rush her to a hospital. By the time I was on a streetcar at three in the morning, headed for downtown Indianapolis to get a culture, she was beyond saving. When the hearse drove away I vowed I would never be broke again.

If I was spoiled, I was not as spoiled as many others I knew; for success is hard to wear and harder to live with. But I managed. I did no great foolish thing, I made no mad headlines. If I hurt myself, I tried to hold back the yelp of pain. If I hurt others, it was not intentional.

In some ways I've never changed from the boy in Indiana; his scar tissue still ached in certain emotional weather, his shy retreat from the world often overcame me during some particular odd agonizing moment, and often I could walk outside myself and look at myself and say: What the hell are you doing here, Hoagy;

or what damn fool thing are you acting out now? With few satisfying answers.

There are things no man can write down, and yet I must say one more thing about my personal life, not as one wanting to confess or explain or refute, but to fill out these records so I can present an image a little more in the round.

My marriage ended with the 1950's. It had a great many strong wonderful years, it produced fine children, and then it broke up. I do not know how real I see things, how true what I call facts are to actual events. But of the image that I call myself, I see a man who has his own secret core and perhaps I never let anyone come in and share it with me.

There are those who thought I made a pretty good husband— I had patience. Perhaps I provided too much in the material sense. The best thing about it was two wonderful sons, Hoagy, Jr., and Randy, both of whom can beat me at golf today. But the marriage ended and it would be foolish to talk fully about where the fault was, unless I were trying to write a novel, which I'm not. The boys were old enough to understand what was happening. And the worst of our dislocation was their loss of a house, to which we had all become attached. As Randy said, "Some day when I'm twenty-one, I'll get married and build a house just like it."

In the wee hours of the morning, while tossing and turning, faces appear, either as I saw them last or as I saw them at their best. I see my sister Martha gently brushing a tenor drum, her dark eyes glowing in ecstasy at every beat. Or as she read a beautiful passage from the pen of John Bell Clayton. He was her husband and her life. When he died, she gathered up his papers and manuscript and made another book for him, and then one night while still young and healthy she very quietly let go.

That made the house too much for Georgia, what with looking after Mother and teaching Religious Science, so I found a cozy little apartment with a front yard and back patio and broke the news to Mother. There was silence. A couple of days before she was to move, she called us to her bedside. Although weak, her faculties were crisp and clear and she told us in no uncertain terms that we ought to know she didn't want to ever move again, and she added other remarks that implied she was getting out of our way. Georgia and I were crushed. I was so broken up and ashamed that I didn't feel privileged to kiss her.

At four-thirty on that same day I finished signing contracts to appear in the "Laramie" series as "Jonesy." At five came a frantic call and at five-fifteen I was holding Mother in my arms. In two minutes she was gone. Of course Eva was there. She had come to California with us and had raised our two boys. She had also been Mother's pal and helpmate. She tied a ribbon under Mother's chin while Randy Bob played *The Lord's Prayer* at the upright and I, in turn, played Mother's favorite of mine, *One Morning in May*. Mother had told Georgia a few days before that she didn't mind going at all. "I feel as though I will be able to reach out and take hold of Dad's hand." Being a practical minded person, the will to die, the beauty of it, and the easy manner of its accomplishment was all too much for me. I can only say it was another example of ruggedness I may never attain.

Yes, Randy Bob was given piano lessons at an early age and in no time at all he was looking at the music pretending he was reading it and all the time playing by ear. He regrets this now, but he does play well, sometimes professionally, and he has written a few tunes of which I am proud. Hoagy Bix took to the drums—Stan Levey's old set, no less—and before I knew it he was sitting in with some of the best progressive artists. A two or three handicapper at golf, he became sales manager of a Manhattan brokerage office at the age of twenty-five.

Since my sons are grown up and living their own lives, we talk out many things together, and while I have never set myself up as a prime example of wisdom and knowledge, I can at least sandpaper some of the bumps they will have to slide over.

Besides Eva, there was Miss Ada to help keep the family going, and now there is Bessie Pickett to boss me around, gorge me with vitamins, and make my life as comfortable and gastronomically pleasant as possible.

2

I do not know what the world of tomorrow will do to itself, but I know I shall go on with my work as long as there are reflexes enough in me to make the sound of music, hoping that unlike some people of my generation, I have not become hardened and walled off from new ideas, fresh forms, today's discoveries— and that I do not live too much in the past. I would also like to believe in the future, and that isn't easy as picking peas these days. Or listening to good tunes. But I still feel young.

Sometimes what we are told is to be the future doesn't seem to have the proper jet fuel to propel itself forward. In my day we walked but we got there. I had to be in San Francisco this year and I thought I'd take a gander at the beatniks, the readers of poems to Zen and jazz (not mine I hoped), those who had their own answer for the mid-century. I'm a good listener and have a pretty good deadpan expression.

San Francisco—upper Grant Avenue—is the Paradise Found, I was told, of the Beats. I wandered on from the foot of Telegraph Hill to the North Beach section of a city that still, to me, appears to be built up and down and not from north to south or east to west. The narrow houses in North Beach are old and weathered and their bay windows protrude like fat gals peering into the street, watching the passing scene. It's not a fashionable neighborhood. It's far from the lush hotel and night-club life of Top O' The Mark, the Fairmont, and Sheraton-Palace. It has been spared the shine and chi chi of modern plate glass, stainless steel, and roofs like derby hats. These are solid houses I remembered from other visits, gone a little to ruin in the sun and salt-sea fog of San Francisco. But here, I was told, shout the Beat Generation, a collection of young people talented in some ways, rejecting the moral values of our society as we did in our early days, but accepting as freedom the need not to shave too often, bathe regularly, work for a weekly salary, or take an interest in politics, baseball scores, stock market prices, balanced diets, PTA meetings, or popular motion picture or TV stars.

The Beat Generation are no strangers to me. I have known them for a long time, and under other names. Sandals and long hair had been worn by Greenwich Village characters in the twenties as they listened to fairly bad poets, drank red wine in a damp cellar, and gave the impression that they were in rebellion against conformity, good tailoring, and Main Street's social behavior. I myself had sat at the Café Dôme in the thirties on the Left Bank in Paris, where the rather addlepated goddess, Gertrude Stein, sprinkled us with her blessing.

I was part of a Beat Generation in the twenties that rebelled against being forced to study the classics in ivy-walled colleges, take jobs in old firms, or live in a square world. We feared settling down with a girl who could bake a cake, crank a Model T, and had been our sweetheart since our high school days. I didn't follow up the doings of the Beatniks of the forties, who had a new name: Social Protest.

3

I found out that a few years ago, the poet Kenneth Rexroth began to publicize the young Beats of San Francisco and to recite his own poetry to jazz music. Rexroth is a big shaggy man with a face of much character that looks as if it were carved with an axe out of a block of wood. He is in his fifties, and thus has never claimed to be more than a forerunner and not wholly approving sponsor of the beat poets. But he did help the younger poets to an audience by lending them the weight of his twenty-odd years of prominence as a poet and critic.

The new kicks I was told were often found at Lawrence Ferlinghetti's City Lights Book Shop in North Beach. Hunting the beats, I went there—the usual small bookshop without fancy fixtures. The only difference was that it also published poetry, beat poetry, which the owner had to defend in court as not being obscene. He, like some other Mahatmas of Beat, was no longer young, being an ex-subchaser commander and a Ph.D.

As I walked in I saw a tall thin man wearing no socks, his

feet in Mexican woven leather, his yellow corduroy jacket not matching his unpressed green pants, and his chin failing to grow a beard. I could tell from the trumpet under his arms that he was probably an unemployed musician short of bread.

"Looking for a gig?" I asked.

"Man," he said, "you'd think they were past getting gassed at Stravinsky. I mean, how square can the critics get?"

"You're a Dixieland man?"

I gave him a cigarette and we talked beat music. He was twenty-eight years old, married to a woman who painted modern art on the walls of the beat dives. They had two children and he had been playing bop for ten years. We went over to the place where some of his wife's painting were hung. It was a dingy expresso joint, with some red electric light bulbs trying to fight off the gloom of a thick Frisco fog.

"The creeps are resting."

There were several couples bent over the coffee, smoking very short cigarette stubs, listening to some old recordings of King Oliver playing 1920 jazz. The records were so worn that only fragments of music came through. The joint was, as I found out, a typical beat hangout. Beats can't afford the real night clubs like Bimbo's Club, Shanghai, or John's Rendezvous. My guide pointed to some paintings on the wall. "The wife's."

"Has she sold anything?" I asked, looking away from the paintings.

"I trade some off to some hipster who has the know. For a bag of potatoes. If you want to buy one . . ."

I ordered two expressos and shook my head. "Why is this beat stuff—you have a philosophy?"

"Beat?" He sat sipping his drink, holding the glass with both hands. "Being beat, we're in it for kicks. I mean, man, it's a jungle out there and everything is square."

He closed his eyes, took a drag on my cigarette and addressed the ceiling. "We beats believe it's a waste of time trying to make this cornball world over. It's going over the falls, and it's all only a big ride. You dig me?"

"And the beat—what does he do lots of other people don't do?"

"He's free—loud and clear—the way he wants to be."

"Don't you conform to the beat pattern? Aren't you hogtied to beat conventions like the kook punching the time clock? Suppose you didn't like expresso, red wine, cupino fish stew, jazz records, beards, dives like this, unpressed clothes? Wouldn't the beats toss you out?"

"Be seeing you," he said sadly, and went out with my pack of smokes, leaving me to pay for the drinks. Somehow it was a little like the taste of the Book Nook back in Bloomington, only not as clean and hopeful. And I liked our racoon coats and bell bottom pants better than levis and Hawaiian sport shirts. And the flappers were more desirable than the chicks in black cotton stockings.

4

Back on the street, I went down past the shadows of the Coit Tower and into a cafe called The Place. It needed paint, sweeping, and more lights. It didn't look much different than the last place or any other beat place. A tall pale girl in very tight yellow Capri pants, heavy earrings, and long dark hair combed back in a Charles Addams cartoon hair-do, was standing by a pay phone, hunting in her red shirt pocket for a coin. I handed her a dime and she nodded, recognized me, and said, "Thanks the most, Hoagy."

She made a call and spoke to somebody named Nina about meeting her at The Zen at seven. She hung up and turned to me as she patted her hips. "You can't carry coins in these pants."

I said politely, "They fit fine for beat."

"Who, me? I'm not beat. I work in the big record shop on the corner, nights. All I'm interested in is real gully low jazz. I mean the real thing, not just cool or progressive riffing. The poetry-and-jazz crumbuns around here, they're from Weirdsville if you ask me.

I found out she was nineteen. She had been married to a drummer in a jazz combo that had played jazz and recited poetry, but they had broken up long before he went to the federal hospital in Kentucky to take a drug cure.

"I don't blast," she said. "It disgusted me. I didn't know Sam was main-lining, and when I found out he was an addict that tore it. Besides he was going more and more for modern concert jazz, that Ravel, Stravinsky beat. And that's not real jazz. Not to me."

"What's the beat thing really about? They sincere?"

"Well," she said, "I'll tell you. You're a playing composing cat. Maybe twenty people in San Francisco are sincere about this beat kick. And they all make a buck out of it. Know what I mean? They give lectures or concerts or they write poems or novels. And they try to say, what's the use, it's never going to get any better, and maybe a lot worse. So let's have some fun, let's say and do what we want and let it go at that."

I went back to my hotel, remembering how it was when I was young, in the can houses on an old upright, in the speaks, the football weekends, the tin lizzies: it was all as far away as the Ark. I sat in the window and looked down at San Francisco. The fog was walking up the hill and rows of little pearls lit up the Golden Gate Bridge crossing the bay, and out by Alcatraz a boat hooted and the night smelled of old walls. The world still puzzled this Hoosier, but I remained as full of curiosity as an unborn egg. So, having nothing to do in the day (I was appearing at the Italian Village night club), I painted a picture of the roof top next door with air vents that looked to me like knights in armor. The rusty one became King Edward I; the painting's called *The Crusades*. Last Christmas it was sold throughout the country as a Christmas card.

Going back to Los Angeles I remembered the line that my friend Bix used to recite when the blues were on him: 'I am not a swan."

I looked about me. The Film and TV industry have a grip on people that does not appear as yet to be breakable. Frustration in the studios is plentiful, and like all frustrated people, they like to talk about it, always ready to talk things out without really reaching the core of any problem. There is a constant worry in the town about being discarded, about being used, being fired.

I do not willingly, I think, join in the town's condescension, contempt, and the hostility of those outside the industry and its morals. Many see nothing wrong with the studios, networks, or agents and their contempt for people as property, and would welcome a seven-year contract with all its slave-class clauses. None of them will see, or cannot, for their thinking is in the hands of their agent and soothsayer. Good work cannot remain second-rate, but will become third-rate unless they lift themselves from the rut into which their lack of strength has put them.

As my friend, the unemployed director, said: "You come out here young and able and enter a studio. Then you look around you one day, and suddenly, overnight, you're sixty years old."

You can catch the lost souls in front of Schwab's drugstore, picking unfed teeth with free toothpicks while reading the trade papers; they appear at the Academy or TV re-runs of pictures they did years ago; they are arrested driving an old car without brakes; sometimes they appear in court for an hour and some reporter remembers them. They are living on their own tails, like wrecked monkeys, all along the beaches at Santa Monica and Topanga and Malibu, aging, wrinkling, souring, lamenting, and *waiting*. They never give up waiting for the town to make that one phone call, for the agent to say, "Hang on, you're hot at Paramount, Ziv, Four-Star. . . ."

In this way they become conditioned to unreality. When I find myself involved with them or their problems, I escape by writing a song.

5

As I sorted out my impressions of the beats, I wanted to check a little further into their world, find a clue as to what they were after. Jazz was part of it, but I wondered just how they used jazz.

A Los Angeles newspaper reporter I knew called me. "Hoagy, there's a beat place you ought to make."

"I've made them."

"No, this place is out further than any place."

"I'm far enough out now."

"Beachwood Drive, to listen to records. Progressive stuff."

I weakened.

We drove up Beachwood Drive to a simple house and walked up two flights of wooden stairs into a large room overlooking the city below us. Since there were no chairs, everyone sat on the bare wooden floor. There were several dim red bulbs burning in lamps made of driftwood, and a lot of people were drinking cheap red wine from dime store glasses. Almost everyone was smoking and the air was blue in layers of tobacco fumes. It was a listening crowd and the music was good—good in the sense that the musicians teamed well together. The Cole Porter or Gershwin tune they were playing was made barely recognizable by their subdued manner of flat-toned improvisation, particularly from the trumpet. They seemed to be saying things like, "We know the truth, we are not extroverts." But in the main, they were very interesting musically because they used and re-used phrases in fugue-like ways over the constant but quiet left-hand counterpunches of the drummer. The string bass seemed to sing his heart out rather than finger-pluck each note. The alto sax was rather a bore. He wailed away and got no place, really, trying to find that forbidden note. I'm sure that in his young mind nobody had ever played those notes before. All in all, a lot of progressive jazz has proved very interesting to me if played by artists like Dave Brubeck, Chico Hamilton, Oscar Peterson, Miles Davis, and others. A step forward until something new comes along. As I listened, the music grew louder and one of the bulbs went out, making me aware of young people all around me in the gloom, and of some not so young, all trying to capture a personal kick, hanging on to an oddball way of seeing and doing because it made them a little different from the unhep.

I said to the reporter, "Just what do the beats say?"

"Trying, they say, to break away from doing what everyone else does. Me, I think most of the beat rebels will become middle-class conservatives in a couple of years."

It was too dark to see if he was smiling. The jazz was very solid, the riffs were perfect, and the Beat Generation sat and listened. I had an idea that already they were too old, already old-fashioned squares.

6

Later, alone, I felt neither old nor out of fashion. I had my memory of my father and mother, and many good and great band men. I wasn't worried about the future of jazz, popular music, or the beats; there would be other rebel generations.

I know that some people think of the jazzman as being poor in education and background, but he is often working for a new ideal in music, a closer view of truth, and a fuller meaning of life —trying to absorb them into his music, to make of his work something always new, yet always creative. Jazz drops tired stuff overboard, for it is willing to face the difficulties of original work, rejecting easy ways out and going beneath the surface of things.

Looking at myself in the mirror I can see jazz has come a long way since my stone-age days of early Dixieland, the Chicago school, and Bix and his horn. But somewhere hidden in it have remained the notes and the echoes of what it started with. First came swing to dilute it, and then came bop and bebop to give it a new pace. Then came the cool and the progressive. It's all been a long march, an evolution of a pure American music. I've never taken sides, joined the cults, or given out fat fancy statements of why it was good, why it was bad, or why some was better than others.

I can quote Whitman, "I was the man—I suffered—I was there." It was not too long ago, and I don't think the music has reached its peak yet. It has been thought fancy and avant-garde by some, and lamented as lost and perverted by others. But the deep dark blue center of it can't be contaminated, not for long.

West Coast jazz during the fifties caught on, and the studios, before TV drove them from their high place, brought together the best jazzmen around. There were times up and down the coast when the San Francisco Dixielanders caught fire, as did the modern at the Monterey Jazz Festival. The cool school was represented by the Lighthouse, where you could hear the best of it being brewed and created. Kid Ory, Benny Pollack, and lots of the old-timers made the scene, while the new sounds came from Turk Murphy, Brubeck, Kenton, and Coltrane.

Nothing was really lost, and a lot was found in the past to renew the music. Maybe some of us fought the change a little, for we were getting on, and the past always took on a glow that wasn't there when we were living it.

Are the sides of the twenties classics because they are old? Or because they are often still fresh, strong, and real? The classic babies had once been the moderns—and romantics, too. Only old age had made them classic.

The limits of jazz? In most jazz, the actual performance is important in itself, so that one must accept or reject it on that basis. The long-hair composers sometimes try to take over some of jazz's vitality; sometimes they reject it altogether. Whatever they do, the scalar, rhythmic, and harmonic power of jazz will last a long time. For me Bix is still alive when I hear the progressive stuff, and jazz has roots as long as Louis Armstrong brings the crowds into the arenas to let him blow that horn.

Louis has done over six-hundred sides in his time—maybe more by now—with Oliver, Tate, Henderson, and lots of others. Hearing him today, I feel he's no longer a great horn, but a complex virtuoso. Mr. Personality. Full of fun, full of mood.

They all had it: Bolden, Oliver, Morton, Bix, Armstrong. They all understood that living in an ivory tower was a hell of a good way of identifying yourself with the tomb. They went out among people, made mistakes, and got better. They learned the hard way.

In the newer mood, mention should be made of the Sauter-

Finnegan groups, Stan Kenton and his personal approach, and if I may mention a name the critics overlook—Ray Noble, who has manner and style. And how many of us still hear the echoes of Bob Crosby and his Bobcats, or Red Nichols and his various Pennies?

Five

"The Purple Dusk of Twilight Time"

XXIX

There is a point in any life where one can look back and add up a few simple heartfelt things. I don't want to say them too fancy. I leave that for the professors.

Glib generalities on jazz are the result of ignorance. Real creators are terrible folk when gripped by passions. We can only see them clearly, as with Bix, when the flames of their creation have burned down a little.

Ordinary people want popular music merely for its surface; the jazzman wants his music for its content. Basic to jazz music is a harmony of shapes, broken often by dissonance, sometimes with blaring, repeated discords. These crescendos rise to a climax, followed by a diminuendo of color and form, then another crescendo, another climax. And sometimes in the right place, in the right man, it comes out right.

The jazzman is, at his best, a free agent. His forms, his tones when concentrated and distilled. become a private world he offers freely. It has a sympathy with all that lives, stirs, feels. It reconciles us, as all good music does, to our reality—even that of an aging man walking on an old street of memories.

If, as some very bright men think, all events occur in cycles, and every ending is a new beginning, then maybe that kid from Indiana, who once was me, is still circling around there some place in space, waiting to begin all over again.

I want to end the book with him, as he was the time he first heard the music he was going to give his life to. A band had come to play at the high school fraternity dance, a hot-shot

Negro band from down in Louisville that we had signed sight unseen. The coming of Jordan's band had exploded in me almost more music than I could consume.

I remember the September morning of 1919 that followed the big dance. I was cutting the grass for Ma and Pa Robison, trying not to run the lawn mower into Ma's nasturtium bed, trying to trim neatly around the little circular basins that held her long-stemmed roses.

As I wrote about it years later. . . .

The blade of the mower purred in an uneven pattern of rhythm—monotonous, yes, but crisp and real. The events of the night before were real enough—didn't I run into the clothesline pole thinking about them?—but they were difficult to recapture in all their obscenity as I glanced down the street a block or two and saw Aunt Sadie's house standing there in quiet honesty. Simple, unchanged and unmoved. That other world, the one I didn't quite belong in was going along just the same. Jordan's orchestra hadn't made a dent in it. Inside Aunt Sadie's house were two newborn cakes; one for the Ladies Exchange and one for the neighbors and relatives to sample if they chanced to drop in:

("Why don't you go down and sample her cake, Hoagland? She'd appreciate it. She lives in a kitchen, clean and respectable. Doesn't care one iota about your shindig last night—only cares about your health. She loves you because you are one of the men of the family. Young yet, but she doesn't see you that way. She sees you as the future president of the Monon Railroad, the one her Uncle Billy has worked on for twenty years. Go see her but don't tell her about last night. She won't understand.")

Grass grows green and deep and the harder you push the faster the mental processes work too. Energy is sapped and there I lay in the shade of a quilt that hangs on the line. Took Ma ninety-four days to make that quilt. Could have won a prize. Didn't even enter it. Took me three hours to make five dollars playing a dance. Aunt Sadie got fifty cents for her cake and her two hours' work. It made me think. There will be lots more dances and lots more dollars. Whistle while you work, too. ("No, Aunt Sadie, I don't think I'll ever be president of anything. Mother named me after a railroad man, I know, but it is too late now, I'm afraid.")

Much, much too late. . . .

And now, how appropriate Mitchell Parish's opening words seem as I sit here trying to "dig" the future—"Sometimes I wonder. . . ."